Keech

LEGISLATIVE INSTITUTIONS AND IDEOLOGY IN CHILE

This is a book about the guarantees demanded by authoritarian governments that voluntarily cede power to democratic successors, employing Chile as a case study. It shows that such guarantees are a special case of a much more general problem of constitutional design: how to constrain future decision makers to do what the authors of a constitution would want while still delegating to them the flexibility to adapt to a changing world.

The work extends the spatial model of policy preferences by incorporating a valence approach to policy choices. This valence component allows an agenda setter – in Chile the democratically elected president – to overcome some objections by veto players to proposed reform. The book also introduces a new methodology for analyzing roll-call voting data and employs Senate Committee voting records to study the impact of human rights concerns on the political debate.

John B. Londregan is Associate Professor of Political Science at the University of California, Los Angeles. He has previously taught at Princeton and Carnegie Mellon Universities. Professor Londregan has authored numerous articles in well-known publications, including the *American Political Science Review*, *The Journal of Politics*, *International Studies Quarterly*, *World Politics*, and *Public Choice*.

POLITICAL ECONOMY OF INSTITUTIONS AND DECISIONS

Series Editors
Randall Calvert, *University of Rochester, New York*
Thráinn Eggertsson, *Max Planck Institute, Germany and University of Iceland*

Founding Editors
James E. Alt, *Harvard University*
Douglass C. North, *Washington University of St. Louis*

Other books in the series
Alesina and Howard Rosenthal, *Partisan Politics, Divided Government and the Economy*
Lee J. Alston, Thráinn Eggertsson, and Douglass C. North, eds., *Empirical Studies in Institutional Change*
Lee J. Alston and Joseph P. Ferrie, *Southern Paternalism and the Rise of the American Welfare State: Economics, Politics, and Institutions, 1865–1965*
James E. Alt and Kenneth Shepsle, eds., *Perspectives on Positive Political Economy*
Jeffrey S. Banks and Eric A. Hanushek, eds., *Modern Political Economy: Old Topics, New Directions*
Yoram Barzel, *Economic Analysis of Property Rights, 2nd edition*
Robert Bates, *Beyond the Miracle of the Market: The Political Economy of Agrarian Development in Kenya*
Peter Cowhey and Mathew McCubbins, eds., *Structure and Policy in Japan and the United States*
Gary W. Cox, *The Efficient Secret: The Cabinet and the Development of Political Parties in Victorian England*
Gary W. Cox, *Making Votes Count: Strategic Coordination in the World's Electoral System*
Jean Ensminger, *Making a Market: The Institutional Transformation of an African Society*
Kathryn Firmin-Sellers, *The Transformation of Property Rights in the Gold Coast: An Empirical Analysis Applying Rational Choice Theory*
Clark C. Gibson, *Politics and Poachers: The Political Economy of Wildlife Policy in Africa*
Anna L. Harvey, *Votes Without Leverage: Women in American Electoral Politics, 1920–1970*
Murray Horn, *The Political Economy of Public Administration: Institutional Choice in the Public Sector*
John D. Huber, *Rationalizing Parliament: Legislative Institutions and Party Politics in France*
Jack Knight, *Institutions and Social Conflict*
Michael Laver and Kenneth Shepsle, eds., *Making and Breaking Governments*
Michael Laver and Kenneth Shepsle, eds., *Cabinet Ministers and Parliamentary Government*
Margaret Levi, *Consent, Dissent, and Patriotism*
Brian Levy and Pablo T. Spiller, eds., *Regulations, Institutions, and Commitment*
Leif Lewin, *Ideology and Strategy: A Century of Swedish Politics (English Edition)*
Gary Libecap, *Contracting for Property Rights*

Series list continues on page following Index

LEGISLATIVE INSTITUTIONS AND IDEOLOGY IN CHILE

JOHN B. LONDREGAN

CAMBRIDGE
UNIVERSITY PRESS

PUBLISHED BY THE PRESS SYNDICATE OF THE UNIVERSITY OF CAMBRIDGE
The Pitt Building, Trumpington Street, Cambridge, United Kingdom

CAMBRIDGE UNIVERSITY PRESS
The Edinburgh Building, Cambridge CB2 2RU, UK   http://www.cup.cam.ac.uk
40 West 20th Street, New York, NY 10011-4211, USA   http://www.cup.org
10 Stamford Road, Oakleigh, Melbourne 3166, Australia
Ruiz de Alarcón 13, 28014 Madrid, Spain

First published 2000

Printed in the United States of America

Typeface Sabon 10/12 pt.   *System* LATEX 2_ε [TB]

A catalog record for this book is available from the British Library.

Library of Congress Cataloging in Publication Data
Londregan, John Benedict.
   Legislative institutions and ideology in Chile / John B.
Londregan.
         p.   cm. – (Political economy of institutions and decisions)
   ISBN 0-521-77084-X hb
   1. Legislative bodies – Chile.   2. Democratization – Chile.
   3. Constitutional history – Chile.   4. Separation of powers – Chile.
   5. Chile – Politics and government – 1988 – Decision making.
   I. Title.   II. Series.
   JL2654.L66   2000
   328.83 – dc21   99-33216
                                                             CIP

ISBN 0 521 77084 X hardback

This book is dedicated to my parents:

Marjorie and Edward.

Contents

Contents

Acknowledgments

Work on this book began with a six-month sojourn in Chile in 1994, which was made possible by a Richard Allen Lester Preceptorship from Princeton University. In Chile my work was facilitated by the hospitality of the Centro de Estudio y Asistencia Legislativa (CEAL) of the Catholic University of Valparaíso. This research also benefited enormously from a year of unfettered time spent as a National Fellow at the Hoover Institution, in 1966 and 1997. I am also grateful to UCLA for an academic Senate grant that made it possible to do some follow-up field work in 1997. The initial logistics of field work in Chile benefited from the advice and intervention of Paul Sigmund, while I thank Sybil Abarca, Jesica Fuentes, and Marcela Villegas of the Catholic University of Valparaíso for helpful research assistance, and Carlos Hoffmann and Mariana George Nacimento for access to Senate committee records. I have also benefited from the openness and patience of politicians across the ideological spectrum who were willing to make time in their demanding schedules for interviews.

This work has benefited enormously from the persistent encouragement and advice of James Alt, who read multiple drafts in their entirety. I have also benefited from critical readings of the entire manuscript by Avinash Dixit, Barbara Geddes, Keith Poole, Howard Rosenthal, Susan Stokes, and two anonymous referees, and from partial readings by Jim DeNardo, Susanne Lohmann, George Tsebelis, and John Zaller. Parts of the book were presented at the annual meetings of the American Political Science Association in 1994 and 1997, and the annual Political Methodology meetings in 1996, where I received useful comments. Parts of the work have also benefited from comments by seminar audiences at Cal Tech, the University of Chicago, Columbia, Duke, New York University, Princeton, Stanford, UC Berkeley, UCLA, and Yale. While visiting at MIT in Fall 1993 I benefited from conversations with Whitney Newey, who helped me to understand the need for a statistical estimator adapted to small legislatures, and with Jim Snyder, who helped to shape my thinking about valence issues.

Most importantly, I am grateful to my wife, Victoria, and my children; Megan, Mateo, and Eduardo (listed in order of arrival). Without their patience and understanding and their tolerance of more than normally idiosyncratic behavior on my part, this book would never have been written.

Introduction

Constitutions provide structure for two kinds of activity: solving problems about which there is consensus, and mediating conflict over policy choices about which there is not. Moreover, the structure of constitutions is not assembled behind a Rawlesian veil of ignorance. Those who write constitutions, whether they are the elected democratic representatives of a free people or the agents of an authoritarian government, are often partisans in the policy conflicts the constitution will resolve, ready and willing to manipulate the institutional structure on behalf of their policy goals. This lack of innocence produces a tension between the problem-solving and conflict-mediating features of constitutional design. The best structures for solving problems about which there is consensus delegate considerable flexibility. This is what we see in the world of commerce; when all of the stockholders of a firm share the goal of earning higher profits, they delegate considerable decision-making authority to the company's manager. In contrast, when there is conflict about policy goals, those whose grip on power may subsequently slip will seek to "lock in" concrete policy choices, denying flexibility to future decision makers who may not share their objectives.

Yet even the most guileful partisans will perceive some cost in fully constraining future decision makers. Future politicians constrained from increasing spending on public health cannot expand medical subsidies as a way to redistribute income to the poor, but neither can they raise spending to combat an unforeseen epidemic. Constitutions embody tradeoffs made by their authors between locking in their vision of good government and permitting future decision makers to adapt to a changing world.

In this book I develop a model of executive legislative relations that illuminates the balance between delegation and constraint that the Pinochet government imposed on Chile as the price for that country's transition toward democracy. This model challenges the common wisdom that gridlock is the inevitable result of a legislature and an agenda-setting executive

1

who seek to move policy in opposite directions from the status quo. Central to the model is a recognition of the often neglected concept of policy "valence." This term, coined by Stokes (1963), pertains to policy objectives such as highway safety and low crime, about which there is consensus. An agenda-setting executive can pry grudging legislative approval for ideological reforms that a majority of the legislature oppose in exchange for improvements in valence that are advantageous for both the executive and the legislature.

A chief source of the executive's ability to make proposals with higher valence than the status quo is the inevitable tendency of any set of laws to "lose touch" with their environment. Several economists (Schultz, 1968), (North and Thomas 1973) have argued that institutional change occurs in response to a change in "relative prices." The agrarian revolution at the end of the neolithic era and the industrial revolution of the past several hundred years both created pressure for major institutional changes. But as with earthquakes, not all social and economic changes are cataclysmic. Government policy can be fine-tuned to a steady stream of microtremors, such as changes in the moral content of popular culture that increase the number of single-parent households, the arrival of cable television technology, and the invention of effective but expensive prescription drugs that change the optimal mix of medical expenditures away from doctor visits and toward drugs. Social and economic tremors like these create an asymmetry between constitution writers and the policymakers who follow them. It would have been impossible for a constitution writer fifty years ago to anticipate computer vandalism by "hackers," while contemporary policymakers can easily draft antihacker legislation. In a rapidly changing environment, constitution writers can be sure that it will be increasingly easy for future policymakers to formulate high-valence alternatives to any policies put in place today, but they cannot anticipate the substance of the changes. This is why the need for constitutions to delegate grows over time.

The constitution left behind by the Pinochet government creates a tension between a powerful, democratically elected executive, and numerous "authoritarian enclaves," centers of administrative, judicial, and legislative power insulated from direct electoral control. This arrangement is the Pinochet government's solution to one of the fundamental dilemmas of military government: how to disengage from direct rule. Samuel Finer compared this to the problem of dismounting a tiger (Finer 1962). The enclaves are a tranquilizer that keeps democratic politics inert while those close to the military government climb down. In the early years of the transition the struggle between the enclaves and the executive favored the former, which act as veto players, locking in numerous policy guarantees demanded by the Pinochet government, most notoriously in the ambit of

2

human rights. Over a longer time horizon the executive is increasingly able to bundle high-valence alternatives to an increasingly obsolete status quo with changes in the ideological position of policy more to the liking of the president, and the electoral majority that put him in power, and less appealing to the defenders of the authoritarian enclaves. The institutional tranquilizer is beginning to wear off. In contrast with the stereotype of strong presidents as antidemocratic, the powerful Chilean executive is the main avenue by which the voters are able to influence government policy.

The potential for the Chilean experience to provide general lessons about democratic transitions has been recognized by academics (Przeworski 1991) and politicians (La Tercera 1998) alike. Here the analysis provides guidance about the circumstances in which the institutions that shape Chile's democratic transition are most likely to lead to an eventually stable democratic outcome, and when they are not.

The plan of this book is straightforward. First I develop a model of the constitution writer's tradeoff between allowing future decision makers the flexibility to implement policies that improve valence on the one hand, and constraining future decision makers from altering the ideological content of government policy on the other. I then use this model to clarify the mechanisms affecting the balance of power in executive legislative relations, a balance that largely determines the speed of Chile's democratic transition.

Actually carrying this plan through is not a trivial task. First a detailed roadmap of Chile's constitution is needed to verify the adequacy of the characterization of the Chilean president as the agenda setter in the legislative process. Then there is the even knottier task of charting the ideological landscape. This is done by using roll-call votes cast in Senate committees. While these votes have a number of properties that make them very useful measures of members' policy preferences in the various issue areas dealt with by the committees, they also require that the analysis overcome some serious technical hurdles that are guaranteed to thwart the standard techniques used to analyze the U. S. Congress when the number of voters is small. The methodological approach I develop to deal with these problems in the Chilean context is easily and widely adaptable to other settings in which a small number of decision makers take positions for and against a stream of agenda items. Potential applications include the U. S. Supreme Court, the U. S. International Trade Commission, and party whip votes in which the number of independent decision makers corresponds to the number of parties rather than the number of legislators.

This analysis results in a three-part payoff. First there is a model of the tradeoff between flexibility and constraint faced by constitution writers, which will find useful applications far beyond the western coast of South

America. Second there is a statistical model of roll-call voting in small legislatures. While this model was essential to mining ideological gold from the committee roll-call vein, it is also likely to prove useful to analysts in a variety of other contexts. Finally, this book offers guidance on when the "Chilean way" of military extrication from power leads out of hell, and when a framework of institutional guarantees such as those imposed by the Pinochet government as its price for ceding power will simply delay the onset of a new round of breakdown and military rule.

THE PLAN OF THIS BOOK

The first two chapters present a model of constitution writing. In Chapter 1, I introduce a spatial model that recognizes that public policy questions involve a combination of valence issues, such as honesty, efficiency, and safety, about which there is a consensus, and position issues, such as abortion and gun control, about which people disagree.[1] Most public policy involves elements of both valence and position. Consider the development of financial transactions via the internet. Virtually all would agree on the importance of regulating internet transactions to reduce fraud and abuse, but we would expect that the left and the right would disagree on the details of those regulations, and how their costs should be born. Should companies making financial transactions on the internet place interest-free deposits with the Central Bank, and if so, how large should the deposits be? How large a processing fee should such companies be allowed to charge? Should financial transactions on the internet be taxed? The greater the weight people place on the valence elements of policy relative to the position elements, the more scope there is for compromise.

When the executive has agenda-setting power and is able to propose policy reforms with higher valence than the status quo, the resulting outcome departs from the standard predictions of the agenda-setter model (Romer and Rosenthal 1978). Even when the executive and the legislature cannot agree on the preferred direction for ideological change, the executive can make the legislature a take it or leave it offer that gives the median legislator something he or she and the executive both want: higher valence, in exchange for the legislature giving the executive something he or she wants, and the median legislator does not; policy that is ideologically closer to the executive and farther from the median legislator.

This simple model of public policy captures the crucial tradeoff constitution writers must make between entrenching specific policy positions and allowing future policy to adapt to changing circumstances. At one extreme one could make the the entire legal and administrative code part

---

[1] This useful terminology was developed by Stokes (1963).

of the constitution, so that any change, whether an expansion in the band of frequencies broadcasters are allowed to use or an adjustment in the tariff on imported blue jeans, requires a constitutional amendment. At the other extreme, a constitution could provide a very simple framework for choosing decision makers, and then leave these decision makers great leeway in their choice of policies. In the Chilean case the solution imposed by the Pinochet government was somewhere between these two poles, with an executive agenda-setter able to propose policy reform, and a legislature capable of blocking it.

Chapter 2 provides a brief account of the circumstance in which the military government's dual legacy of institutional structure and unresolved human rights abuses came about. This account begins with the conflicting histories that are remembered on the left and the right. Each has its own version of the fall of the Popular Unity government. The chapter goes on to show that the institutional framework that emerged was in part a by-product of Pinochet's struggle to consolidate power within the military government. The model developed in Chapter 1 is extended to account for constitution writers' uncertainty about the future and then used to analyze the military government's extrication problem. Most analysts emphasize the importance of growing opposition to the Pinochet government in spurring the democratic transition: forced to choose between withdrawal or killing large numbers of demonstrators and facing a downward spiral of civil opposition to military rule at home and pariah status abroad, the armed forces withdrew. While foreign and domestic opposition were important, the analytical model developed here shows that under plausible assumptions about the Pinochet government's uncertainty about its electoral appeal, powersharing with the civilian opposition could have resulted in a more favorable ideological outcome from the standpoint of Pinochet supporters than would unfettered delegation to Pinochet! The chapter concludes with a brief description of the surprising success of the opposition to the military government in uniting to defeat Pinochet in a plebiscite on his continued rule, thereby hastening the resumption of civilian rule.

Attention in Chapter 3 turns to the details of the institutions left behind by the military government when it ceded power in March 1990. The institutional battlefield of the transition is the Senate. The Concertación, an alliance of parties that opposed Pinochet, controls the presidency and the lower legislative chamber, while the opposition, which is sympathetic to the Pinochet government, account for a majority in the Senate, thanks to the presence of the so-called institutional senators, who are appointed mostly from within the institutional enclaves. The analysis of the Constitution in Chapter 3 confirms that, despite many twists and turns in the legislative process, the president's monopoly over certain types of proposals, and his constructive veto powers over all proposals, leave him as the de facto agenda setter, while the opposition delegation in the Senate must decide between the status quo and the president's proposals. This institutional analysis also identifies some powerful "proposal germaneness" restrictions, to use Shepsle's terminology (Shepsle 1979), that are at work in the Chilean constitution. These have the effect of limiting changes in the ideological content of policy to a single-issue dimension at a time.

In Chapter 4 attention turns to measuring issue positions and calibrating the relative importance of issue positions and valence. These are empirical questions about preferences. In this analysis I exploit the information to be found in voting records from Senate committees. To learn about underlying preferences from voting records it is customary to assume that legislators vote "sincerely" for the closest alternative. Chapter 4 identifies the conditions under which we may expect this behavior: public votes, and an agenda that is difficult to predict or manipulate, and that includes a wide array of proposals, not merely those crafted by floor managers to have the best chance of passing. As shown in Chapter 4, these conditions are all closely approximated when committees of the Chilean Senate cast votes on proposals at the second readings of bills.

The discussion then turns to the key issues involved in analyzing roll-call voting data, and it shows how these data can be used to estimate the parameters of the analytical model developed in Chapter 1. It discusses the details of the voting data analyzed here. This analysis is extended beyond the standard agnostic approach of estimating the characteristics of proposals to overcome the serious statistical problems to which the standard models are prey, problems that become even more serious when, as in this analysis, the number of voters is small. Beyond the importance of the statistical issues, I argue that proposal making is intrinsically important, and that our empirical methods have heretofore accorded it too little attention.

The subsequent three chapters focus on three important legislative committees: Constitution,[2] Education,[3] and Labor.[4] In each chapter the statistical analysis is integrated with a discussion of some of the votes that divided Senators in order to put their estimated ideological locations in a substantive context.

This committee-specific analysis is restricted to the revealed preferences of the senators who actually participated in the deliberations of these three standing committees. However, committee assignments are closely controlled by the parties. At any time during the legislative session Senators can be replaced on committees, something that happens routinely when Senators must be away from Congress on the day of a committee meeting.

[2] The Comisión de Constitución, Legislación, Justicia, y Reglamento.
[3] The Comisión de Educación y Monumentos.
[4] The Comisión de Trabajo y Prevision Social.

A renegade committee member who pursued an agenda distinct from his party caucus would quickly find himself reassigned. The policy preferences exhibited by Senate committee members must reflect the views of at least a substantial portion of their party delegations.

What emerges from an analysis that encompasses the details of Chile's legislative institutions and a careful mapping of Senators' ideological positions is a clearer picture of the pressure points in Chile's democratic transition. At one extreme voting records from the Constitution Committee indicate the human rights issue is highly polarizing, with members of the Concertación and the opposition Senators each taking a unified position against the other group. The analysis indicates little scope for compromise, and a very high level of cohesion, especially among the Concertación Senators. The Concertación formed around the human rights issue, and this continued to be a significant source of unity for the coalition until Pinochet stepped down as commander in chief of the armed forces to become Senator for Life. The seating of Pinochet in the Senate, and his subsequent October 1998 arrest in London on Spanish charges of murder, torture, and genocide, divided the Concertación, with some grudgingly accepting the Faustian bargain they had struck in allowing Pinochet impunity from prosecution while others could no longer contain their disgust and wanted him punished. The distances among members of the Concertación on these issues should not be exaggerated. The Concertación's Senate delegation voted in block and against the opposition on a pair of resolutions addressing the government's response to Pinochet's arrest, and the official positions of all of the Concertación parties have been supportive of the government in these matters. Shared disgust with the human rights legacy of the military government continues to be an important part of the Concertación's system of beliefs.

At the other extreme, the Concertación are deeply divided on social legislation, with a significant segment of the Christian Democratic party aligning with the parties on the right on social issues such as drug abuse and divorce. In part, this is a byproduct of the electoral system. In order to win the second seat in Chile's two-member Senate districts, one of the Concertación candidates must win the allegiance of some very conservative voters. One way to do this is to offer the electorate a candidate who is on the left on economic issues, but on the right on social issues. However, these candidates, who are competitive in the general election, tend to do badly in the internal politics of the Christian Democratic Party.

While Chile has been characterized as a blocked transition, in which the "authoritarian enclaves" of power have checked all meaningful attempts at reform, the picture that emerges here is more complex.

On human rights issues the characterization that the military and its political allies retain a policy veto is fairly accurate. The highly cohesive

7

issue position shared by the opposition Senators means that most human rights initiatives from the president are dead on arrival in the Senate. On education policy the lower degree of polarization and the executive's ability to bundle high-valence reforms with proposals that move education policy leftward mean that over time the Concertación has been able to move education policy steadily in their preferred direction.

On labor and social issues the picture is more surprising. The moderate position of institutional Senator William Thayer combined with the razor-thin majority enjoyed by the opposition in the Senate place the median Senator somewhere between the preferred issue positions of the Concertación and the policy advocated by most of the opposition Senators. This has given the government leeway to move labor policy leftward on this issue, which has traditionally divided the right and the left.

On social policy the conservative position taken by several of the Senate's Christian Democrats has meant that the opposition Senate majority has been redundant; even without it leftward reforms of social policy would be checked by an alliance between the socially conservative Christian Democrats, with their deep roots in Catholicism, and the Senators of the opposition.

The eighth and concluding chapter compares Senators' estimated preferred outcomes across issue areas and provides evidence that there are at least two issue dimensions to Chilean politics. The first concerns welfare state issues such as labor relations and education, but it also encompasses human rights, while the second is associated with Senators' stands on social issues including divorce, drug abuse, and other issues concerning personal morality. This second issue dimension harks back to the late-nineteenth-century divisions in Chilean politics over relations between the Catholic Church and the state. Because the Concertación divide on the social issues, the opposition has an incentive to focus on this issue area in an effort to pry apart the Concertación alliance on the welfare state, while those on the left have an incentive to keep the human rights issue alive as a means of reenforcing the beliefs that hold the Concertación together.

Consistent with the theoretical analysis of the conflict between the executive and the institutional enclaves, the highly polarized question of how to deal with the human rights abuses of the former military government has not been resolved. There is a high level of polarization, and high salience on the position issue of pursuing those guilty of human rights abuses committed under the auspices of the military government (on the left this issue is called "justice," while on the right it is referred to as "revenge") relative to the valence issue of reconciliation and reduced risk of future civil war. As the model predicts under such circumstances, the civilian government that took power in Chile in 1990 has done almost nothing to punish the human rights abuses committed under the auspices of the military regime; doing so would require repeal of the military's "self amnesty," which covers the vast majority of the unresolved human rights cases. During the first ten years of civilian rule in Chile the human rights issue has followed the recipe for gridlock; a policy area with high-salience polarized policy positions relative to the weight accorded to valence. However, this is a policy area in which the terrain may change very dramatically. While at this writing ten years of civilian rule have gone by with little progress toward solving the human rights crimes committed during the period of military government, these have also been ten years during which few new human rights abuses have been committed. If the current stalemate persists for another decade or two, those with direct personal involvement in the conflicts of the 1970s, when human rights abuses committed by the armed forces were most numerous, will no longer constitute a significant part of the voting public, nor will the officers who ordered extrajudicial executions and torture remain in powerful positions within the institutional enclaves. A generational change in leaders, and voters, may be expected to reduce the salience of justice, in the form of investigations and trials, relative to reconciliation, in the form of reduced willingness to risk Chile's partial democracy in order to arrest, or protect, the guilty.

To assess the lessons offered by Chile's ongoing transition we must first ask how well the Faustian bargains Chileans struck during the 1980s have served them during the 1990s. A useful anecdote helps to illustrate the question. A very energetic and talented young economic theorist went shopping in an antique store, and found a lamp he liked. He and the store owner haggled a while, and settled on a price of $100. As the store owner was writing up the sale, the economist interrupted; "I'll give you $99 for it!". "What do you mean?" replied the owner, with enraged surprise, "We agreed on a price of $100!". The economist then patiently explained that since the store owner had been willing to sell for $100, and he would have to wait to sell the lamp to someone else, tying up valuable space in his store and wasting time haggling with someone else, his reservation value for the lamp was certainly at least a bit under $100. Although his understanding of bargaining theory was impeccable, the economist soon found himself standing in the parking lot, sans lamp.

Like the antique dealer, the military government would probably have been willing to relinquish power on at least somewhat less favorable terms than it did. Many opponents of the former military government note this and argue that it proves the transition was a failure, that the Concertación sold out to the armed forces. But ex post regret at not pressing for more favorable terms must be weighed against ex ante uncertainty about how far the military government could be pushed. With the clarity of hindsight

9

it seems very probable that if the Concertación had insisted on a few more concessions the armed forces would have been willing to accede. But at the time this was far from obvious, while the improvements in Chilean society, notably a nearly complete end to further human rights abuses, at least by the second or third year of civilian rule, are not to be dismissed lightly.

While the Chilean transition toward democracy remains unfinished, leaving many frustrated with the slow pace of events, it compares well with alternatives such as civil war and continued military rule. Moreover, if social peace can be maintained for another decade or two, with no new round of military intervention in politics, the salience of the human rights issue may be expected to decline, opening the door to further reform.

A common view of the Chilean transition is that the institutional enclaves have prevented a full transition to democracy, saddling the country with "Pinochet without Pinochet." But when the powerful executive is weighed in the balance, the incompleteness of the transition from military rule can be seen as temporary. The speed with which the executive is able to move policy depends on the salience of conflict vs. the consensus elements of policy. In the Chilean transition this salience can be expected to fade as the generations that lived through the coup age, allowing further reform.

While it is clear that Chile is undergoing a transition from military rule, it is less obvious what sort of government this will be a transition to. As the Concertación gain control of the institutional enclaves, they will face a moment of truth. Thus far the coalition has been united around the objective of reforming the constitution to eliminate the institutional enclaves. As the opportunity to actually do so presents itself there will be a strong temptation to keep the institutions in place, using them to defend the Concertación's own policies, much as it has been used up to now to protect the status quo left behind by the military. That final chapter of the transition has yet to be written, and for now we may only speculate as to how the Concertación will choose. But much can be learned from what has already transpired.

How readily can the Chilean example be followed by other countries undergoing transitions from authoritarian rule? Chile's institutions, which have the effect of preventing change in some key policy areas, may be expected to work best when the issues dividing the sides are currently intense, but they can be expected to fade in importance over time, as with the importance of human rights prosecutions in Chile. The Chilean approach will not work so well when divisions will remain, or worsen. If an authoritarian government has targeted its victims along ethnic or religious lines, then we may expect that time will do little by itself to reduce the rancor that divides societies that come under authoritarian rule. Future generations with the same ethnic or religious identities as the victims may continue to identify with them and to seek "revenge" against their coevals with the ethnic or religious affiliation of the authoritarian government, who may in turn be inclined to take "preemptive" action, perpetuating a chasm of mistrust and fear into the indefinite future. Consider the attempt in Lebanon to guarantee mutual policy vetos for the Christians and the Muslims, or the attempts by Yugoslavia's Tito to repress ethnic conflict. In each case these measures simply delayed civil war for a generation, but they failed to prevent it.

The U. S. Constitution built in a series of guarantees dealing with the regional conflict over slavery, including the apportionment of extra seats in the House of Representatives for states with large numbers of (nonvoting) slaves, and for the continued importation of slaves until 1808. Later there was the implicit bargain to balance the entry of new states where slavery was illegal with states in which it was permitted, thereby giving the slave states a veto over policy at the national level. These institutions, like those left behind by Chile's military government, were designed to keep a dangerously polarizing issue off the agenda. However, over time the conflict between the slave states and the rest of the U. S. became more rather than less intense, and the institutional guarantees built into the constitution failed to avert civil war. Countries with deep and persistent ethnic, religious, or regional conflicts should be cautious about adopting the Chilean model, while those that can look forward to a reduced salience for the most divisive issues may find parts of the Chilean model worth adopting.

A PERSONAL NOTE

The democratic transition in Chile strains the boundaries between positive political science, which is concerned with why things happen, and normative politics, which concerns itself with what is right. This strain is always present in any scientific analysis of politics, but it is particularly intense here because moral arguments are part of the process one is trying to explain. The moral outrage felt by many Chileans over human rights abuses committed during the period of military rule is an important factor in their ideological belief systems, and it exerts a (partially) predictable influence on their political behavior. The importance of the use of ethical arguments by political actors during the transition makes it both more important and more difficult to draw the line between positive political science and normative politics.

It is impossible to remain neutral about either Chile's transition toward democracy or about the importance of the human rights violations of the military regime. For all its faults, democracy is the best form of government known, and it should be encouraged everywhere. The human rights record of the military regime is a part of the extensive weight of evidence for the superiority of democracy. Even if one were to accept the contention of those close to Chile's military government that in 1973 the country was already in the early stages of civil war before the military coup occurred, the vast majority of those killed by the armed forces, and of course all of the people whom they tortured, were prisoners who posed no immediate threat to their captors.

Some might point to the wretched human rights record of Communist regimes as a justification for the behavior of the military toward its prisoners. But this is no justification at all. The human rights record of many Communist governments is the most compelling indictment of that ideology; it does not constitute a reason to imitate those governments' worst features in the name of preventing their emergence!

But good intentions and a sense of moral outrage are of little use in preventing human rights abuses or nondemocratic rule, just as outrage at the ravages of disease does nothing by itself to prevent or cure sickness. Without scientific understanding, good intentions would never have eradicated smallpox. The politics of democratic transitions is vastly more complex than the lifecycle of the smallpox virus, but the importance of a clear understanding of the process is just as great. Without it those who are involved in democratic transitions would fare little better than our medieval ancestors when they faced epidemics armed only with their good intentions and quirky superstitions.

The effort here has been to focus on positive political science. If it is not possible completely and hermetically to seal off one's own sympathies from positive political analysis, it still doesn't hurt to try, and that is what I have done here. At the very least I hope that my own opinions on what should have happened, and what ought to happen, in Chile do not cloud the analysis.

1

Ideology and Valence

Legislators and their constituents alike weigh policy alternatives in terms of ideology, about which they disagree, and on the basis of shared public policy values, such as a desire for efficiency. The initial section of this chapter sets forth a simple model of policy preferences that incorporates both sets of considerations, policy position, and what Stokes (1963) referred to as policy "valence," and it helps to illustrate how the balance individuals strike between them can facilitate or prevent agreement on policy choices.

The second section of this chapter builds on the basic model of the first to analyze an important source of agenda control in legislative politics: the ability to formulate policies that mix controversial ideological departures from the ideological status quo with high valence. This is largely dependent on the ability of policymakers to deploy large expert staffs to help them formulate policy initiatives. In all presidential systems the executive enjoys an advantage on this score, an advantage that is substantial even in the U. S., where Congress is sometimes able to act as a "policy incubator." In Latin America, where legislatures must cope with very sparse infrastructure, the executive's advantage at formulating high-valence proposals is overwhelming. The ability to formulate high-valence proposals magnifies the executive dominance over the policy agenda that is written into many constitutions, while legislators' influence over the agenda can be severely curbed by their inability to formulate proposals with valence high enough to compete with the status quo.

1.1 A SIMPLE MODEL OF PUBLIC POLICY

The spatial model of politics can be traced back at least as far as the French Revolution, when legislative factions were ordered from those on the left, who wanted the revolution to proceed quickly, to those on the right, who advocated a more cautious pace. However, the spatial analysis

13

of policy preferences came into its own with the work of Harold Hotelling (1929), who exploited the analytical potential of the spatial analogy, while Anthony Downs brought this powerful tool to the notice of political scientists (Downs 1957). Since Downs there has been an explosion of theoretical and empirical work using the insights afforded by this framework.[1]

Spatial models emphasize peoples' disagreements over policy, with preferences being characterized in terms of an individual's most preferred policy outcome, which is represented by a spatial location, and policy being represented as a location in the same "space." Divergent policy preferences are represented by differences among individuals' most preferred locations. Romer and Rosenthal (1978) use the spatial framework to analyze the politics of school operating budgets. In their model people's preferred policies are characterized by the size of the budget they would like to see approved, while the policy "location" is simply the size of the budget actually passed. In this context the spatial analogy is straightforward; we can represent preferences graphically as locations along a line stretching from $0 at the left to some very large amount on the right. In this simple setting it is convenient to add the assumption of "Euclidean preferences," meaning that individuals prefer the policy option closest to their most preferred outcome. In the school budget setting this means that an individual will be indifferent between underspending his or her preferred level by an amount such as $100,000 and overspending by the same $100,000. While this may not be exactly the case for most people, departures from this approximation are likely to be fairly minor in the application to school budgets, and in many other interesting cases as well.[2] Euclidean preferences are not required to operationalize the spatial model, but they make the analysis more transparent, and they have the added advantage that they make empirical applications much more straightforward. The analysis here will adopt the additional structure contained in Euclidean preferences.

While the spatial model provides a versatile framework for analyzing political choices, it has become influential primarily for empirical reasons. It has long been noted that individuals' preferred outcomes tend to align across issues. For example, a Democrat serving in the Eighty-First Congress of the U. S. who voted not to recommit a bill to repeal the Taft-Hartley Act and for the extension of rent control could be confidently expected to have favored both the National Science Foundation and the Jensen amendment limiting strikes against the government, to have

[1] Those interested in a now slightly dated but illuminating introduction to the literature on spatial models are referred to Krehbiel (1988).

[2] At least over the range of alternatives actually considered by the voters; the parallel can be pushed to the level of absurdity by considering the possibility of spending negative amounts, or sums which exceed the U. S. GNP.

opposed creation of a Department of Health, Education and Security, to have voted to override President Truman's veto of the Communist Control Act, and to have taken a whole range of issue positions associated with being a moderate conservative on MacRae's (1958) "Fair Deal" scale. This predictability arises because people subscribe to ideological world views that shape their preferences across a wide range of specific policies.

There is no lack of controversy over just what makes up an ideology. Hinich and Munger (1994) provide a workable definition:

> Ideology: an internally consistent set of propositions that makes both proscriptive and prescriptive demands on human behavior. All ideologies have implications for (a) what is ethically good, and (therefore) what is bad; (b) how society's resources should be distributed; and (c) where power appropriately resides.

What is left ambiguous in their definition is the meaning of "internally consistent." Certainly in a strictly logical sense most ideologies contain self-contradictions. For example, the three basic principals of liberty, equality, and brotherhood espoused by the French Revolution not only contradicted many of the policies of the revolutionaries – beheading one's political opponents was unbrotherly even by the standards of the most dysfunctional family – they often stood in direct conflict with one another; respecting liberty is often impossible unless one is willing to tolerate inequality.

But an ideology is not a scientific theory; it is a set of core beliefs and emotional responses. Asked whether hourly employees should be made to "punch out" before taking coffee breaks, so that they receive no pay, a liberal Democrat does not need to make an involved calculation about the trade off between lost wages and the increased competitiveness, nor to make a careful comparison between the quality of free time spent sitting on a mud-covered wooden bench sipping coffee and breathing dust at a construction site relative to recreational time spent outside the workplace. The reaction is a visceral: "That's not fair!" Likewise for a conservative Republican, there is an immediate emotional response: "It's already scandalous how much employees get paid when they're pretending to work; paying them to loaf openly would be an outrage!" Adherents of ideologies share a series of emotional responses to issue positions.

The internal consistency of a successful ideology has two parts. First, it is perceived by adherents as being internally consistent, and second, adherents will react similarly to newly encountered issues, so that the ideology provides the same guidance (or nearly so) to its adherents. A conservative who prefers reduced workplace safety regulation by the government on the grounds that consenting workers and firms should be allowed to reach mutually acceptable working arrangements, arguing that the government should not impede individuals' freedom to choose, is

15

also very likely to favor vigorously enforced laws against the distribution of pornography by businesses to consenting adult customers. While the second issue position is logically inconsistent with the doctrine of government noninterference in voluntary exchanges used to justify the first, both issue positions are entirely consistent with a system of conservative values. For a political conservative the prospect of workplace safety inspections evokes an image of harassment and humiliation by arrogant and combative bureaucrats who would just as soon see businesses fail. Likewise, conservatives reject pornography as immoral, and are disgusted by what they view as sleazy opportunists who violate natural law by distributing and consuming it. Both reactions emerge from a set of beliefs and feelings about the world shared (with some variation) by adherents of an important strand of conservative political ideology, in Chile as in the U. S. A doctrinaire libertarian arguing for both less safety regulation and repeal of antiobscenity laws on the grounds both entail less government meddling is seen by mainstream conservatives as utterly out of touch and somewhat surreal. For its adherents an ideology is not a book full of rules, logically consistent or otherwise; it is simply common sense.

Twenty years ago no political party in the world had an AIDS policy, for the simple reason that the disease was as unknown then as its cure is today. However, as the disease emerged during the early 1980s in the U. S., the political ideologies of the left and the right provided quick and ready policy guidance, with the right favoring prevention while the left favored intensely funded medical research and subsidized intervention. This response to a previously nonexistent policy challenge was hardly a logical outgrowth of the ideologies of the left and right. In fact, the left often tended to favor prevention over intervention in other areas, such as anticrime policy, while the right often took the opposite position. Yet there was little confusion or discord among people at either end of the political spectrum over how to respond. The association of AIDS with homosexuality and drug abuse meant that prevention via abstinence from high-risk behaviors reenforced the right's preexisting opposition to homosexuality and drug abuse. Those on the left sought to intervene massively against the disease and to protect those infected from mandatory testing because the victims tended to be poor and/or to be the objects of discrimination. While neither response was a logical outgrowth of the ideology that spawned it,[3] both "made sense" to adherents and both emerged with little need for coordination.

---

[3] It is an interesting "thought experiment" to ask how the U. S. political parties would react to a widespread epidemic of the BCGE virus, commonly known as "mad cow disease," which is potentially as fatal as AIDS but is transmitted to humans by eating red meat.

This means that, while the spatial model provides an enormously useful framework for analyzing political choices, it also raises its own set of questions. The most fundamental of these is why people use ideologies at all. Why not simply calculate one's self-interest in a given policy question, and advocate policies accordingly? The reason why not probably has to do with the limited cognitive power of human beings. The "metamodel" of public policy that accurately predicts the social and economic consequences of each policy option has thus far eluded the combined efforts of the world's social scientists, so it is hardly realistic to expect voters and politicians to be able to make such predictions routinely when evaluating policy options. This is the point of departure for the literature on "bounded rationality" ignited by Simon (1982). Simon noted the difficulty individuals have in processing even fairly simple information, observing that they instead rely on heuristic rules of thumb for making decisions. These rules of thumb are used *instead* of fully rational and calculated decisions, and decision rules used by a boundedly rational individual may embody logical contradictions.

There are important connections between ideology and bounded rationality. Ideology simplifies complicated policy positions into positions in ideological space. The constellation of social and economic costs entailed by limiting the number of hours an interurban bus driver may remain at the wheel, from reduced traffic accidents, to higher bus fares, to changed bus schedules with extra stops, and labor market spillovers to the markets for truck drivers and urban bus drivers, are all reduced to an ideological position on a spectrum running from "extremely pro-labor" to "extremely pro-business." The status quo policy is likewise converted into an ideological location, and then voters and politicians alike compare these policies in ideological terms. As with any heuristic decision rule, this entails some loss of information; the policy does not affect all workers with the same allegiance to a pro-labor ideology equally. However, while ideology has practical consequences that resemble boundedly rational decision-making rules, this is not how it is perceived by adherents, who experience their ideologically colored world view as common sense.

Ideology has an additional practical effect – making it easier for voters (and interest groups) to monitor politicians (Lott 1992), and so easier for politicians to commit to policy positions. The empirical regularity is that politicians who change their ideological positions do not linger long in office. It is somewhat difficult to trace a politician's performance on a specific policy question; did he or she really do all that he or she could to change the "no strike" provision in a law? The monitoring problem for self-interested voters is a difficult one to solve. However, when a politician is committed to an ideological agenda rather than to a lengthy laundry list of unconnected promises, he or she becomes much easier to monitor.

If a politician claiming a pro-labor ideology abandons one group of workers, say longshoremen, this information can be easily summarized and shared – "The Senator took a pro-business stand; he was lying when he said he adhered to a pro-labor ideology." While this will be reason enough for voters with pro-labor ideologies to stop supporting the politician, it would also signal to a purely rational and calculating copper worker or public school teacher that the politician is not constrained by a pro-labor ideology, and might well abandon their interests as well once outside the public spotlight. Although ideologies are substitutes for rational pursuit of calculated self-interest, they can have practical effects that align with adherents' self-interest.

To be sure, the connection between self-interest and ideology is more than mere coincidence. Among respondents to the 1996 National Election Study, older respondents were less likely than others to favor reductions in Social Security, with only 1.7% of respondents over 55 years of age favoring reductions as opposed to 8.2% of those under 55.[4] Likewise, poor respondents were more likely to favor aid to the poor than were wealthy ones, with 60.8% of those with incomes below $9,000 per year favoring increased aid to the poor as compared with only 37.8% of those with incomes above $120,000.[5] Asked to locate themselves on a seven-point scale, on which a 1 corresponded to strong agreement with the statement that "The government should assist African-Americans" while 7 indicated agreement with the statement that "African-Americans should help themselves," 22% of African-American respondents located at 1

---

[4] Respondents were asked whether they wanted to see spending on Social Security reduced, maintained, or increased. Among 1,550 respondents providing sufficient data to permit the calculation, eighty-nine of those under age fifty-five wanted to see spending reduced, and 489 favored maintaining the current level, with the remaining 503 backing increased spending. Among the respondents aged fifty-five and over, eight favored reductions, 242 wanted the status quo levels continued, and the remaining 219 favored increased spending. A χ_2^2 test of the null hypothesis that age and the preferred direction of change in Social Security spending are independent yields a test statistic of 25.0792, corresponding to a p value of less that 0.00001 and leading to rejection at all standard significance levels.

[5] Respondents were asked whether they wanted to see spending on the poor reduced, maintained, or increased. Among 1,203 respondents providing sufficient data to permit the calculation, seven of those with annual incomes below $9,000 wanted reduced aid, thirty-one favored maintaining the status quo, and fifty-nine preferred increased spending. Among those with incomes in the $9,000 to $27,500 range, twenty-eight favored reductions, 134 the status quo, and 124 wanted increased spending. For those in the $27,500 to $120,000 range, 124 wanted reductions, 356 liked the current spending level, and 266 supported increased spending. Even among those with incomes of $120,000 and over, only eighteen favored reductions, while twenty-eight backed the status quo and twenty-eight favored more spending! A χ_6^2 test of the null hypothesis that income and the preferred direction of change in spending on the poor are independent yields a test statistic of 35.6962, corresponding to a p value of less that 0.00001 and leading to rejection at all standard significance levels.

18

while fewer than 1% of white males did so. At the same time, a larger fraction of white males, 21.5%, located at 7, while only 15.5% of African-American respondents did so.[6] Similar examples abound. In each case the margins respond to what most would recognize as self-interest. The elderly are less likely to favor reductions in Social Security, the poor are more likely to favor income redistribution to the needy, and African-Americans are more likely than white males to agree that government should assist African-Americans.

Yet people's policy preferences are not entirely driven by self-regard; in each of the cases mentioned above some individuals advocated policies that ran counter to their narrowly defined self-interest: three-eighths of those earning more than $120,000 per year favored increased aid to the poor even though they would likely enjoy none of the direct benefits of such a policy, while bearing much of its additional cost. The fraction of people under 55 favoring an increase in Social Security benefits, 46.4%, is virtually identical with the 46.6% of those above 55 who favor such an increase, while even among the elderly a few respondents favored benefit reductions. Similarly, while the fraction of African-Americans who located themselves at 7 (the "African Americans should help themselves" end of the scale on the question about government assistance for African-Americans) was lower than it was for white males, one-seventh of African-American respondents nevertheless took this position, which would seem at odds with their narrowly defined self-interest. Although ideological beliefs are not independent of individuals' personal stakes in policy, neither are they mere masks for self-interest.[7]

Given that people have ideologies, the web of connections linking ideology with policy choices becomes part of what North (1990) refers to as the "informal institutional structure," and it is as integral a part of the institutional framework as the formal written Constitution. Like the formal institutional constraints, ideologies change over time. Consider the odd swap of free-trade positions in the U. S. between the Democrats, who have become protectionist, and the Republicans, who now favor free trade, although historically these parties long held just the opposite set of beliefs.

---

[6] Among 608 respondents who were African-Americans or white males, and who provided sufficient data to permit the calculation, twenty-six African-Americans and only one white male placed themselves at 1, the "pro-aid to African-Americans" end of the spectrum, while eighteen African-Americans and 106 white males identified with a location at 7, the "African-Americans should help themselves" end of the spectrum. Based on the data for all seven possible response categories, a χ^2_6 test of the null hypothesis that the preferred level of government intervention on behalf of African-Americans and ethnic identity are independent yields a test statistic of 129.0241, corresponding to a p value of less that 0.00001 and leading to rejection at all standard significance levels.

[7] For a more extended discussion of the limited responsiveness of attitudes toward capitalism to one's personal economic circumstances, see McClosky and Zaller (1984).

However, as with major constitutional reforms, political realignments are infrequent. In the short run ideological preferences are stable.

At this point it is worth noting that, although much informal discussion of politics implicitly presumes that politicians align neatly from left to right along a single ideological dimension, it may be that individuals' policy preferences are informed by a mixture of several distinct ideological perspectives and are best represented in two or more dimensions. For example, we might expect that some policy areas, like labor policy, will cleave along a single dimension of conflict, with a spectrum of preferences running along a continuum from a prolabor outlook to a probusiness perspective. Likewise, we might expect environmental policy to cleave along a "conservationist" to "pro-user" dimension. Both of these policy areas would then be divided ideologically, with the degree to which one was pro-labor determining one's outlook on a host of workplace policy choices, while one's conservationist stand likewise implied a list of specific environmental policy choices. Yet there is no a priori reason to expect positions on labor policy and the environment to line up perfectly. A factory worker who enjoys hunting may simultaneously have pro-worker preferences on labor policy and yet favor pro-user environmental policies. Whether ideology reduces political conflict to one dimension or several is an empirical question.

While the map of the political battlefield is drawn in terms of ideology, Stokes (1963) noted that not all political issues were of the conflictive variety the standard spatial model handles best. He divided issues into two types: "position issues," which resemble the school bond example of the preceding discussion, and "valence" issues, such as honesty and integrity, about which voters all agree: all would agree that scandal is undesirable, and virtually all would agree that a hard-working politician is preferable to one who is not. Nor do valence issues pertain only to characteristics of candidates. In fact many legislative votes are unanimous ones – including very important decisions such as increases in the debt ceiling or declarations of war.

While some issues fit neatly into Stokes's dichotomy of valence and position issues, many others contain elements of both. Consider the example of the public's shared interest in vaccinating children against infectious diseases. Because inoculation does not confer perfect immunity, all are better off if every child is required to be vaccinated.[8] However, there may be less agreement about how the costs of vaccination should be born; wealthy parents and childless adults may be expected to prefer requiring parents to pay for their children's vaccinations, while less affluent parents might prefer a state subsidy for the inoculation. A proposal to

[8] Of course the benefit to childless adults with little contact with children may be very small.

subsidize vaccinations will resemble a valence issue (all will approve of the minor improvement in public health) and it will also resemble a position issue (people will disagree about the desirability of the small amount of income redistribution it implies). As with many issues, the proposal to subsidize vaccinations combines elements of position and valence issues, which we may view as idealized types. Most issues, no matter how consensual, can be translated into policy in different ways in order to appeal to different groups; most issues, no matter how divisive, leave politicians with some areas of agreement.

A simple analytic model that combines the valence and position aspects of issues represents policies in two dimensions. Along the first, or position dimension, preferences are represented as in the standard spatial model; all else being equal, the closer a policy is to an individual's preferred outcome along this first dimension, the better the individual likes that policy. Along the second dimension, all individuals agree about what makes for better policy; for example, all would find a given level of environmental protection more attractive if it could be achieved at a lower economic cost.

A simple model that captures these basic features represents an individual's preferences as separable between position and valence:

$$U(p, v; x, \alpha) = -\text{dist}(x, p) + \text{val}(\alpha, v) \tag{1.1}$$

where dist represents[9] the individual's preferences on the position issue and depends on the distance between the individual's most preferred outcome, x and the position content of the policy, p. The second element, val, represents[10] the impact of the valence content of policy, with higher values being more desirable, while high values of α represent greater intensity of caring about the valence aspect of policy, relative to the position element.

For the sake of illustration, it is convenient to work with some particular choices for dist and val. Here I will use the following linear-quadratic utility function:

$$U(p, v; x, \alpha) = -\frac{1}{2}(x - p)^2 + \alpha v. \tag{1.2}$$

The linear-quadratic functional form has the advantage of being readily adaptable to empirical applications, as will be seen in several subsequent chapters.[11] To illustrate the factors at work, consider the hours of workers employed in public transportation. There is a powerful public interest in

---

[9] Which is taken to be an increasing convex function of the distance between x and p.

[10] Which is supermodular.

[11] This model is very similar to a model of U. S. Congressional campaigns proposed by Londregan and Romer (1993). It is also related to the model of voting used in Alesina, Londregan, and Rosenthal (1993), though in that application the valence issue is economic growth, while inflation is treated as a pure position issue.

drivers being awake at the wheel, so that limits on the length of time a driver is permitted to remain at the wheel between rest spells lead to consensus improvements in the public good of road safety, represented by a high and positive v in the model. At the same time, the right and the left disagree about the details of how to implement such hourly limits. Should the limits that apply to interurban bus drivers also apply to truck drivers? Should train crews be included in the limit? What about drivers in urban public transit? Should drivers be paid for the time they spend in mandatory rest spells between turns at the wheel?

When the Labor Committee in the Chilean Senate considered these questions in March of 1993 as part of a series of proposed reforms to the Labor Code, Senators on the right and the left all agreed on the importance of keeping tired drivers off the roadways, but they balanced this shared concern against different ideological preferences. On the right Senator Miguel Otero, of the National Renovation Party, proposed strict hourly limits for interurban bus drivers, with a limit of four hours of continuous driving between rest periods (of at least an hour's duration) during daylight hours, and a three-hour limit on nocturnal driving. He also proposed that bus and train crews finishing trips of more than twelve hours should have a minimum rest period of at least eight hours before returning to work (Biblioteca del Congreso Nacional 1993a). A similar proposal was forthcoming from Senators Hormazábal and Palza, from the left-of-center Christian Democratic Party. However, these Senators proposed including truck drivers as well as bus drivers in the hourly limit (Biblioteca del Congreso Nacional 1993a).

Senator Palza argued the status quo of no regulation over the working hours of truck drivers was a dangerous factor contributing to Chile's high rate of traffic fatalities, adding that he had been lobbied to legislate limits on work hours by the truck drivers themselves. Senator Otero, for his part, argued that hourly limits for truck drivers would be all but impossible to enforce, given the solitary nature of truck drivers' work. He argued instead that special courses in road safety should be offered for truck drivers, contending that unprofessional drivers would pose a risk to public safety with or without legislated limits on their hours. The subtext was that mandatory rest hours would mean higher wage payments to truck drivers for a given trek, for example, bringing a truckload of goods from Concepción to Santiago, which with a mandatory rest period would represent more hours, and so a higher payment, for the driver. From the standpoint of the right, higher labor costs are in themselves undesirable, while there was scepticism about whether drivers would actually take the additional rest periods, or instead simply continue to work the same brutal hours and pocket the extra payment. Viewed through the pro-labor ideological prism of the left, higher payments to the truckers would represent an unambiguous improvement, however the drivers allocated the extra resources between more rest periods, leading to improved road safety, or higher earnings for their status quo work schedule.

A similar tradeoff between the valence concern with road safety and the ideological labor policy position emerged over an amendment proposed by Senator Otero, which, among other provisions, would have prohibited urban bus drivers from simultaneously acting as fare collectors. He argued that the proposed change would improve traffic safety by freeing drivers to focus all of their attention on the road (Biblioteca del Congreso Nacional 1993a). Of course, this policy would have required either a switch to a system of automated fare collection, not an inexpensive undertaking, or the presence of a fare collector on every bus, a change that could badly erode the earnings of the drivers. Mr. René Cortázar Sanz, the Concertación's Minister of Labor, expressed serious concerns about the effect the proposal might have on drivers' earnings, counseling against approving the amendment until the drivers' opinion had been canvassed. In this case it was the left for whom the proposal placed the valence and position elements of policy in conflict – Otero's proposal offered greater safety at the price of lower earnings for the drivers.

Equation (1.2) says that the farther the position p diverges from the individual's preferred outcome, x, the less the individual will like the proposal. The square term has the effect of penalizing both proposals that overshoot the individual's preferred outcome and those that fall short of it. The parameter α measures the relative importance of the valence element of policy and the position element. The higher the value of α, which we will take to be positive, the more the individual cares about the consensus element of the proposal, for example traffic safety, and the less weight he or she places on the position element, for example, the treatment of workers.

Now consider the choice of whether to support the proposal by Senators Palza and Hormazábal to include truck drivers among those subject to mandatory rest periods.[12] Suppose for the moment that if the proposal is not approved then only interurban bus drivers will be covered, an outcome represented in Figure 1.1 by a position of x_0 and a valence of v_0. As a member of the National Renovation Party, Senator Miguel Otero will prefer fewer fetters on the managers of trucking firms, and so he will tend to prefer narrower applicability of limits on the hours drivers can spend behind the wheel without rest. In order to comport with the convention that pro-labor policies lie to the left while pro-business policies are associated with the right, the axes are drawn with 100% of drivers covered on

---

[12] The graphical analysis in Figures 1.1 and 1.2 builds on the exposition in an earlier and unpublished version of Londregan and Snyder (1994).

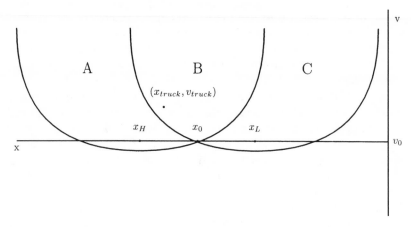

Figure 1.1. Hypothetical Policy Preferences: High Salience on the Valence Dimension.

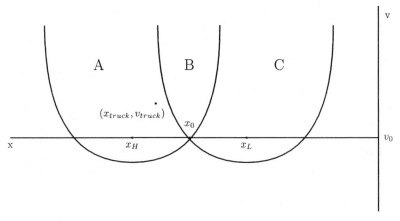

Figure 1.2. Hypothetical Policy Preferences: Low Salience on the Valence Dimension.

the left, and 0% of drivers covered on the right. We can represent the pro-business preferences hypothesized for Senator Otero as corresponding to a low level of regulation, represented by x_L in Figure 1.1. Senator Otero will prefer any proposal (x, v) that lies within the regions marked "B" or "C" to the reference policy. Thus he would prefer greater road safety than under the reference policy of covering only bus drivers, while at the same time he would like to see less constraint on business than under the reference policy. The curved lower boundary of the Senator's preferred region corresponds to the set of policy proposals (x, v) that leave Senator Otero just indifferent between the proposal and the reference policy (x_0, v_0) of

24

mandatory rest periods for bus drivers only.[13] Notice that Senator Otero is willing to approve measures that would shift policy "against" business, provided such policies compensate with sufficiently improved road safety. In contrast, Socialist Rolando Calderón is likely to prefer widespread coverage, corresponding to the policy position x_H, while he would agree with Senator Otero that, all else held equal, greater road safety is to be preferred. The set of policy proposals preferred by this Socialist Senator to the reference policy corresponds to the regions marked "A" and "B" whose lower boundary consists of the set of proposals that would leave him indifferent between the proposal and the reference policy.[14] As with Senator Otero, Senator Calderón is willing to accept a less favorable outcome on the position issue, but only if it yields a compensating increase in safety. The proposals that would meet with the approval of both Senators correspond to the region marked "B." This area of mutual acceptability consists of proposals that would result in sufficient improvement in road safety relative to the reference policy to compensate both Senator Calderón or Senator Otero for having to accept an extent of coverage at odds with his preferred outcome. Notice that the breadth of region B is greater at higher levels of valence. This is because both Senators are more willing to compromise when there is a large improvement in valence at stake. Thus we see that, with the hypothetical preferences shown in Figure 1.1, the policy of extending the restrictions on working hours to truck drivers lies within region B, meaning that both Senators prefer it to the policy of only restricting hours for interurban bus drivers. For Senator Calderón the choice is an easy one; extending the restriction to bus drivers moves policy to the left even as it improves road safety, at least somewhat. Given the hypothesized preferences, Senator Otero's decision is more difficult; on the one hand, he is attracted by the increase in road safety, but on the other, the restriction moves policy leftward, farther from his preferred position at x_L. However, because he places high weight on the valence issue of road safety relative to the position issue of labor relations, his hypothetical indifference curve through the policy of restricting hours for interurban bus drivers only has a very shallow slope, and the proposal lies above it, near the left-hand edge of region B.

Changes in the relative weight legislators place on the valence issue, road safety in this example, change the scope for compromise. Consider

---

[13] Formally we can express the set of points Otero, with a hypothetical preferred outcome x_L, prefers to the status quo as

$$P(x_0, v_0 \mid x_L, \alpha) = \{(x, v) \mid -(x - x_L)^2 + \alpha v \geq -(x_0 - x_L)^2 + \alpha v_0\}.$$

[14] Formally we can express the set of points Rolando Calderón with a hypothetical preferred outcome x_H prefers to the status quo as:

$$P(x_0, v_0 \mid x_H, \alpha) = \{(x, v) \mid -(x - x_H)^2 + \alpha v \geq -(x_0 - x_H)^2 + \alpha v_0\}.$$

the case portrayed in Figure 1.2, in which the preferred outcomes for Senators Calderón and Otero are still taken to be x_H and x_L, respectively; but now both Senators place less weight on the valence dimension of safety relative to their respective ideologies. We can represent this in terms of Equation (1.2) by their having lower values of α. This means that both individuals are less willing to accept ideological compromise on the question of rest periods. In the graph this reduced willingness means that for each the set of (x, v) pairs that are preferable to the status quo shrinks, with the lower boundaries sloping up more steeply as policy moves away from individuals' preferred policy outcomes. Consequently, the set of mutually preferred proposals, marked "B" in Figure 1.2, also shrinks; for a given level of safety gains the region of proposals that both Senators prefer to the status quo narrows. The policy of extending mandatory rest periods to cover truck drivers does not meet with the approval of both Senators with these more polarized preferences. While Senator Calderón continues to prefer the change, which from his perspective results in improvements on both valence and policy content, Senator Otero no longer attaches as much weight to the valence dimension relative to proposals' ideological content, represented by the steeper indifference curver, which now leaves the proposal point $(x_{\text{truck}}, v_{\text{truck}})$ beyond the edge of region B.

In this setting the level of political conflict depends on how dispersed individuals are on the position issue, and on how much weight they place on the position issue relative to the valence issue. If the differences among individual's desired regulation levels are relatively small, so that the two Senators differ little in the fraction of drivers they would like covered, represented by x_L and x_H being fairly close together, while the weight they place on the consensus issue of safety is relative great, so that α is large, then politics will tend to be consensual, with individuals agreeing about most proposals; those that fall short of the status quo for one Senator will usually do so for the other; those representing a policy improvement for one will usually entail better policy for both. But as either of these conditions changes, politics become more confrontational; when individuals place relatively little weight on safety levels they become less willing to compromise on other aspects of working conditions. Likewise, the larger the differences in their preferred levels of pro-labor regulation, the smaller the set of proposals that will meet with consensus responses.

Why Valence Varies

If politicians were able to freely choose the valence of their proposals, there would be no limit to the consensus appeal of their ideas. Because all agree that higher valence makes any proposal more attractive, authors of bills and amendments would always choose "infinite" valence if they could. Of course, this is not an option. Instead politicians search for proposals that combine desirable position content with high valence. However, not all politicians are equally successful at generating high-valence proposals, nor do all proposals written by the same author exhibit equal consensus appeal. The variation among proposals' valence is attributable to several sources, including differences in authors' substantive expertise, and heterogeneity in their ability to communicate persuasively. While some proposals handily trump the valence of the status quo, some mediocre amendments garner only the vote of the authors who spawned them.

Part of the reason high-valence proposals are hard to formulate is the complexity of legislation's "side effects." Consider the recent controversy over the effects of minimum wages. In the U. S. Democrats, and the unions that support them, typically prefer to see higher wages; Republicans, and the business enterprises that support them, typically would prefer wages to be low. Minimum-wage legislation is designed to increase wages, a subject about which Democrats and Republicans disagree. However, economic theory tells us that price floors, such as minimum-wages, can dampen demand. In the context of minimum-wage legislation this means reducing employment, a valence issue; politicians of all tendencies would prefer low unemployment to high unemployment. In deciding whether to support an increase in the minimum wage from, say $4.50 per hour to $5.15, there is little uncertainty about the implied shift on the position issue of higher wages; all politicians recognize that this would represent a shift to the left. At first glance there is much less certainty about the employment consequences. While most would expect some employment losses as the result of such a hike in the minimum wage, it is unclear just how extensive this job loss would be. To alleviate this problem legislators might call upon economists with labor market expertise. To the extent there is professional consensus about the aggregate demand elasticity for labor, the legislators might obtain a fairly precise estimate of the valence outcome. With an accurate unemployment forecast, those willing to pay the price in extra unemployment would prefer the increase; everyone else would vote to reject it. But when expert opinion varies the choice becomes more difficult. Thus the recent flurry of controversy over a series of studies by Card and Krueger (1995) of the impact of the minimum wage. These economists have also reanalyzed earlier work by others, and they find little impact on employment from minimum-wage increases. These results conflict with the standard policy analysis of the unemployment consequences of minimum wages by economists of all political persuasions,[15]

---

[15] See, for example, the literature surveyed in Brown, Gilroy, and Kohen (1982).

and so the new evidence may have led many politicians to reevaluate the impact of an increased minimum wage on the valence policy outcome of employment.

The difficulty of formulating policies without undesirable side effects is by no means restricted to such traditional legislative instruments as minimum wages. Consider a socially conservative legislator who wants to take a sterner stance toward drug abuse by accelerating the priority of cases against people accused of violating the anti-drug-abuse laws and imposing harsher penalties on those convicted. A legislative proposal to do this will move policy rightward on the position issue of social policy, a shift that will appeal to those on the social right and repel those on the left. It will also have an impact on valence issues, such as public safety, prison crowding, congestion of court calendars, and the cost of maintaining the criminal justice system. To at least some extent drug abuse appears to increase the likelihood that someone is involved in other forms of crime, such as robbery. Thus a law that deters drug abuse may also reduce the rate of crimes against people and property. However, without a careful criminological study it is difficult to forecast the precise level of reduction stemming from, say, adding an extra year to the prison sentence meted out for possession of a few grams of marijuana. Offsetting this potentially benign side effect is the question of congestion of the court calendar, which may delay the hearing of cases against robbers and murderers, and the impact on prison crowding. If prisons are crowded to capacity with drug abusers, prosecutors might pursue other types of crime less aggressively. Both the congestion of the court calendar and of the prisons might therefore reduce the effective penalties for other forms of crime, leading to reduced valence. Also, more aggressive enforcement of the laws against drug abuse might be expected to increase the costs of the criminal justice system, another negative valence issue.[16] It is entirely conceivable that when the members of a legislative committee began to study a proposal for harsher enforcement of the anti-drug laws, they might conclude that it actually embodies less valence than the status quo.

Similar examples can be found in almost any policy area. Changes in the tax code can also have undesirable consequences for policy valence: imposing what economists call "dead weight losses," for example, by deterring investment. Tax reductions may also have unfavorable consequences: a reduction of tariffs on imported automobiles may lead to lower valence in the form of increased traffic congestion and lower air quality.

[16] Highly specialized interest groups, such as felons and prison guards, might hold a different view of a reduced deterrent against violent crime or of increased spending on prisons, but these are very close to being valence issues, with the vast majority agreeing on the desirability of keeping both crime and prison spending low, all else held equal.

A bill granting a pay increase for public school teachers may lead to layoffs and larger classes, while a badly written law may create damaging loopholes.

Consider the example of an amendment to article 23-A of the Labor Code proposed by the Socialist Senators Calderón, Gazmuri, Nuñez, and Vodanovic, joined by Christian Democrat Arturo Frei, and by Laura Soto of the Party for Democracy. This amendment had the object of guaranteeing minimum rest periods for workers on factory ships. Among other provisions, it required that workers be guaranteed a minimal rest period of at least eight uninterrupted hours per day. Yet this pro-worker measure had unexpectedly negative valence, and met with the unified opposition of both the worker's association[17] and the association representing the owners of factory ships.[18] This is because the standard work schedule in the industry involved two six-hour shifts of work and two six-hour rest periods every twenty four hours. To change this to accommodate the eight-hour rest requirement would utterly disrupt the ships, a prospect that dismayed the shipowners and met with fierce opposition among the workers, whose earnings were calculated in part on the basis of the quantity of fish processed (Biblioteca del Congreso Nacional 1993a). The authors of this unsuccessful measure had neither the personal acquaintance with the industry to foresee the problems with their proposal nor the staff resources to follow up on even its most direct consequences.

A second and related source of difficulty emerges when everyone recognizes that the policy consequences of a proposal are hard to forecast. Starting from their insight that legislators propose and vote over bills but care about policy outcomes, Gilligan and Krehbiel showed that uncertainty about the ideological content of a proposal, that is, about its position p relative to the status quo, acts like a valence issue. When legislators have quadratic utility over a position issue, and they are uncertain about the policy $\tilde{p}$ that will result if they vote for a bill which yields an expected policy of $E\{\tilde{p}\}$ and variance $\sigma^2 = Var\{\tilde{p}\}$, Gilligan and Krehbiel (1987) show that the expected utility of voting for the policy is equal to the expected utility of voting for a policy with position $E\{\tilde{p}\}$ and valence $-\sigma^2$. This very neat coincidence between uncertainty and policy valence is special to the case of quadratic utility. Suppose instead a legislator cared about the absolute value of the gap between his or her preferred outcome x and the actual policy outcome $\tilde{p}$, as in Equation (1.3):

$$U(p, v \mid x, \alpha) = -|x - p| + \alpha v \qquad (1.3)$$

In this case the effects of uncertainty will depend on the legislator's

---

[17] The Federación Nacional de Tripulantes de Naves Especiales de Chile.

[18] The Asociación de Buques Fabricas Arrastreros e Industrias Conexas.

preferred outcome and the expected policy outcome, as well as on the policy variance.[19] The effects of uncertainty are felt unequally in this case, with those closest to the expected policy outcome μ the most risk averse, while those who are far enough away from it are oblivious to the uncertainty. In general, uncertainty about the policy position that will be implemented by a particular bill is not the same as negative valence, but it is similar, and in some interesting special cases, such as quadratic utility, uncertainty about a policy's position is a valence issue. In general we may expect uncertainty about policy outcomes to work in favor of the status quo. Authors with extensive staff resources may be better able to compensate for this intrinsic disadvantage by adapting their proposals to a changing policy environment; those with limited expertise and small staffs will be less able to compete with the valence of the status quo.

While there may be considerable ex ante uncertainty about the policy consequences associated with new proposals, there is little about the consequences for legislators who are shown ex post to have favored poor policies. Political opponents and journalists have much to gain from bringing these proposals to wide public attention, and few voters will be swayed by an argument that their legislator had simply made a mistake (McGraw 1991)! This means that before making a proposal public its author must consume time and effort to forecast its policy consequences. The costliness of this activity limits the number of proposals that can be made. Experts with greater ability at forecasting policy consequences will be able to achieve a given level of "quality control" over their proposals with a smaller investment in time and energy, and so can be expected to sponsor more frequently.

1.2 LEGISLATIVE COMPETENCE AND AGENDA CONTROL

The central questions during a transition toward democracy revolve around how divergent policy goals among citizens are to be resolved. In authoritarian environments the national leader simply implements his or her most preferred policy options, subject only to the weak and aleatory

---

[19] For example, if $\tilde{p}$ is uniformly distributed with mean $E\{\tilde{p}\} = \mu$ and variance $\mathrm{Var}\{\tilde{p}\} = \sigma^2$ while the valence of the proposal is known to equal 0 and the legislator's utility function is as given by Equation (1.3), then the expected utility of the proposal is

$$E\{U(p, v \mid x, \alpha)\} = -E\{|x - p|\}$$
$$= -|x - E\{\tilde{p}\}| - f^*(x, \mu, \sigma)$$

where

$$f^*(x, \mu, \sigma) = \begin{cases} 0, & \text{if } x < \mu - \sqrt{3}\sigma \\ \frac{[\sqrt{3}\sigma - |x - \mu|]^2}{2\sqrt{3}}, & \text{if } |x - \mu| < \sqrt{3}\sigma \ . \\ 0, & \text{if } x > \mu + \sqrt{3}\sigma \end{cases}$$

constraint that the indulgence of his or her whims does not provoke a coup or mass uprising.

More democratic forms of government employ more inclusive institutions for vetting policy choices. This typically involves popular elections for a legislature, and, in presidential systems, for a national leader as well. Further institutional details specify who may run, how conflicting ballot choices are translated into electoral outcomes, and how conflicts among the goals of elected representatives are resolved.

A key ingredient in the institutional brew is the allocation of agenda control. In parliamentary systems this control lies with the government. In some presidential systems, notably that of the U. S., the executive does not enjoy a monopoly on policy initiatives, and bills originating in the Congress often become law without help from the executive, and in some cases, bills are even implemented over the president's strong objections.

However, in the presidential systems of Latin America the executive typically enjoys a de facto monopoly on legislative initiatives. To be sure, many constitutions, in and out of Latin America, accord explicit monopoly proposal powers in certain policy areas. The French Constitution requires that bills in the "domain of regulation" be sponsored by the government (articles 34 and 41), as must any bills that would lead to either net increases in spending or net reductions in revenues (article 40). These features of the French Constitution are echoed by similar restrictions in the Chilean Constitution, where they apply to the president, for example article 60, which will be discussed in Chapter 3. It is true that institutional guarantees of executive proposal monopolies are not encountered in all of Latin America's presidential systems, and when they are they are often limited to certain policy areas and do not extend across the entire spectrum of legislation. Nevertheless, it is hard to imagine any of the region's legislatures playing the role of "policy incubator" so often taken by the U. S. Congress.

Latin American legislatures lack the resources to act as agenda counterweights to the executive. In contrast to the U. S. Congress, with its lavish staff resources and in-house expertise in the form of organizations such as the Congressional Budget Office, and the world-class research facilities of the Library of Congress, legislatures in Latin America must make due with sparse staffs and austere research budgets. Not only must Congressional staff resources stretch simply to hold committee hearings, reply to mail, and maintain the Hansard, but even more importantly, the executive has vastly greater resources for policy formulation at his fingertips. A determined president can draw on the manpower and experience of entire executive agencies to formulate policy.

While this huge imbalance of resources is not formally written into any constitution, it is a salient feature of what North calls the "informal institutional structure" of these countries, indelibly coloring executive–legislative relations throughout Latin America. A simple analytical model serves to illustrate how the inability to formulate proposals with an acceptable valence can frustrate even a proposer with a formal institutional monopoly over the legislative agenda, while conversely, the ability to formulate high-valence proposals further expands the influence accorded by the ability to put proposals on the agenda. This model shows that even when formal agenda control is shared, if only one proposer is competent to formulate alternatives to the status quo with acceptable valence, that proposer becomes the de facto agenda monopolist.

Starting with the preferences set forth in Equation (1.1) of the previous section, it is convenient to adopt the following functional forms for the distance function and for valence:

$$\text{dist}(x, p) = |x - p|$$
$$\text{val}(\alpha, v) = \alpha v \tag{1.4}$$

so that the preferences of an individual with a preferred policy location x and valence weight α are represented by Equation (1.3) shown in the previous section. The distance function used here differs from the quadratic form set out in Equation (1.2), which makes the results much more tractable, and helps to clarify the focus on the ability to formulate high-valence proposals.

Presidential Agenda Setting

While the model developed here will characterize conditions under which the executive needs no formal proposal monopoly in order to be the de facto agenda setter, it is useful to begin with a reference model in which the executive does hold such formal powers. I will then compare this with the polar opposite case in which it is the median voter in the legislature that enjoys a proposal monopoly.

Suppose that the executive and a unicameral legislature both care about a one-dimensional position issue, for example the degree to which the tax code equalizes the distribution of income, and that in addition policy has a valence aspect about which both agree; think of this as something like the efficiency of the tax code. In the first version of this example, the executive enjoys a proposal-making monopoly and can propose policy to the Congress under a "closed rule." Such constitutional provisions do exist in practice; the Chilean Constitution (article 70) allows the executive to offer a constructive veto in which the executive can introduce new language that is put to an up or down vote against the status quo. Only if the Congress rejects the new language is an override vote taken on the initial segment of the bill passed by the Congress and vetoed by the executive. When the president can count on blocking the veto override, the new language introduced in a constructive veto amounts to a take it or leave it offer vs. the status quo. The package vote in article 44.3 of the French Constitution (Huber 1996) allows the government a similar ability to make a take it or leave it offer.

This stylized constitutional framework corresponds to the setter model of Romer and Rosenthal (1978), save for the addition of valence considerations in the model. For the time being, let's ignore variations among executive proposals' valence, so that all executive proposals enjoy a common valence, q. The executive is free to propose any policy position, y, to be considered against the status quo policy. Thus, the executive proposal is characterized by the pair (y, q), where the valence, q, is fixed, and beyond the executive's control, while the policy position, y, is an element of choice.

When the executive proposes a policy (y, q) it is voted without amendments by the Congress against the status quo, which is also characterized by a policy position, and a valence. Without loss of generality, the position and valence pair for the status quo can each be normalized to equal 0. In this simple setting, suppose that the policy choice is made once and for all, so that neither the president nor the voters in Congress evaluate the policy proposal in terms of its impact on future rounds of executive–legislative bargaining. This means that the median voter in Congress will support the executive's bill provided it yields higher utility.[20]

Substituting from Equation (1.3), this condition becomes

$$\alpha q > |y - x_c| - |x_c|$$

Let $\text{win}(z, r \mid q, x_c)$ denote the "position win set" for a policy with position z and valence r when the proposal has a valence of q and the median voter in Congress has a preferred policy location of x_c. This is the set of policy positions that would prevail against a status quo of (z, r) when the executive can make proposals with valence q. Applying this notation, the win set for the status quo of $(0, 0)$ in this example[21] is written $\text{win}(0, 0 \mid q, x_c)$. Provided the executive can make higher-valence proposals than the status quo, so that $q > 0$, the executive will propose a policy position y inside the position win set for the status quo $\text{win}(0, 0 \mid q, x_c)$ that comes closest to his or her own preferred outcome.

---

[20] Formally the median member of Congress will back the executive proposal provided

$$U(y, q \mid x, \alpha) > U(0, 0 \mid x, \alpha).$$

[21] Formally, $\text{win}(z, r \mid q, x_c)$ consists of the set of all y which satisfy

$$U(y, q \mid x_c, \alpha) > U(z, r \mid x_c, \alpha)$$

substituting from Equation (1.3) this condition becomes

$$\alpha(q - r) > |y - x_c| - |z - x_c|.$$

A minor complication arises when the executive is not able to make proposals with higher valence than the status quo. In this case the position win set may be empty, or it may be that no member of this set represents an improvement for the executive over the status quo. In this case, an executive with an agenda monopoly will simply keep the gates closed and propose nothing, thereby guaranteeing the continuation of the status quo policy.

Consider for now the outcome when the executive is able to improve on the valence of the status quo. The outcome depends on the strength of the executive's valence advantage over the status quo, q, on the preferred policy outcome of the median member of Congress, x_c, and on the executive's own policy preferences, captured by the presidential ideal point x_p. While these outcomes vary continuously, there are five generic types of outcomes.

First, we may observe executive dominance. This occurs when a policy proposal that combines a valence of q with the president's most preferred policy position, x_P, dominates the status quo from the standpoint of the median voter in the Congress. From the perspective of the executive, this is as good as it gets: the president can have exactly his most preferred policy position, and at the same time the valence of policy rises to q. This class of outcomes corresponds to outcomes like the one illustrated in Figure 1.3.

The horizontal axis in Figure 1.3 corresponds to the position component of policy, while the vertical axis measures the consensus appeal of proposals. If we think of the executive and the legislature as setting tax policy, the case illustrated corresponds to a president who is to the left of the median legislator, with a preferred policy of x_P, placing more weight on income redistribution than the congressional median, while the status quo, normalized to equal 0, is to the right of the congressional median, with even less redistributive content than Congress would like to see. Although the position of the status quo is closer to the congressional median's most preferred policy position than is the president's, this is not enough to guarantee that Congress will reject the president's proposal. This is because the valence element of the status quo, which in this illustrative example corresponds to the economic efficiency of the tax code, is lower than the valence of proposals the executive is

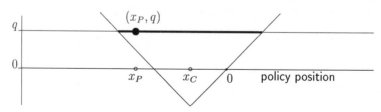

Figure 1.3. Executive Dominance.

capable of generating. This might arise if the status quo involved inefficient inflation taxes, while the executive was able to propose a more efficient but also more redistributive income tax. The median legislator with moderately conservative preferences on economic policy, represented by x_c, then makes tradeoffs between policy valence and the ideological content of policy. The V-shaped pair of lines in Figure 1.3 corresponds to the set of proposals that would leave the congressional median just indifferent between the proposal and the status quo. Notice the contrast with the rounded indifference curves encountered earlier in Figures 1.1 and 1.2. The linearity of the indifference curves in this illustration stems from the linear specification in Equation (1.4) adopted for this example. Because presidential proposals will all have a valence element of q, and so will contribute αq to the utility of the congressional median, we see that the position win set for the status quo corresponds to the thickened portion of the horizontal line at a height of αq. The president will then seek to propose the most attractive element of this set, which from his or her perspective is the point (x_P, q), which gives the executive his or her most preferred policy position. Notice that, in this example, the president uses his or her ability to make proposals with higher valence than the status quo to gain approval of a policy with a position element that is more distant from the congressional median than is the status quo.

A symmetrical type of executive dominance can arise if the president and Congress are both to the right of the status quo, with the president more extreme than the Congress, but not too much more extreme, so that the Congress, when presented with a take-it-or-leave-it offer of (x_p, q), will prefer it to $(0, 0)$.

In contrast with the leeway open to the executive in the example depicted in Figure 1.3, if there is greater divergence between the preferences of the executive and the legislature, as in the case shown in Figure 1.4, the executive will be compelled to compromise with the legislature, adopting a tax policy that is less redistributive than he or she would like. In the illustration all is as it was in Figure 1.3, save that the president is farther to the left, at x'_P.

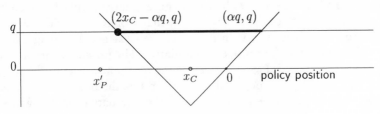

Figure 1.4. Legislative Executive Compromise.

In this case, the president is not able to entice the congressional median into voting for a policy position at x'_p, because this position is simply too far to the left of x_C. Even with the inducement of higher valence, at q, the median legislator still prefers the more proximate policy position of the status quo, at 0, despite its lower valence. However, this does not mean that the president is unable to improve on the status quo. To the contrary, he or she can still propose a policy substantially leftward of the congressional median. The executive can pull policy even farther leftward of the congressional median than the status quo is rightward of it because of the valence advantage. The position win set of the status quo for this situation corresponds to the heavy line segment from $(2x_C - \alpha q, q)$ to $(\alpha q, q)$. From the executive's perspective the most desirable element of this set is found at the its leftward edge, at $(2x_C - \alpha q, q)$. This is still not as far to the left as the executive would like, but it is as far as the median congressional voter can be pushed before he or she rebels, even with the executive's valence advantage at making proposals.

A similar outcome of executive–legislative compromise mirrors that illustrated in Figure 1.4. In this second type of compromise the president is far to the right of Congress, which in turn is located rightward of the status quo. This case is symmetrical with that shown in Figure 1.4; the executive can induce Congress to cooperate in moving policy rightward as far as $2x_c + \alpha q$ before Congress loses its appetite for further compromise. The Congress is grudgingly willing to let policy "leapfrog": its preferred outcome of x_c, to a point on its right. With the added inducement of a higher-valence proposal, the executive can even extract congressional approval from a policy that moves somewhat farther rightward of Congress than the status quo is to its left. However, as in the symmetrical case illustrated in Figure 1.4; the executive cannot parlay this into congressional approval for the president's most preferred policy position, which from the perspective of Congress is too extreme to accept in exchange for the status quo even with the higher valence the president is able to offer.

Another possible outcome is shown in Figure 1.5, with the status quo located between the executive and the median member of Congress. With no valence advantage this would lead to pure gridlock, with the executive unwilling to propose any policy option that Congress would prefer to the status quo. However, with the executive's valence advantage, there remains some scope for presidential initiative. The president can procure congressional approval for any point in the position win set of the status quo[22] win $(0, 0 \mid q, x_c)$, depicted in Figure 1.4 as the heavy line segment from $(-\alpha q, q)$ to $(2x_c + \alpha q, q)$. Among the alternatives in the win set

---

[22] As in the other examples, the position of the status quo is normalized to equal 0.

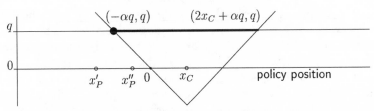

Figure 1.5. Near Gridlock.

$(-\alpha q, q)$ comes closest to the executive's preferred policy position of x'_P. At this point the extra valence just compensates Congress for the leftward shift in policy. However, the executive is not able to move policy as far to the left as he or she would like; the best attainable point in this situation is still to the right of x'_P, the preferred policy position of the executive.

A similar case of near gridlock arises when the status quo is bracketed by the president's most preferred policy on the right, and the congressional median's ideal policy position to the left. This case is symmetrical with that shown in Figure 1.5; the executive can pull policy rightward as far as αq but no further. The logic is the same; the Congress would prefer to see policy move closer to its ideal point, and farther from that of the executive. All of the president's leverage comes from his or her ability to offer higher valence; as soon as this currency is expended, by moving policy αq toward the executive, there is no further room for compromise.

There is also a special case of executive dominance, in which the president's most preferred policy corresponds to a point such as x''_P in in Figure 1.5 that is between $-\alpha q$ and 0. When this happens the president does not need to use all of the leeway his or her ability gives to make high-valence proposals, and instead of proposing a policy of $(-\alpha q, q)$ the president is able to propose his or her most preferred policy of (x''_P, q). This can happen whenever the executive and the legislature are on opposite sides of the status quo and the president's preferred position is close enough to the status quo so that the higher valence of presidential proposals is able to compensate the legislature for the policy shift away from their most preferred outcome.

The results from the preceding discussion are summarized in Figure 1.6, which shows how policy outcomes respond to the preferences of the executive, x_p, and the legislature, x_c. The different qualitative results discussed above correspond to different regions of this figure. For preference parameter pairs (x_c, x_p) in region F_2, below and to the right of the line $x_p = 2x_c - \alpha q$ and to the left of the x_p axis,[23] we have outcomes of executive–legislative compromise, including the case depicted in

[23] The x_p axis consists of all the points for which the congressional median has a preferred outcome equal to the status quo; $x_c = 0$.

37

Figure 1.4. The region marked D_2, to the right of the x_p axis and below the line $x_p = -\alpha q$, corresponds to cases of near gridlock such as the one portrayed in Figure 1.5, with the executive able to move policy only αq leftward of the status quo. The very extensive region marked E corresponds to preference parameter pairs that result in the executive's being able to propose and get his or her most preferred policy position. Regions D_1 and F_1 correspond to regions of near gridlock and executive–legislative compromise when the executive's preferred policy is to the right of that of the legislature.

As the president's ability to make high-valence proposals increases, the preference parameter pairs that result in the executive getting his or her most preferred policy position, corresponding to the region marked E in Figure 1.6, expands, while the regions of executive legislative compromise, and of near gridlock, become smaller, and arise only when presidential

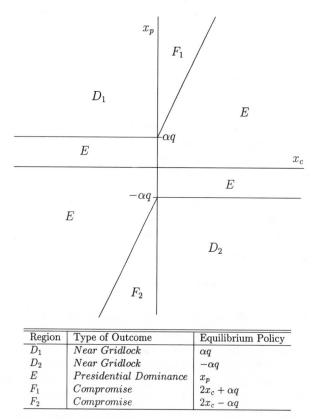

Region	Type of Outcome	Equilibrium Policy
D_1	*Near Gridlock*	αq
D_2	*Near Gridlock*	$-\alpha q$
E	*Presidential Dominance*	x_p
F_1	*Compromise*	$2x_c + \alpha q$
F_2	*Compromise*	$2x_c - \alpha q$

Figure 1.6. Presidential Preferences, Congressional Preferences, and Policy Outcomes: $\alpha q > 0$.

preferences are more distant from the status quo. For a president with an agenda-setting monopoly the ability to make high-valence proposals enhances the executive's ability to influence the outcome. The greater the valence advantage, the wider the range of presidential dominance, and the more favorable the compromises that can be made with the legislature.

Congressional Agenda Setting

Taking this example of presidential agenda setting as a benchmark, let us now turn our attention to what we may think of as the polar opposite case, in which the constitution makes the congressional median the agenda-setting monopolist. In technical terms, this description perfectly fits the U. S. case, in which the executive is not allowed to initiate legislation and is presented with bills that have passed both houses of Congress, which the executive must either accept or veto without amendment. Of course, U. S. presidents have substantial de facto proposal-making capacity, and they never seem at a loss for members of Congress willing to act as formal sponsors of presidential initiatives. However, to understand better the role of the ability to formulate high-valence proposals, it is useful to analyze a hypothetical example in which the legislature does enjoy such a proposal monopoly.

Formally, suppose the median member of a unicameral legislature proposes a policy pair (y, q^*), where y is the position element of policy, which the legislative median is free to choose, while q^* is the valence of policy proposals made by the legislature. As in the analysis of the presidential proposal monopolist, the valence of proposals is taken to be fixed at q^*: all proposals from the congressional median have the same valence. The congressional proposal is then presented to the executive as a take it or leave it offer. Think of this as a Congress with a sufficient minority of executive supporters to sustain presidential vetos reliably. In this case, the executive will support the bill if it provides higher utility.[24]

Substituting from Equation (1.3), this condition becomes:

$$\alpha q^* > |y - x_p| - |x_p|$$

With the use of the previously developed notation for the position win set, the set of policy positions that will escape presidential veto when the status quo is normalized to have a position and valence of 0 is $\text{win}(0, 0 \mid q^*, x_p)$. If the valence of congressional proposals, q^*, were the same as the valence of presidential proposals in the preceding example of a presidential proposal monopolist, then the qualitative outcome would

---

[24] Formally the condition is

$$U(y, q^* \mid x_p, \alpha) > U(0, 0 \mid x_p, \alpha).$$

be the same as well, with the labels for the president and the congressional median switched to reflect the change in proposal power. Yet the assumption that congressional proposals will enjoy the same valence advantage over the status quo simply because the constitution is amended to accord Congress monopoly proposal power is an optimistic one. Only if the change is accompanied by a substantial reallocation of resources will the median member of Congress be able to duplicate the proposal-making capacity of the executive.

Suppose that in contrast with the previous example of a presidential proposal monopolist, the valence of congressional proposals is below that of the status quo, so that $q^* < 0$. This example is useful in that it illustrates the most extreme disparity with the proposal-making competence of the executive. However, while it helps to clarify the issues, it is not entirely farfetched as a characterization of some real-world legislatures. We might expect to see low valence relative to the status quo in a legislature with limited staff resources and a small or nonexistent research budget, the typical case in Latin America. It is one thing to propose lower taxes, it is quite another to calculate the margins. Which taxes should be cut? By how much? How will these changes affect revenues? Which tax brackets should be reduced? Should sales taxes adjust to offset part of the revenue loss? For a host of policy questions, from harsher prison sentences to reform of the laws governing workplace safety, the devil is in the details. Keeping the details under control requires a large and expert staff. When the president decides to cut taxes by 3% he or she can set entire executive agencies to work on the details, forecasting and minimizing the deadweight costs of adjusting various margins of the tax code to rebate money to the electorate, targeting political friends, and limiting the inefficiencies of the tax code. Tiny congressional staffs, no matter how insightful or hardworking, simply cannot overcome the enormous volume of research required to formulate efficient policies of this type, or even credibly to forecast their actual impact. This limitation on the valence of congressional proposals substantially curbs the legislature's ability to mount successful policy initiatives.[25]

As with the presidential proposal monopolist, the policy outcome depends on the preferences of the median legislator, x_c, on executive preferences, x_p, and on q^*, the valence of congressional proposals. Because accepting a congressional proposal means a reduction in policy valence from 0 to q^*, with a loss in utility of αq^*, the congressional median will never propose reforms if his or her most preferred outcome is within a

---

[25] Of course, if the legislature were powerful enough it could remedy this lack of staff by voting itself a larger budget for that purpose, something Latin American legislatures don't do.

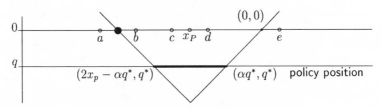

Figure 1.7. Congressional Proposals.

radius of $-\alpha q^*$ of the status quo.[26] This is because the most advantageous policy Congress could possibly propose, with a position of x_c and a valence of q^*, would result in an improvement in the utility of the policy position of $|x_c| < -\alpha q^*$ and a loss in utility of $-\alpha q^*$. By similar reasoning, if the executive's ideal point is within a radius of $-\alpha q^*$ of the status quo he or she will be guaranteed to veto any congressional initiative. The best Congress could offer would be the executive's most preferred outcome of x_p, but when x_p is close to the status quo of 0 even this complete concession on the position issue would not be enough to compensate him or her for the reduction in valence.

Figure 1.7 shows several possible outcomes with a congressional policy monopolist. Only when the executive and the legislature are both sufficiently far from the status quo will there be potential for Congress to find attractive reforms that will avoid a presidential veto. Suppose that the president's most preferred policy of x_p is to the left of the status quo position, here normalized to equal 0. The dilemma faced by Congress stems from the low valence of its own proposals. The position win set for the status quo is shown in Figure 1.7 as the dark line segment from $(2x_p - \alpha q^*, q^*)$ rightward to $(\alpha q^*, q^*)$. These points are sufficiently close to the president's ideal point to compensate for their lower valence as compared with the status quo at $(0, 0)$. If the congressional median has a preferred point such as a or b in the diagram, to the left of the position win set, the best that the congressional median can do is to propose a policy position of $2x_p - \alpha q^*$. This corresponds to executive–legislative compromise, with Congress succeeding in moving policy somewhat closer to its preferred outcome than the preferred point of the executive, but nevertheless facing a serious obstacle in the form of the low quality of the proposals it is able to formulate. At points such as the ones marked c and d, with the congressional ideal point sufficiently close to that of the executive, Congress is actually able to dominate the policy process, proposing and getting its most preferred position. Notice, however, that the possibility of

[26] Recall that q^* is negative, so that $-\alpha q^* > 0$.

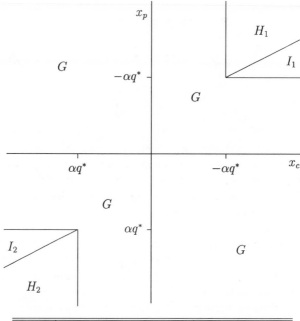

Figure 1.8. Congressional Counterproposals and Policy Outcomes with $\alpha q^* < 0$.

Region	Type of Outcome	Equilibrium Policy
G	*Gridlock*	0
H_1	*Congressional Dominance*	x_c
H_2	*Congressional Dominance*	x_c
I_1	*Compromise*	$2x_p + \alpha q^*$
I_2	*Compromise*	$2x_p - \alpha q^*$

replacing the status quo fades to the vanishing point as the quality of the proposals Congress can make falls below $\frac{x_p}{\alpha}$, the valence that corresponds to the apex of the V-shaped presidential indifference curves in the diagram. Finally, even if the president and the Congress are both distant from the status quo, gridlock may still arise if Congress's preferred policy position is to the right of the edge of the position win set. In this case Congress prefers the status quo to any proposal that could escape a presidential veto.

The relationship between the equilibrium policy position, the valence of congressional proposals q^*, and the preference parameters for Congress, x_c, and the executive, x_p, are summarized in Figure 1.8. The most striking contrast between Figure 1.6, which illustrates outcomes when the executive is the dominant proposal maker, and Figure 1.8, in which Congress has the proposal franchise, is the immense region of complete gridlock, labeled G, that arises when Congress is the proposer. Whenever the president and the congressional median are on opposite sides of the status quo, gridlock is guaranteed. In contrast, when the executive is the proposer, his or her ability to formulate higher-valence proposals parlays into an ability to nudge policy in his or her preferred direction. Moreover, the region of complete gridlock with Congress as the proposer is even larger, expanding as the valence of congressional proposals falls. This additional region of gridlock, which can emerge even when the Congress and the executive are on the same side of the status quo, for example when they would both prefer a policy position to the left of the status quo, emerges when the preferred policy of either the Congress or the president is sufficiently close to the status quo that even the prospect of shifting the policy position to match their most preferred outcome is not enough to compensate for the low valence of congressional proposals. The lower the valence of congressional proposals, as measured by q^*, and the higher the weight members accord to policy valence, the larger will be region G of preference parameter combinations leading to gridlock. As congressional proposals become more mediocre, the regions of congressional dominance, H_1 and H_2, and of executive–legislative compromise, I_1 and I_2, recede further and further from the origin. When Congress is only able to make very low-valence proposals, even a proposal-making monopoly may not suffice to permit Congress to move the policy position.

Of course, the institutions of the preceding examples, with either executive or legislative proposal monopolies, are extreme cases. Even constitutions that give the executive monopoly control of some aspects of the agenda, such as the Chilean and French constitutions, nevertheless leave substantial policy areas within the ambit of congressional proposals. But even without formal exclusivity for the executive, the preceding examples show how limited legislative staff resources can enable the president to dominate the policy debate. Even with a proposal monopoly the Congress is unable to formulate policy initiatives in region G of Figure 1.8. If the formal institutional structure is more symmetrical, allowing some proposal-making power to both the Congress and the executive, congressional counterproposals in region G will still be dead on arrival because of their low valence. When the legislature is restricted to making only very low-valence proposals and counterproposals, so that the spectrum of political opinion lies within region G, legislative proposals are doomed to failure, and we can restrict our analysis to executive proposals. To paraphrase the former Russian Czar, "Not the constitution, but 10,000 clerks make the president agenda monopolist." At least, they do so when, as is the case throughout Latin America, the Congress does not have similar resources. If the president is the only source of viable proposals it matters little whether or not the constitution formally allows Congress to initiate legislation. In either case the executive enjoys a de facto agenda monopoly, and in either case something like the model in Figure 1.6 with presidential agenda control describes the legislative process.

Competence and Agenda Control

The preceding examples illustrate the importance of being able to make high-valence proposals. Even if it were armed with a proposal monopoly, Congress's capacity to direct the agenda would be very limited unless it could also formulate high-valence alternatives, an option that is mostly out of reach for legislatures with limited staff resources. The impact of limited staff resources is particularly heavy when, as in Chile, proposals must be made and adjusted on short notice and according to a timetable fixed by the president. If a legislator cannot predict the revenue losses stemming from a bill to reduce the sales tax, or tailor a tariff increase so as to minimize the distortions to incentives given the revenue being generated, the legislator has little chance of persuading others to vote for it, and even less of escaping a presidential veto if against the odds her or his proposal does win the support of her or his colleagues. This is what is being captured by the low-valence term of legislative bills in the model of the preceding section.

This rolls the question back a level: given that small legislative staffs allow the executive to dominate the legislative process, why doesn't the legislature respond by voting itself more staff resources? This is what has happened in the U. S., where individual members of Congress have extensive personal staff and can also draw on the resources of the standing committees and of organizations such as the congressional Budget Office. In Chile, as in almost all of Latin America, the situation is different, and the staff resources of the executive dominate those of the legislature.

A potential answer to why the Chilean legislature allows itself to be outgunned by presidential staff resources probably has two parts. First, article 60 of the Constitution of 1980 requires that all bills that would entail a spending increase must be sponsored by the president. This means that the Congress could not take the initiative in proposing more extensive staff for itself; it would instead have to persuade the executive to do so. Given the likely effects on the executive's ability to dominate legislation, this is something most presidents would be loath to do in the absence of considerable pressure from public opinion. Although once armed with serious staff resources Congress could become a substantial adversary to the executive, article 60 of the Constitution enables the president to keep the congressional genie bottled.

The second part of the explanation for scant legislative staff resources must answer the question: "Why does public opinion not rally to the idea of increasing legislative staff?" For members of the Concertación, presidential dominance is appealing while they continue to control the presidency. With the backing of a substantial majority of the population and direct popular election of the president, the Concertación can confidently look forward to controlling the executive for some time to come. For the foreseeable future executive dominance of staff resources means Concertación dominance of staff resources. In contrast, and for the time being, much of the opposition's legislative mission is to blockade changes to the status quo that was left in place by the military government. While being able to formulate effective counterproposals would be useful in this effort, it is not vital to their success, and explaining to their voters why they should press for more staff resources does not resonate well with their ideological message that spending should be reduced.

A Comparison with Other Spatial Models

The incorporation of valence into the one-dimensional spatial model leads to somewhat different predictions than those generated by spatial models without valence considerations, whether they are of the one-dimensional or multidimensional variety. Because these other models are widely applied, it is useful to compare the qualitative predictions made by the model with valence used here with the predictions that would be made by these other models.

The most straightforward comparison is with the one-dimensional model without valence. This is really just a special case of the model set forth in Equation (1.1), with the valence set equal to the status quo for all proposals:

$$\text{val}(\alpha, v) \equiv 0.$$

This leads to equilibrium outcomes shown in Figure 1.9 that are intermediate between those depicted in Figure 1.6, where even partial gridlock is rare, and the equilibria shown in Figure 1.8, where full gridlock is the rule rather than the exception. However, when proposals lack any valence advantage over the status quo, we will observe full gridlock whenever the status quo policy position lies between that preferred by the agenda setter, which in Chile means the president, and the preferred outcome of the veto player, here the Congress.

If this one-dimensional agenda-setter model with no valence applied during the Chilean transition, what would we expect to observe? With a Concertación president and an opposition Congress we might expect to see many cases in which the preferred outcome for Congress lay slightly to the left of the status quo and considerably to the right of the president, leaving us in the region marked H_2 in Figure 1.9. This would lead to

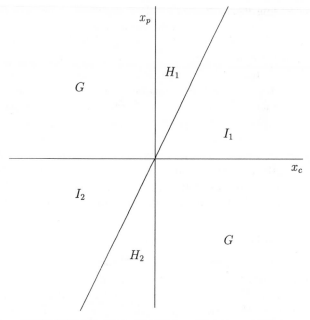

Figure 1.9. One-Dimensional Agenda-Setter Model Without Valence.

Region	Type of Outcome	Equilibrium Policy
G	*Gridlock*	0
H_1	*Presidential Dominance*	x_p
H_2	*Presidential Dominance*	x_p
I_1	*Compromise*	$2x_c$
I_2	*Compromise*	$2x_c$

a number of one-time-only legislative executive compromises, involving policy shifts from a status quo at 0 to a new point, at $2x_c$, to the left of the congressional median. After that we should observe gridlock, with the status quo policy between the preferred outcomes of the president and the legislature. With the exception of the annual budget, this gridlock would entail the passing of virtually no bills.

A more complicated equilibrium would result if instead the status quo were subject to what we might view as random ideological drift, with old policies, for example, tariffs once favored by the right to protect import competing industries, taking on new ideological coloration, as, for example, when trade unions defend tariffs on labor intensive imports. While this process may proceed glacially, it complicates the executive agenda setter's decision of when to propose a legislative–executive compromise. If the status quo were to drift rightward then an executive on the left could extract even more favorable concessions from the median

46

member of Congress; leftward drift would correspondingly undermine the executive's bargaining position. The decision of how and when to time proposed reforms would then turn into what is known as an "optimal stopping time" problem. While this possibility is not fully modeled here, with slow and ideologically neutral drift in the status quo, so that leftward drift is as likely as rightward drift, we might expect to see a flurry of proposal activity as soon as the Concertación came to power, followed by large spans of time with no legislative activity beyond the annual budget.

While the subsequent chapters will provide considerably more detail, it is safe to say that the observed regularity of a steady stream of legislation coming from the executive and gaining approval in the legislature is inconsistent with the predictions of the one-dimensional model with no valence. In contrast, as will be made clear by the discussion in Chapter 8, we can expect a very different set of outcomes when valence is part of the picture, with a steady stream of presidential proposals chipping away at the status quo, gradually reforming policy in the executive's preferred direction. The observed steady stream of legislation since 1990 is at variance with the long spells of complete gridlock predicted by the one-dimensional model with no valence, while it is entirely consistent with what we would expect from the model that does incorporate valence.

A second problematic implication of the one-dimensional model without valence is its interpretation of unanimous votes. The model with valence can readily explain unanimous votes in favor of or against a policy option as resulting, respectively, from very high or very low levels of valence. In contrast, without valence a unanimous vote must be explained in terms of the relative locations of the proposal and the status quo. Barring an unusual string of idiosyncratic preference shocks that all line up heavily against a proposal, something that by definition will be a rare occurrence, proposals that are unanimously rejected must have been farther than the status quo from each of the legislator's preferred outcomes. Likewise, unanimously accepted proposals must have been closer than the status quo to each of the legislator's preferred points. Yet we observe substantial variation in the reception given proposals from the same legislator. Moreover, this is observed for authors across the political spectrum. For this to occur in the one-dimensional model would require, among other things, that authors near the center of the spectrum routinely make proposals with such radical ideological implications that even voters at the extremes of the spectrum prefer the status quo to the proposal. This seems less plausible than the notion that authors simply have the occasional bad (low-valence) idea, such as the failed amendment regarding work schedules on factory ships discussed earlier.

Multidimensional spatial models are more difficult to analyze. McKelvey (1976) showed that except in very special circumstances that are extremely unlikely to hold in practice, no proposed policy is stable, and with an open agenda all are subject to an endless and chaotic stream of successful counterproposals. With a monopoly agenda setter this chaos disappears as long as the same agenda setter retains the proposal monopoly, and provided the congressional median is well defined across issue dimensions.

The key qualitative difference between the multidimensional spatial model and the single-dimensional version is the potential for logrolling across issue areas, with the agenda setter offering to move policy away from the veto player's most preferred outcome on some dimensions, which are less important to the veto player than to the agenda setter, in exchange for shifting policy closer to the outcome the veto player would most like on other dimensions, which matter less to the agenda setter than to the veto player.

If such multidimensional logrolls were taking place, one would expect to hear complaints from at least some politicians; those for whom the dimension on which the agenda setter demanded concession was important, as well as from politicians seeking to stake out a clear ideological position. Occasionally this happens. Consider the reaction of Christian Democratic Senator Lavandero to a proposed constitutional amendment that would have abolished the institutional senators, an outcome favored by the left, in exchanged for a series of supermajority thresholds for reforming laws in sensitive areas such as taxation, an outcome preferred by the right. The Senator complained that the bargain was unfavorable, saying "I know how to fight the Institutional Senators, and we can win, but this proposed constitutional amendment is forever" (interview with Jorge Lavandero, May 20, 1997). The proposed amendment failed.

Rhetoric suggesting multidimensional logrolls, with rightward movement on some policies combined with leftward movement on others, is rare. Part of the reason for this is that Chile's legislative institutions make such multi-issue logrolls difficult. Article 66 of the 1980 constitution forbids amendments that are not germane:

> Every bill may be the object of additions or corrections during the legislative process, in the Chamber of Deputies as in the Senate; but in no case are admissible those that do not have direct relation with the essential or fundamental ideas of the bill.

This germaneness requirement is usually enforced by committee chairs, or on the occasions on which germaneness questions arise during a debate on the Senate floor, by the president of the Senate. However, these decisions can be appealed to the Constitutional Tribunal, which is still heavily influenced by the former military government. The right can use article 66 of the Constitution to object to amendments that add an additional issue dimension, and they can expect a sympathetic hearing by the Constitutional Tribunal if the issue is contested.

If the appeal process does not serve the left they have other means to block an amendment they view as not germane. To begin with, the Chamber of Deputies, where the Concertación are a majority, can reject the amendment, forcing formation of a conference committee. If this fails, there remains the stopgap of the president's veto power. Article 70 creates a line-item veto option for the president, allowing the president to strike parts of a bill that he or she does not like, and even to offer amendments, called "observations," which must themselves be germane to the bill. Congress must then consider these observations under a "closed rule," that is, without further amendment. While this veto power is much more general, it allows the president to block any amendments he or she does not consider germane, even if they are not blocked by the Constitutional Tribunal.

Any bundling of issues by way of a nongermane amendment is subject to reciprocal vetos by the left and the right. As a practical matter, this means that either side can force a policy bargain that is as favorable as the one it would get by voting on the issues one at a time. Only if a single bill tapped several distinct issue dimensions from the outset could multidimensional amendments be considered germane. Even in this case the various veto players might succumb to the temptation to declare hostile amendments not germane. Otherwise, the institutional framework will slice up a multidimensional environment to be voted one issue at a time. With the issue space voted one dimension at a time, the behavioral implications of a multidimensional spatial model without valence considerations closely resemble those of its one-dimensional counterpart. For the reasons already mentioned, if issues are voted one dimension at a time, the high rate of unanimous votes is hard to explain without appealing to valence.

2

Accident and Force

For the first two-thirds of the twentieth century, Chile enjoyed perhaps the most stable democracy in South America. All of this changed in the early 1970s after Salvador Allende became president at the head of a leftist coalition that included both Socialists and Communists. His administration, which came to power by perfectly legal means, sought to carry out socialist policies that created sharp divisions among Chileans, with some embracing his plan for a "Chilean Way" to socialism while others viewed Allende as a stalking horse for an eventual Communist dictatorship. Because the electorate divided fairly evenly between enthusiastic supporters of Allende's Popular Unity (UP) government and its determined enemies, democratic resolution of this conflict was difficult. By the third year of the Allende administration the country was in crisis, with increasing levels of violence and a collapsing economy. At this point the military intervened, as it had done twice before in the twentieth century. But this time several thousand of their real and suspected enemies "disappeared" or were killed, and the armed forces remained in power for over sixteen years.

The crisis of the early 1970s and the long period of military rule that followed had a profound effect on both the ideological climate and the institutional environment. Since the early 1970s there have been two histories of Chile. On the political right, people recall takeovers of farms and factories by groups of workers, and the economic collapse and civil unrest of the UP government's final year, which they perceive as the inevitable result of an attempt by the UP government to impose a Marxist dictatorship on Chile. From their perspective the military takeover came at the last possible moment and barely saved the country from plunging into an abyss (Allamand 1989). On the political left, the economic privation and civil unrest of the Allende years are thought of as the work of "the facists on one side and the agents of the CIA on the other,"[1] while

[1] From the pro-Allende newspaper *La Nacion*, quoted in Biblioteca del Congreso Nacional (1973).

the entire political right are seen as accomplices in the killings and disappearances perpetrated during the period of military rule. These distinct histories have percolated into the ideologies of the right and the left and continue to influence Chilean politics.

During its years in power the military government sought to "lock in" guarantees against a return of the crisis of the early 1970s. The most important of these guarantees came in the form of a new Constitution, which the military government promulgated in 1980. While it has much in common with Chile's earlier constitutions of 1831 and 1925, its authors wanted to make it impossible to construct a socialist state within the Constitution of 1980. In the words of Sergio Diez, one of its authors, "The tome is not neutral because Allende wanted to impose socialism, as he said in his speech of May 21, 1973. It [the Constitution of 1980] contains anticommunist values" (interview with Sergio Diez, May 27, 1997c). On the left many would agree with Senator Diez's assessment of the Constitution as locking in policy, though they do not share his enthusiasm for the policies that it has entrenched, glumly referring to the status quo as "Pinochet without Pinochet." In the words of Alexander Hamilton, Chileans have joined the many who have been "destined to depend for their constitutions on accident and force" (Cooke 1961).

This chapter sets the stage for an analysis of legislative institutions in Chile's transition. The first two sections discuss the ideological legacy of Allende and Pinochet, and the military government's search for legitimacy, which led it to write a new constitution. The fourth section of this chapter discusses the surprising electoral reversal suffered by the military regime in the plebiscite it held in 1988. Pinochet's defeat astonished the aging dictator, if not those around him, while the willingness of the armed forces to accept defeat was a surprise for many on the left. However, the armed forces did not leave power without first locking in a final round of institutional guarantees that continue to influence Chilean politics long after their departure.

The third section of this chapter extends the formal model of Chapter 1 to encompass the framing of the Constitution by the military government to provide a preliminary analysis of the nature of the policy guarantees set forth in the Constitution of 1980. This analysis shows that the non-neutrality of the Constitution is very real, and that it takes the form of a built-in tendency toward partial gridlock, with the president's ability to make high-valence proposals partially alleviating the intensity of the gridlock. The discussion also takes up the puzzle of why the military government agreed to the Constitution's provision for a plebiscite to be held in 1988, a plebiscite which Pinochet lost. While many attribute this decision to hubris, the analysis here indicates that the special nature of the gridlock built into the Constitution of 1980 could actually provide the

51

military government and its supporters with greater policy guarantees than they could extract from any dictator, even Pinochet, who remained free to change his mind. This tendency to gridlock built into the Constitution continues to preserve many of the policies of the military government long after its departure.

This preliminary analysis of the Constitution makes some heroic assumptions; the democratic opposition are treated as all sharing the same policy objectives, as are the armed forces and their political allies, and the president is treated as an agenda setter able to make high-valence proposals. The analysis of the subsequent chapters goes into the details of the institutional foundations of the president's agenda-setting power, in Chapter 3, and policy objectives of the executive and the legislators, in Chapters 4–7. As the subsequent analysis will show, the characterization in section three of this chapter of the president's agenda-setting power is a reasonable approximation, at least during the Aylwin administration, which corresponded to the initial years of the transition. The highly polarized preferences, with the government and opposition each uniting around closely shared policy objectives, is a better characterization of some policy areas, notably education policy and human rights, than others, such as legislation concerning labor policy and social issues. Likewise, the executive's ability to make high-valence proposals varies across issue areas. A more detailed analysis of the workings of the policy guarantees embedded in the Constitution, in Chapter 8, must await the more detailed description of the institutional constraints and politicians' policy preferences in the intervening chapters.

2.1 THE IDEOLOGICAL LEGACIES OF ALLENDE AND PINOCHET

Salvador Allende and the man who seized power from him, Augusto Pinochet, have come to symbolize two competing histories,[2] histories that now divide the right and the left in Chile. To be sure, neither of these histories is a balanced account. But the purpose here is not to sort out the relative merits of these competing versions of the tragic events of the 1970s and the 1980s, but to examine how they influence the ongoing transition toward democracy. What is important for an analysis of the ongoing democratic transition is not whether these different accounts are correct, but that they are each believed by different segments of Chilean society.

[2] For those interested in forming their own judgments, there are probably more shelf feet of library space devoted to the events leading up to the 1973 coup than to any other period of Chilean history. For a concise analysis of the breakdown of democracy in Chile in the early 1970s, see Valenzuela (1978); a more detailed account can be found in Sigmund (1978). Readers interested in a general account of the period of military rule might start with Constable and Valenzuela (1991), or Spooner (1994).

Accident and Force

The View from the Right

On the political right Salvador Allende is demonized as a man who abused his position as President of the Republic by trying to impose socialism on Chile, with or without the consent of the governed. The memory of the Allende years continues to haunt those on the political right, and they are resolved to never again allow totalitarians disguised as democrats into power. From this perspective the military regime saved the country at the brink of disaster, and any blame for the harsh measures it took should be placed at the doorstep of the left for leaving democrats with no other alternative short of supporting military intervention. From the viewpoint of many on the right, complaints about the human rights record of the military government hold people coping with a mortal crisis to an inappropriate standard. As a one-time supporter of the military coup put it shortly after the military intervened: "It is very easy to turn oneself into a judge of others who are fighting while one is comfortably seated at the desk" (El Mercurio 1997).

People on the right recall the economic collapse and civil unrest of the UP government's final year, which they perceive as the inevitable result of an attempt by the UP government to impose a Marxist dictatorship on Chile. The UP government went forward with extensive nationalizations of private businesses. Not only did it "intervene" in such foreign enterprises as Anaconda, ITT, and Kennacott, but many domestically owned companies were taken over as well, notably those with connections to the political opposition, such as the Edwards Bank, and the country's largest publishing house (Sigmund 1993). However, the UP government's success in running these businesses did not match its zeal in taking them over; by 1973 these enterprises were losing large amounts of money (Urzua 1975). Opposition to the UP government greatly intensified when many small-business owners, notably the independent truck drivers, began to suspect that even their enterprises were on the UP government's list of eventual targets for expropriation.

There is little doubt that during the early 1970s policymakers in Washington were hostile to Allende and wanted to "make the economy scream" (Staff Report of the Select Committee on Intelligence Activities 1976). Yet despite U. S. Ambassador Edward Korry's threat that "not a nut or bolt would be allowed to reach Chile under Allende" (Staff Report of the Select Committee on Intelligence Activities 1976), the Allende government successfully renegotiated payments on $800 million in debt with a group of creditors that included U. S. banks (Staff Report of the Select Committee on Intelligence Activities 1976). The overall effectiveness of the U. S. effort to make Chile's economy "scream" has been called into question (Sigmund 1993).

53

Whether as a result of U. S. sanctions or not, it is clear is that by mid-1972 the Chilean economy was in trouble. Food imports soared in 1972 and 1973 (Sigmund 1993). Inflation, which had averaged 38.5% during the period 1950–1970, shot up to 205.2% in 1972 and 599.4% in 1973 (Urzua 1975). As with inflation, so deficit spending, which had already become a chronic problem during the preceding decades, worsened during 1972 and 1973: by 1973 the fiscal deficit was equal to 53% of total government expenditure (Urzua 1975). The combination of high inflation and price controls led to food shortages and a thriving black market (Sigmund 1974).

The legitimacy of a coup was enhanced by increasingly open exhortations from politicians for the military to intervene. On August 22, 1973 in the Chamber of Deputies Hermógenes Pérez de Arce, a member of the politically conservative National Party asserted "the executive branch has ceased to contain itself within the Constitution and the law, which has given rise to the illegitimacy of the President of the Republic, whom Chileans cannot continue to obey," remarks which found attentive listeners among the armed forces (Huidobro 1989). The resolution subsequently adopted by the Chamber was somewhat more temperate, calling on the government not to appoint military men to the cabinet, and on the soldiers in the government to resign from their cabinet posts (Junta Militar 1973), but it was nevertheless interpreted by some as lending at least tacit support for a military coup against the UP government (Sigmund 1974).

The armed forces moved closer to the brink of insurrection when, in August 1973, the Navy announced it had uncovered a conspiracy involving several active-duty sailors and three prominent figures associated with the UP government: socialist Senator Carlos Altimarano, Oscar Garretón, a member of the Chamber of Deputies, and Miguel Enriquez, Secretary General of the leftist organization MIR (Huidobro 1989). The conspiracy allegedly involved plans for a mutiny aboard a Chilean Naval vessel. Rather than denying the accusations outright, Altimarano enraged many in the armed forces by saying that the discussions were meant to undermine the military chain of command in the event the armed forces attempted a coup. But when a coup followed the next month, only the crucial topmost link in the military chain of command was interrupted – the link between President Allende and the armed forces. Senator Altimarano narrowly escaped the country, but many other UP participants were not as lucky.

When asked about the military government's human rights violations, Andrés Allamand, a prominent civilian politician on the right, responded that the UP government would have done the same had they been able. When journalists Florencia Varas and Mónica González followed up by asking whether the UP government had treated street protesters as the military government did he replied: "No. Because they could not, not because they didn't want to. We were treated badly to the extreme that they could reach. It wasn't benevolence; they went as far as they could." (Allamand 1989).

The View from the Left

On the left the same history is remembered very differently. The predominant view of the UP government is that it was a noble attempt at implementing "social justice," an attempt that was given little or no chance to succeed because of strident opposition aided and fomented by the United States. To the extent that they are critical of the "mistakes" of the UP government, many still view it as the last legitimate government of Chile. Their post-coup experiences have further served to stir their anger and harden their resolve against anything associated with the military regime.

On the left, the economic privations of the Allende period are blamed on a U. S.–led "invisible blockade" of Chile. There is certainly evidence that trading with the U. S. became more difficult during the Allende years. Consider the U. S. Import–Export Bank's refusal to extend Chile credit to buy three Boeing passenger airplanes (Farnsworth and Feinberg 1973). Moreover, there was a wider decline in the availability to Chile of short-term U. S. commercial credits, which by 1972 had fallen 90% from their level during the Frei years. The U. S. government opposed the emergence of another socialist government in Latin America, in addition to that in Cuba, and the fact that it had been selected through a democratic process did not dispel the concerns of presidential advisor Henry Kissinger, who remarked, "I don't see why we need to stand by and watch a country go Communist because of the irresponsibility of its own people" (Hersh 1983).

A strike initiated in October 1972 by independent truck drivers in Chile's southern Aysén province snowballed into a national confrontation, with truckers and large segments of the middle class joining the truck drivers. To at least some extent, this strike appears to have received support from the U. S. government. One report asserted that "the majority of the $8 million authorized for clandestine C.I.A. activities in Chile was used in 1972 and 1973 to provide strike benefits and other means of support for anti-Allende strikers and workers" (New York Times 1973). However, the precise magnitude of support for the truck drivers' strike is hard to measure. The "Committee of 40" that oversaw covert U. S. operations never approved direct aid to the striking truckers (Staff Report of the Select Committee on Intelligence Activities 1976), neither during their 1972 strike nor in a subsequent stoppage that began in July 1973. Yet as the Senate Committee Staff Report on covert action in Chile noted, "all observers agree that the two lengthy strikes ... could not have

Table 1. *Party strength and human rights violations*

Party	Vote share in the 1969 deputies' elections[a] (%)	Vote share in the 1973 deputies' elections[a] (%)	Victims of human rights violations[b]
Political Right			
Nacional	20.0	21.3	4
Democrata Radical	0.0	2.3	0
Political Center			
Democrata Cristiano	29.8	29.1	7
Democratico Nacional	1.9	0.4	0
Radical	13.0	3.7	15
Izquierda Radical	0.0	1.8	0
Political Left			
FPMR	0.0	0.0	19
MAPU	0.0	0.0	24
MIR	0.0	0.0	384
Socialista	12.2	18.7	405
Comunista	15.9	16.2	353
Izquierda Cristiana	0.0	1.2	5
Others	2.2	3.6	15
Political Affiliation Unknown			1,048

[a] Comisión Chilena de Derechos Humanos (1978).
[b] Comisión Nacional de Verdad y Reconciliación (1991) at 885.

been maintained on the basis of union funds" (Staff Report of the Select Committee on Intelligence Activities 1976).

The coup changed everything. What little resistance the military encountered was crushed, and real and suspected opponents were dealt with harshly. Nor was the intervention shortlived. After seizing power to "restore" democracy, the military government remained in place for over sixteen years. While military rule affected everyone, it did not do so equally. Table 1 highlights just how heavily the military government targeted the political left for repression. The Rettig Committee, set up by President Patricio Aylwin in 1990 to document human rights abuses during the period of military rule, from September 1973 until March 1990, was able to come to conclusive findings that 2,279 deaths and disappearances were in fact human rights violations. Of these, 1,231 were people whose political affiliations the committee was able to ascertain, and this information is summarized in the third column of the accompanying table. To place the deaths and disappearances in the context of the relative sizes of the political parties, the preceding columns report the political parties' vote shares in the two elections that selected the Chamber of Deputies during the UP government. As can be seen, almost all of the victims came from political parties and organizations on the left. The leadership of the Christian Democratic and National parties initially expressed support for the coup, and members of their parties were relatively scarce among the dead and the disappeared.

Repression by the military government had a particularly pernicious effect on the Communists, whose pre-coup leaders had been voices of comparative moderation within the UP government. During the Pinochet years the party was driven into hiding. Those who rose through the underground party hierarchy to replace the leaders killed by the military government viewed the failure of Chile's UP and the seeming success of the Nicaraguan Sandinistas as a "natural experiment" on the relative merits of democratic vs. violent social change, and opted for the latter (Constable and Valenzuela 1991). Of course most on the left did not agree with the Communist leadership that democracy had been discredited, and the question of whether and when to participate in plebiscites and elections organized under the rubric of the Constitution of 1980 became an issue that divided them. But the entire left, democrats and would-be totalitarians alike, are marked by the military's use of torture and killing as political weapons.

The View from the Barracks

The other group that continues to be most affected by the military's human rights abuses is the military itself. As Finer (1962) has observed, "the military that have intervened in politics are in a dilemma: whether their rule be indirect or whether it be direct, they cannot withdraw from rulership nor can they fully legitimize it. They can neither stay nor go." Instead the armed forces find themselves caught between the fear of reprisal and a return to the political conditions that brought on their intervention in the first place, should they relinquish power, and the difficulty of ruling with little legitimacy and limited expertise if they remain.

The large number of victims of the coup meant that the fear of reprisal was well founded. The military personnel involved in killings and disappearances during the first months of military rule were in no hurry to see an independent civilian judiciary resume its jurisdiction. One can interpret the "hardening of October" (Comisión Nacional de Verdad y Reconciliación 1991) in this light. In early October, several weeks after the coup it became clear that in some areas the military was committing relatively few human rights abuses. In response, emissaries of the high command went to these areas to oversee summary executions and encourage a harsher stance by the local authorities (Comisión Nacional de Verdad y Reconciliación 1991). The Rettig Committee interprets the

intent of this program as having been to show that there was a single policy, and that it would be exercised harshly (Comisión Nacional de Verdad
y Reconciliación 1991). An alternative interpretation is that those who
had already crossed the point of no return by committing human rights
abuses did not want to stand alone. By pushing as many others as possible
to cross the threshold as well, they ensured a more unified interest among
the armed forces in avoiding the threat of human rights prosecutions an
unconditional return to civilian rule would entail.

Both the Allende government and the military regime have had lasting
effects on the ideologies of the left and the right in Chile. Measuring the
extent of these effects, and the ways in which they have interacted with
the more customary differences between the left and the right over labor
relations, public vs. private education, and social policy will occupy our
attention in several of the following chapters. But before we turn to these
questions, it is important for us to examine the institutional legacy of
military rule in Chile.

2.2 THE MILITARY GOVERNMENT'S SEARCH FOR LEGITIMACY AND THE CONSTITUTION OF 1980

From the day of the coup onward the military sought legitimacy on two
fronts; first there was the need to justify the coup itself, which was complicated by the extreme violence of the undertaking, and then there was
the problem of justifying its continued hold on power. The two questions
were related; the large number of people killed during the coup and its
immediate aftermath made returning power to civilians more difficult,
because of fears of reprisal under civilian rule, while at the same time the
regime was indelibly tarnished by having overthrown a democratically
elected government.

As the military remained in power its claims to legitimacy had to
change; the arguments used to justify intervention were not arguments
that could explain years or decades of continued rule (Garretón 1983).
The military needed a "narrative" to explain its continued presence in
power. Even as he consolidated power within the regime, Pinochet began
to construct such a rationale, warning that without fundamental changes
to Chilean society, civilian rule would lead to recurrence of the same type
of crisis that had precipitated the 1973 coup. The alleged need to transform Chilean society became key to the military government's claim to
legitimacy. Its continued grasp on power was asserted to be essential to
the salvation of the country.

The self-description of the military government changed over time. In
the *pronunciamento* it issued on the day of the coup, the military claimed
to be responding to "the clamor, repeated and multitudinous from the

grand majority of citizens," and to be saving a country overcome by anarchy, which "was precipitating into the darkest abyss in which reigned only chaos, misery, and hatred" (Contador 1989). However, there was little detail on just what it was the armed forces intended to do once in power. Moreover, the internal structure of the military government remained somewhat fluid. Interviewed by the press shortly after the coup, the president of the Junta, Augusto Pinochet, declared "the Junta works as a whole unit. I was elected because I was the oldest ... But not only I will be president of the Junta; after a while it will be Admiral Merino, later General Leigh, and so successively. I am a man without ambitions, I don't want to appear as the one holding power" (Arriagada 1989).

In its initial years the military government emphasized its anticommunist orientation and gave the moral, economic, and institutional reconstruction of the country as its agenda, and it was prepared to stay in power for however long this diffuse agenda took to implement (Arriagada 1989). During this period the existence of violent opposition from the far left made life more dangerous for the armed forces, but it also made it easier for the junta to claim that it needed to remain in power to combat this opposition. Moreover, while the military were amateur politicians, they were professionals at the use of force – armed resistance meant trying to beat the armed forces at their own game.

All the while Pinochet increased his dominance over the Army. Through control over retirements and promotions he was slowly but steadily able to bring the entire organization under his control. In June of 1974 a new agency, The National Directorate of Intelligence (DINA), was formed to consolidate the intelligence-gathering and secret-police activities of the military regime. This agency was nominally under the control of the Junta, but increasingly Pinochet gained personal control over its operations.

When U. S. President Jimmy Carter took office in 1977 he began a foreign policy that placed considerable weight on human rights. In May and June of 1977 this translated into high-level meetings with members of the opposition to Pinochet, and a plea by Secretary of State Cyrus Vance for an end of the state of siege the Junta had imposed since the day of the coup (Sigmund 1993).

The Chacarillas Plan

The following month, in a speech delivered in the town of Chacarillas, Pinochet outlined in much greater detail than before just what sort of "social transformation" the regime sought. This speech seems to have served multiple purposes: justifying the regime's continued hold on power, answering international critics, and significantly, outlining an institutional framework solidifying Pinochet's primacy within the military government.

59

The speech described a three-part timetable for the writing of a new constitution and the incorporation of civilians into the government. Pinochet referred to these three phases as "recuperation," "transition," and "consolidation" (Contador 1989). The inclusion of civilians in the first two stages of this timetable was essentially symbolic: the military government, with Pinochet at its head, would retain an exclusive grasp on real power through the end of the "transition" phase.

The recuperation phase, which Pinochet characterized as already in progress, involved the repeal of all vestiges of the Constitution of 1925, which had been in force at the time of the coup. Among the many edicts issued by the Junta, most characterized as "decree with force of law," there had been several dictums labeled "constitutional acts." Pinochet asserted the time had come to "complete the dictation of the Constitutional Acts, in whatever material of Constitutional importance still not considered by them, as well as various transitional laws, such as security, labor, social welfare, education and others that are studied in parallel" (Contador 1989). He saw the recuperation phase continuing until December 31, 1980 at the latest, which he set forth as a deadline for the adoption of a new set of constitutional acts.

Pinochet offered a sketch of what he saw as some important features the new constitution should include. During the transition phase, sovereignty lay with the Junta, though it should, Pinochet said, first consult with the Council of State. Executive power would reside with the president of the Government Junta, who would be called President of the Republic, with the faculties already invested in him,[3] while legislative power would reside with the president and a "Chamber of Representatives," "without prejudicing the legislative faculties that, in this stage of the transition, will have to be maintained by the Government Junta, in extraordinary character" (Contador 1989). What were these "legislative faculties of extraordinary character"? First that each member of the Junta could propose legislation, through the intermediation of the president, and second, that any member of the Junta could ask that any law be "reviewed" by the Junta before being promulgated. This review came with an absolute veto over legislation, with no possibility of an override, if the "prevailing opinion" in the Junta was that the law would be harmful to "national security."

The legislature he foresaw as eventually consisting of two parts. The first of these would control one-third of the seats in the legislature and would consist of "persons of national prominence," who would hold office by right, or by presidential appointment. The other two-thirds would be representatives of regions or groups of regions proportional to the population (Contador 1989). This idea of including unelected

---

[3] Meaning at the time of the speech; Pinochet was thus claiming already to wear the presidential sash.

legislators in the Congress led eventually to article 45 of the Constitution of 1980, which calls for the inclusion of nine unelected Senators in the upper chamber, or just under a fifth of the total membership of the Senate. While no earlier Chilean Congress had included unelected legislators, the idea was not a new one, nor was it peculiar to Chile. Former president Alessandri had advocated constitutional reforms to allow a large fraction of unelected Senators, chosen for their distinction in other walks of life (Alessandri 1967), while both Britain and France have provisions for appointing members of their upper legislative chambers.[4]

Pinochet also called for the adoption of legislative rules, such as a presidential veto, that would avoid the "demagogic excesses that characterized the final periods of our last parliament" (Contador 1989). He thought it worth special mention that the legislative chamber have "technical committees in which regularly participate the people most qualified, on the scientific, technical and professional plane, with the right to be recognized" (Contador 1989), meaning that experts would have a right to express their opinions on the record, though just which experts these would be, or how they would be chosen, was not made clear in the Chacarillas speech.

During the transition phase the legislature would not only be subject to the "national security veto" by the Government Junta; it would also be nonelected (Contador 1989)! Pinochet called for the legislature to serve an initial term of four or five years, starting in 1980, but "given that holding elections is not feasible, the representatives of the regions will have to be designated by the Government Junta" (Contador 1989).

Finally, after this four-or five-year period, the consolidation phase would begin; and with it the inclusion of legislators elected by direct popular suffrage, "in accord with electoral systems that favor the most capable, and that avoid the political parties again converting themselves into monopolistic machineries of citizen participation" (Contador 1989). After the election of the "regional representatives" the newly reconstituted legislature would designate the President of the Republic for a six-year term. Also at the beginning of the consolidation phase, a new Constitution would be set forth, a constitution that would incorporate the lessons learned during the transition phase (Contador 1989).

Shortly after the Chacarillas speech Pinochet had become strong enough within the Junta to consolidate his power by controlling the writing of a provisional constitution, one which left the remainder of the governing Junta with little real power (Arriagada 1989).

Pinochet followed up this bold grasp of agenda control the following month, on August 12, 1977, when the DINA was renamed the CNI,

---

[4] While neither the British House of Lords nor the French Senate can do much more than delay legislation approved by their respective lower chambers, this was not always the case for the House of Lords.

Centro Nacional de Informaciones,whose charter placed it squarely within the jurisdiction of the Interior Ministry. This meant that it was answerable to the Interior Minister, who in turn served at the pleasure of Pinochet. Unlike the DINA, the CNI was not answerable to the Junta (Arriagada 1989).

In December of 1977, Pinochet announced a plebiscite for January 4, 1978, on the ballot a statement of personal support for "President Pinochet" and an affirmation of the legitimacy of the government. Voters could choose the "yes" option, marked by a Chilean flag, or the "no" option, beneath a black flag. There was widespread evidence of electoral fraud; ballots were translucent so that polling officials could see how people voted, and voters were not compared to electoral registries (Spooner 1994). The outcome, in which Pinochet received 75% of the vote, was denounced by the U. S. Department of State (Sigmund 1993). While fraudulent, the plebiscite demonstrated how strong Pinochet had become within the Junta; no longer was he a "man without ambitions" who did not "want to appear as the one holding power," as he had stated at the time of the coup (Arriagada 1989). The day after the ballot he boasted to reporters that he had become the most important man in the Junta: "now I go ahead and the other three go behind" (Maira 1984).

Taking control over the CNI meant an enormous centralization of power in the hands of the president, and it was followed the next year by the removal of Pinochet's one remaining rival: Air Force General Gustavo Leigh. All four of the members of the Junta were said to serve on equal terms and could only be dismissed for "death, resignation, or whatever class of absolute incapacity of the member" (Arriagada 1989). Nevertheless, on July 24, 1978 the Ministry of the Interior issued a decree removing Leigh on the grounds that he was "absolutely incapacitated" (Arriagada 1989). Somewhat surprisingly, the rest of the Junta went along with Leigh's removal. It would be a decade before anyone within the governing Junta again challenged Pinochet's authority.

The Constitution of 1980

In August 1978 the committee Pinochet appointed to draft a constitution, known as the Ortúzar Committee, recommended a constitution with extensive presidential powers; this draft of the constitution was then referred to the Council of State, headed by former president Arturo Alessandri. The council redrafted the document and presented their proposed constitution on July 8, 1980. While the two constitution-writing committees were composed of Pinochet's political allies, the committee members did not have identical objectives to his. Sergio Diez, one of the members of the Ortúzar Committee, remarked that the Constitution's provisions for a strong executive were intended to apply in "two situations, whether

Pinochet were to continue, or no" (interview with Sergio Diez May 27, 1997). The writers of the constitution had policy goals of their own, and they recognized that institutional guarantees were more secure than faith in a particular individual, even when that individual, Pinochet, shared many of their objectives.

While Pinochet approved much of the draft presented to him by the Council of State, which included an ad nominum reference to himself as the president during the transition period, he was uncomfortable with some of its provisions, notably the five-year timetable it set forth for a return to electoral selection of the chief executive (Constable and Valenzuela 1991). Pinochet then appointed a "study committee" made up of a group of trusted advisors (Blanc et al. 1990). Unlike the Ortúzar Committee, the minutes of most of whose meetings were made public, and the Council of State, which invited public input, the "study committee" worked quickly and secretly, modifying many of the Constitution's provisions, including an extension of the transition period. Instead of the five-year timetable recommended by the Council of State, the final version of the constitution extended the transition period period to eight years (Blanc et al. 1990), during which time twenty-five "transitory" articles of the Constitution held force. The combined effect of these transitory articles was to leave the status quo of the military government mostly unchanged, with Pinochet firmly in control until at least 1989.

The Constitution left many details unsettled, for example the workings of the electoral system, the means of guaranteeing central bank independence, and many of the details of legislative procedures. But the document also left the Junta in possession of a large quantity of wet concrete, in the form of its ability to adopt "organic constitutional laws." Article 63 of the Constitution established that, once Congress began functioning, these laws could only be modified with the approval of three-fifths of the entire membership of both Chambers (that is, absences and abstentions would count as "no" votes). The Ortúzar Committee had recommended that these organic constitutional laws require an absolute majority of both Chambers, but the "study committee" boosted the threshold to three-fifths. This was the same threshold set out in article 116 for Constitutional amendments. Thus, the Constitution of 1980 treated the amendment of organic constitutional laws symmetrically with amendments to the Constitution itself.[5]

However, the transitory articles of the constitution in force during the transition period made it much easier for the Junta to pass organic

[5] In 1989 the constitution was amended, reducing the threshold to pass and amend organic constitutional laws from three-fifths of the total membership to four-sevenths, still a significant supermajority hurdle, while the threshold needed to amend some articles of the constitution increased to two-thirds.

constitutional laws than to amend the constitution. Whereas the twenty-first transitory article of the constitution gave the Junta a monopoly at proposing constitutional amendments, it also required that such amendments be approved by plebiscite. During the early 1980s, plebiscites were inconvenient, while after the Tribunal Calificador de Eleciones (TCE) began functioning independently, plebiscites began to present a genuine democratic hurdle. In contrast, the eighteenth transitory article, letter B, gave the Junta leeway to dictate organic constitutional laws. Thus it was easy for the Junta to lay down organic constitutional laws, while it would be difficult for the elected Congress and President who succeeded them to amend these same laws.

The version of the constitution reported by the "study committee" introduced a convoluted procedure for choosing the president at the end of the transition period. First the Junta would nominate a candidate, who would stand for election without opposition in a plebiscite. Only if this candidate was rejected by a majority of the voters would a presidential election with other candidates be held (Blanc et al. 1990). Regardless of the outcome of the plebiscite, at the end of the first eight-year transition period the constitution provided for the election of a bicameral legislature to serve during the second transitional term.

The new arrangements also defended Pinochet's personal grasp on power in other ways. If the Junta was unable to agree on a presidential candidate for 1988, the choice was to be made by a majority in the National Security Council (CSN). The CSN included the four heads of the armed services, Pinochet himself, the president of the Counsel of State, the Controller General of the Republic, and the president of the Supreme Court. Of these the Army Chief of staff and the president of the Council of State served at Pinochet's pleasure, while the Controller General was a Pinochet appointee, as were all replacements for retiring members of the Supreme Court. A majority on the CSN were almost sure to vote to nominate Pinochet, should he want them to. Thus the inclusion of civilians in the CSN had the effect, at that stage, of providing Pinochet with a counterweight to one of the few powers remaining in the hands of the Junta (Arriagada 1989). While expanding CSN membership beyond the commanders of the armed forces served to bolster Pinochet's power at the time, since his departure from the presidency the presence of civilians on the CSN has had the opposite effect;   diluting Pinochet's influence.

Yet even as Pinochet was consolidating his power, and tailoring the Constitution to his liking, events began to turn against the military government on both the economic and political fronts. Economically, high U. S. inflation rates during the late 1970s meant that dollar-denominated debts looked cheap to many borrowers who expected that double-digit inflation was going to become a normal part of economic life in North as well as in South America. This led to a borrowing frenzy throughout Latin America, which then precipitated a regionwide crisis in the early 1980s as U. S. inflation fell, transforming high nominal interest rates into high real rates. On the political front, the very success of the military regime at consolidating its power, and the increasingly permanent nature of the armed forces' presence in power, alienated the Christian Democrats, who had initially lent at least lukewarm support to the military government. Given the history of animosity between the Christian Democrats and the Socialists, this shift of position by the Christian Democrats probably caused the military government little worry at the time. Few observers would have predicted that these traditional enemies would be as successful as they eventually were at forming a united and effective political opposition to the military government.

2.3 CONSTITUTIONAL POWERSHARING: BLUNDER OR CALCULATED RISK?

Many observers have attributed the provisions in the Constitution of 1980 calling for a plebiscite in 1988 on whether the Junta's candidate (almost guaranteed to be Pinochet) would continue for another eight years in power as evidence of hubris. In this version of events, Pinochet was surrounded by sycophants who exaggerated his popularity, and so he allowed the provision blindly thinking that he would win.

But this version ignores the remarkable success of the Constitution of 1980 at locking in the substantive policies adopted during the Pinochet years. As one Christian Democrat complained (interview with Jorge Lavandero, May 20, 1997) "now we have Pinochet without Pinochet!" While this may be cold comfort to the personal ambitions of Augusto Pinochet, many around him were committed to a policy agenda "whether Pinochet were to continue, or no" (interview with Sergio Diez, May 27, 1997). Nevertheless, one's initial intuition is that while sharing power with its opponents may have been an important means for the Junta to increase its perceived legitimacy, the presence of the left in the decision process can't have improved the policy outcome from the perspective of the right. However, this intuition is based on a perception of democracy as a zero-sum game, which it is not.

In addition to its role in promoting the legitimacy of the Constitution of 1980, sharing real power with the opposition also served to institutionalize a number of important policy guarantees for the right in ways they could not have achieved with the same degree of confidence with their own dictator Augusto Pinochet. A clearer idea of how these policy guarantees work can be had by drawing on the model of legislation set forth in section Section 1.2. The Constitution of 1980, and the Organic

Law of Congress[6] create a legislative framework in which the President enjoys something close to a de facto proposal monopoly. There are measures to help the President speed legislation he favors: article 71 of the Constitution, and articles 26 through 29 of the Organic Law of Congress, allow the President to impose time limits within which legislation must be passed or rejected, while article 53 of the Constitution sets the cloture threshold for both the Senate and the Chamber of Deputies at a simple majority, thereby preventing filibusters. Articles 65, 67, and 68 of the constitution permit the President to pass legislation despite opposition by a majority in one chamber, provided the President meets with the support of a supermajority in the other, while article 70 of the Constitution and articles 32 through 36 of the Organic Law of Congress contain powerful veto provisions that allow the president to have the last word in the legislative debate by introducing amendments along with his or her veto, amendments which must be voted up or down without further change by the Congress. As if these presidential powers were insufficient, articles 62 and 64 of the Constitution permit the president to propose and amend legislation, while the same articles, plus article 24 of the Organic Law of Congress, limit the ability of members of Congress to do so. Moreover, as with most Latin American legislatures, the Chilean Congress is starved for staff and infrastructure, and so lacks the administrative and research capability needed to formulate high-valence proposals independently.

To a first-order approximation, we can model the Chilean Congress as lacking the ability to initiate significant reforms independently. To be sure, presidential proposals are modified, sometimes in significant ways, as they pass through the Congress, but much of this modification takes the form of reintroducing elements of the President's bill rejected at an earlier stage of consideration, or restoring elements of the status quo derogated by the bill changes that require little initiative on the part of Congress. Moreover, article 70 of the Constitution allows the President a last move. Along with permitting the President to approve parts of a bill and veto others, the President can also offer amendments, called "observations," that would make the vetoed portions of the bill acceptable, and these must be considered by Congress under a closed rule. Moreover, the President can decide how to bundle these observations. He or she can force them to be considered as a package, or each one can be voted separately; this is the President's choice. Only if the "observations" are rejected does Congress go on to attempt to override the veto. If the President can count on at least one-third of at least one Chamber of Congress, then presidential observations are essentially take it or leave it proposals, and the President

[6] Ley Organica Constitucional No. 18.918.

66

can act as an eleventh-hour agenda setter at the final stage of consideration of any bill.

Key Features of Constitutions

There are two key elements at work in the evaluation of constitutions that distinguish them from laws: uncertainty about what policies will work best in the future, and uncertainty about the objectives of future policy-makers. First consider uncertainty about what policies will work best. While laws can be readily changed to adapt to changing circumstances, constitutional reform requires supermajorities, and so we may expect a constitution written today to remain in force even when the laws that work well now have fallen out of phase with the policy environment of the future. The best tariff policy for the current mix of industries may not work well a decade or two hence. Likewise, new challenges emerge: financial regulations have to be adapted to cope with the electronic transfer of funds via the Internet, and new technologies develop that change the way one thinks about core policy areas such as public health and national defense. The "perishability" of policy checks constitution writers' temptation to embed thousands of pages of detailed statutes into the constitution. We may expect that simply by dint of having seen how the policy environment will have changed, any executive a decade hence, regardless of his or her political outlook, will be able to formulate policy initiatives with higher valence than the status quo that works well today.

A second key consideration in constitution writing is uncertainty about the policy preferences of the individuals upon whom the constitution will confer power in the future. This problem is especially severe in the more distant future; many policy makers who will be constrained by a long-lived constitution will not have even been born at the time it was drafted. However, even within the practical time horizon of a few decades that is relevant to many constitution writers, power may change hands in ways that are hard to foresee. The composition of a legislature depends on how party platforms evolve, and how the electorate react. Moreover, even individual policy makers are unpredictable. The democratic leanings of Spain's King Juan Carlos presumably came as a surprise to those close to General Franco, who had groomed the King as his replacement. A less extreme example of the same phenomenon is the difficulty experienced by U. S. Presidents in predicting the judicial leanings of the men and women they nominate to the bench. When asked whether he felt he had made any errors while in the White House, former U. S. President Dwight Eisenhower quipped that his worst mistakes were sitting on the Supreme Court. Even in electoral politics, candidates' behavior once in office can be hard to predict: consider the bait-and-switch populism of Argentine president

Carlos Menem, who campaigned on a platform of populist government activism but implemented a series of austerity reforms once in office.

Constitution writers are caught between the danger of binding future policy makers in a straightjacket of specific but dated legislation written into the constitution and the alternative risk of delegating to agents who will hijack the agenda and implement distasteful policies. The corrosive effects of time on status quo policy can be captured in the model by recognizing that over the intermediate term, which we might think of as the first few decades after a new constitution goes into effect, the president will be able to make proposals with higher valence than the status quo at the time the constitution is written. Uncertainty about the policy objectives of the executive or the legislature can be represented as probability distributions over decision maker's ideal points.

A Formal Model

In the model of Section 1.2, there is a one-dimensional position issue, which we can think of as corresponding to how redistributive economic policy should be, and a valence dimension, which captures the alignment between legislation and the policy environment. Without loss of generality we can normalize the status quo policy position at the time the constitution goes into force at a location of 0. It seems reasonable to assume that after many years of military rule the status quo matched the policy preferences of the authors of the Constitution of 1980, both because they may have participated in making these policies and because the same government that selected the committee also chose the status quo.

To reflect uncertainty by the constitution's authors about the policy preferences of the political right, suppose that the ideal point for the right is distributed according to a uniform probability distribution with zero mean and unit variance.[7]

This means that on average the right agree with the constitution writers and are sympathetic with the status quo policy position. However, the politicians of the right may prefer policy to be a bit further to the right, or a bit to the left of its status quo location, and the constitution writers do not know and cannot precisely predict their exact policy leanings. As noted in the discussion above, this could arise from unpredicted shifts in the policy outlook of the electorate, from changes in parties' ideologies, or from some mixture of these factors.

Likewise, the policy leanings of the left will be imperfectly predictable. One can certainly look forward to their wanting a large leftward shift in

[7] So $\tilde{x}_R$, the most preferred policy position for the right, is uniformly distributed on the interval $[-\sqrt{3}, \sqrt{3}]$, with a probability density of $\frac{1}{2\sqrt{3}}$.

policy, but just how far leftward? To capture this uncertainty suppose the most preferred policy for the left is uniformly distributed with mean -4 and unit variance.[8]

This treatment of the left and the right is symmetrical; neither is easier to predict than the other. This structure also guarantees that the two distributions do not overlap, guaranteeing that even the leftmost preferred outcome that can be foreseen for the right is to the right of the rightmost policy that might emerge as the preferred outcome of the left. This imposes the reasonable restriction that during the foreseeable future the left and the right won't "change places."

While there is always at least some heterogeneity of outlook even in the most disciplined military Junta and the most doctrinaire branch of the Communist Party, for the sake of illustration it is useful to abstract from these differences by treating the left and the right as each advocating a homogeneous policy agenda.[9]

Suppose further that, as in the case of the Chilean Constitution of 1980, the lower legislative chamber is all but certain to be controlled by the left, while the upper chamber seems all but sure to be in the hands of the right. However, we want to allow for some uncertainty about who will prevail in presidential elections. We can summarize the uncertainty about the president by assuming that the probability the left wins the presidency is p, while the probability of a president on the right is $1 - p$. If the left control the presidency, then the Chamber of Deputies, also controlled by the left, can be expected to ratify virtually all of the president's program, while the Senate, controlled by the right, will be the stumbling block. If instead, it is the right who control the executive, they can expect smooth sailing in the Senate, while it is in the Chamber of Deputies that they will meet with significant opposition. Thus we have a probability of p of observing a president on the left, checked by the need for legislative approval from a legislative chamber, the Senate, on the right, while there is a probability of $1 - p$ of observing the opposite: a president on the right who must contend with the Chamber of Deputies on the left.

The final key element affecting the decision of what kind of constitution to write is the ability of the executive to generate proposals with higher valence than the status quo. This in turn will depend mostly on the speed with which the policy environment is changing. In a very static environment with little technological or social change, the valence of new proposals relative to the status quo is likely to remain more or less fixed for decades or even longer. The prototypical example of this would probably

[8] So $\tilde{x}_L$, the most preferred policy position for the left, is uniformly distributed on the interval $[4 - \sqrt{3}, 4 + \sqrt{3}]$, with a probability density of $\frac{1}{2\sqrt{3}}$.

[9] Several of the succeeding chapters will be devoted to the task of measuring just how homogeneous these policy positions actually are.

be Pharonic Egypt, where the laws governing taxation, water rights, and building construction could remain as unchanged as the society they regulated. In contrast, during crises or periods of rapid innovation, laws will have to be adjusted after even a few years have passed. This effect is most pronounced during crises. Consider the willingness of even some Republicans to go along with Roosevelt's proposed reforms during the early days of the New Deal on the grounds that they might work, whereas the status quo definitely didn't; that is, they had relatively high (expected) valence relative to the status quo. Most societies are somewhere between these extremes, but at the end of the twentieth century a country such as Chile with a small open economy is certainly closer to the rapidly changing end of the spectrum. As they drafted the Constitution of 1980, Pinochet and those around him could reasonably expect that in the 1990's status quo legislation would very quickly go out of sync with the policy environment, so that the executive, whomever he or she was, would be in a position to formulate high-valence reforms to the status quo.

Other factors such as the resources available to the executive for research and how able the executive and those around him or her are at formulating policy are also important, but we may expect these factors to be relatively stable over time, and to resemble those available to the constitution writers' own government. That is, the authors of Chile's Constitution of 1980 probably expected that any civilian successors to Pinochet would have staff resources, motivation, and ability similar to Pinochet's, even if they might not share his policy goals.

Figure 2.1 illustrates the key elements of the decision whether to delegate when the valence of executive proposals represents a moderate but not overwhelming improvement over the status quo, with $\alpha q = \frac{4}{5}$. Given that the Chamber of Deputies was very likely to be controlled by the left, while the Senate was very likely to be controlled by the right, we can focus our attention on the cases of a divided legislature. In this environment the chamber controlled by the president's friends will be all but irrelevant to the bargaining between the executive and the hostile chamber. In practice the friendly chamber provides a forum for public speeches, and it is unlikely to block any initiative that simultaneously meets with approval from the president and the hostile chamber. To keep the model simple the unlikely event of the friendly chamber's blocking a presidential initiative is precluded: the president and the median in the friendly chamber share a preferred policy outcome of x_p. The hurdle for executive initiatives is the hostile chamber, where the median voter has a preferred outcome of x_c. In Figure 2.1 the diagonally shaded regions correspond to preference parameter combinations that could arise with positive probability when neither the left nor the right is sure to win the presidency.

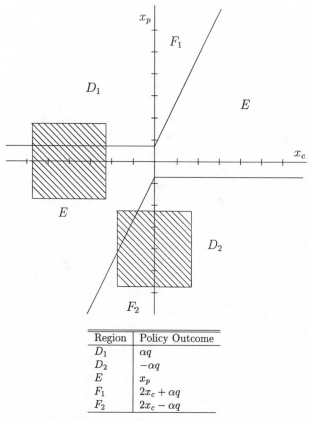

Region	Policy Outcome
D_1	αq
D_2	$-\alpha q$
E	x_p
F_1	$2x_c + \alpha q$
F_2	$2x_c - \alpha q$

Figure 2.1. Presidential Preferences, Congressional Preferences, and Policy Outcomes: $\alpha q = \frac{4}{5}$.

First we must consider whether the constitution's authors want to share power with anybody, even a dictator on the right. Here the alternative is to pour the status quo in concrete by writing it into the constitution. This provides the status quo policy position for sure, but it creates huge obstacles against modernizing policy as the environment changes, so that it also locks in the policy valence of the status quo. In contrast, both dictatorship and delegation to the legislative institutions described above allow policy to adapt. Using the parameter values for the simple model discussed here, delegating to a dictator on the right leaves the constitution's authors better off, in expectation, provided the valence of policy exceeds about $\alpha q = \frac{2}{5}$, while the break-even point for delegating to the legislative institutions comes at just below $\alpha q = \frac{4}{5}$. In the example, $\alpha q = \frac{4}{5}$ and so delegation to either a dictator or to legislative institutions is superior to a constitution containing a "Maginot Line" of specific legislation that entrenches the status quo policy position, but cannot adapt to a changing environment.

There are two shaded boxes in the diagram. The leftmost of the two corresponds to a president on the right, constrained by a Chamber of Deputies on the left. The policy position of the president is measured along the vertical axis, that for the hostile chamber along the horizontal axis. Notice that most of the shaded region lies inside area E, in which the president is able to obtain approval for his or her most preferred outcome. When the president is on the left-hand side of the status quo, corresponding to the region below the x_c axis, this is straightforward: the president's most preferred outcome is left of the status quo, and closer to the hostile chamber, while presidential proposals enjoy a moderate valence advantage over the status quo. Above the horizontal axis the president is to the right of the status quo, while the hostile chamber would like to see policy move leftward. Nevertheless, in the upper portion of the shaded area, which arises with positive probability in this example, the president is able to pry policy somewhat rightward by using the valence advantage his or her proposals enjoy over the status quo. When the president is well to the right, so that we are in region D_1, he or she is not able to gain congressional approval for his or her most preferred outcome and can only move policy rightward as far as αq, at which point the valence advantage of the president's proposal just outweighs the disadvantage, from the standpoint of Congress, of its ideological content.

Notice that in region D_1 the hostile chamber of Congress is better off than it would be if the President were an unconstrained dictator who could simply impose a policy of (x_p, q), which notwithstanding its higher valence would leave the left worse off because of its ideological content on the right. The constitution's authors, with their preferred outcome of $x_A = 0$, are also better off in region D_1, where the president is constrained to offer a policy of $x = \alpha q$, which is closer to their preferred outcome of 0. In contrast, at no point does the constrained president on the right do anything that leaves the constitution's authors worse off than they would have been delegating to a dictator! The key is that the constitution's authors cannot fully predict the policy leanings of their own ally, the future president. However, they can be sure that the left will share their interest in preserving the status quo when the alternative is a policy even further to the right. By making them veto players they prevent large rightward deviations from the status quo that a dictator might impose, but that do not offer a sufficient improvement in the valence of policy to compensate, at least not from the standpoint of the constitution's authors.

Of course, even if the authors of the constitution were sure the president would be on the right, this legislative mechanism does not solve all of their problems: if the president is on the leftward end of the foreseeable range of preferred policies, the hostile chamber will be only too happy to enact his or her proposal with a policy position at x_p instead of the status quo. However, this is the same outcome that world have resulted with a dictator, the legislative arrangement with a president on the right is never worse than delegating to a dictator.

The second shaded box in Figure 2.1, below and to the right of the first, corresponds to a president on the left, constrained by a hostile Senate on the right. This approximates the actual outcome in Chile, in which the Concertación alliance of the Christian Democrats and parties on the left united to capture the presidency. These outcomes are much less appealing, from the standpoint of the constitution's authors. When the political right are farther right than the status quo, the president can only shift policy leftward as far as $-\alpha q$, which just compensates the right for abandoning the status quo by providing higher valence. Regions F_2 and E are another matter. In region E the president implements his or her most preferred outcome, well to the left of the constitution's authors. This happens when there is a combination of a moderate president, and a moderate Senate, in the upper lefthand corner of the box. In region F_2 policy comes leftward until it is blocked by the median Senator, who, in region F_2, is to the left of the constitution's authors.

A president on the left constrained by the Senate on the right leads to a less favorable policy lottery than simply delegating to a dictator. This has led to the common view of Pinochet and his advisors as overconfident dupes expelled from power by their own constitution because they overestimated public support for the policies of the military government. This might be a fair assessment if, in 1980, one could have been certain that Pinochet could not have possibly won the 1988 plebiscite on a second term, and that he would be replaced by a president on the left. However, in 1980 no one could be sure of the outcome of a plebiscite to be held almost a decade later. Simple calculations reveal that for the parameter values used in this example the constitution represents a better lottery over policy, from the standpoint of someone whose ideal point corresponds with the status quo than the alternative of leaving Pinochet with unilateral power provided the probability that the right capture the presidency exceeds 0.791. That is, if Pinochet's advisors placed at least four to one odds on the right's winning the 1988 plebiscite, then the constitution would have resulted in a favorable outcome for them on policy grounds alone.

Of course, the constitution, and its provisions allowing participation by the opposition, had many other benefits as well. By reducing the popular sense of outrage and injustice at policies imposed by a dictatorial government, the constitution also bought some measure of domestic peace. Of course, peace is not infinitely valuable, but it doesn't need to be to affect policy decisions. Accounting for the added legitimacy of the Constitution of 1980 as opposed to the alternative of continued dictatorship from the right, with no prospect for powersharing with the left, the "odds" of a win by the right in the 1988 plebiscite at which the constitution "breaks even" for its authors come down to something less than four to one. If some on the right, including quite possibly Pinochet himself, now experience some ex post regret about the powersharing provisions in the Constitution of 1980, this does not mean that their earlier decision to share power was irrational. Someone who might be happy to bet on a favored horse at ex ante odds of, say, two to one will certainly not want to bet at ex post odds of zero to one after that horse has lost. But this does not mean the earlier willingness to bet was irrational. Indeed, ex ante it may have been very difficult to find anyone willing to bet the actual winner at the ex post favorable odds of a million to one. The decision by the military government to include powersharing provisions in the Constitution of 1980 was a calculated risk, one that turned out serendipitously for the democrats they were betting against.

2.4 THE TIDE TURNS

The military regime was not popularly elected, and probably never enjoyed real support from a majority of Chileans. Nevertheless, they were not without friends. A substantial portion of the public supported their goals and gave them their loyalty. This support, a booming economy at the time he unveiled the Constitution of 1980, and deep divisions among his opponents bolstered Pinochet's prospects for staying in firm control of the constitutional framework he had created until at least the end of 1997. Yet as matters transpired it was the economy that faltered, while the political opposition did not.

Several factors combined to make the opposition much more effective than one might have reasonably predicted in 1980. The most important of these was the role of the Catholic Church as a focus of opposition to the military government. This built bridges of trust between the Church and the suppressed political parties on the left, notably the Socialists, while the Christian Democrats, already closely affiliated with the Church, joined its defense of human rights.

In the initial months after the coup, all but a handful of Christian Democrats, such as Bernardo Leighton and Jaime Castillo, were supportive of the military. This support was echoed by most of the leadership of the Catholic Church (Smith 1986). Yet the Catholic Church consists of more than its leaders. From the day of the coup onward many among the clergy at the pastoral level found themselves in opposition to the military regime, either because they were themselves part of the left, or because of their humanitarian role in helping to shield political opponents of the regime from detention, torture, and execution (Smith 1986). This led the Catholic Church to form an ecumenical Peace Committee, with the notable participation of the Lutheran Church, to intervene on behalf of political prisoners and those persecuted by the regime. However, as time passed, many Catholic priests and the head Lutheran Bishop for Chile were forced out of the country, and the Peace Committee was under increased pressure from the military government. The Committee disbanded in 1976. In its place the Catholic Church established the Vicariate of Solidarity entirely within the Church organization, so that any attack on the Vicariate was an attack on the Church itself. Nevertheless, the military regime continued an increasingly aggressive stance against the Church's humanitarian activities on behalf of political prisoners and regime opponents. There was a notorious incident in which an airport mob that included agents of the DINA hurled bricks and insults at a delegation of Catholic bishops as they returned from a church conference in Ecuador. The effect was to unite the church in opposition to continued military rule (Smith 1986).

At the same time, as the military regime consolidated its power, it became increasingly evident that it was not preparing to turn over the reigns of power after making the Christian Democrats' political opponents on the left "disappear." If the Christian Democrats were to return to power, the military government would first have to go. Moreover, the Christian Democrats' connection with the Catholic Church meant that as the Church moved into opposition to the military government, the Christian Democrats followed. In November 1978 a group of prominent Christian Democrats, including former government ministers Máximo Pacheco and Jaime Castillo, along with other members of the opposition formed the Chilean Committee on Human Rights, meeting publicly in Santiago with UN representative Theodor Van Boven, an event noted in the Chilean press (El Mercurio 1978). What was remarkable about the Human Rights Committee is that it included both Christian Democrats and other prominent opposition figures, such as unionist Clotario Blest. This represented a significant departure from the confrontational stance toward the left that characterized the Christian Democrats during the UP government.

When the constitution was publicly announced on August 11, 1980, a plebiscite to legitimize it was set for September 11 (Blanc et al. 1990), giving very little warning to the political opposition (Garretón 1983). Needless to say, those regime opponents who had not already been killed, imprisoned, or exiled were left with little opportunity to respond (Constable and Valenzuela 1991). Former President Eduardo Frei, a

75

Christian Democrat who had been initially supportive of the coup,[10] spoke against the proposed Constitution. In a public speech delivered two weeks before the plebiscite he spoke mostly in general terms. He noted the illegitimacy of the process by which the Constitution was written, while he characterized the document itself as a work of "science fiction," which "mocked the country" (De la Barra 1982). Substantively he singled out the lengthy timetable for the incorporation of civilians into the process, which was even slower that that set forth in Pinochet's Chacarillas speech:

> For almost a quarter of a century the Chilean people will be maintained in a civic interdiction, deprived of their rights of citizenship. Those who were 18 years old in 1973 will be able to elect their authorities, for the first time, when they have reached 42 years of age.
>
> There is no precedent in the history of Chile of a case like this, neither in terms of length of time, nor of power accumulated.
>
> (De la Barra 1982)

Frei went on to impugn the electoral procedures being used: "the people have already decided 'No', even knowing there will be no genuine control over the electoral lists. Therefore no one has any illusions about the result" (De la Barra 1982).

The plebiscite was held on September 11, 1980, using old electoral rolls and with little opportunity for outside parties to evaluate its fairness. How much direct fraud took place is unknown, but the polling places were under the supervision of the military government, and as with the 1978 plebiscite there are allegations of individuals having cast multiple ballots, while spoiled and blank ballots were counted as votes for the constitution (Spooner 1994). The constitution was reported to have met with the approval of 67.04% of the voters, and this victory became a part of the regime's claim to the legitimacy of the 1980 Constitution. Enemies of the regime were unimpressed and pointed out the questionable nature of the result, but the authoritarian government had little interest in winning over its enemies, and scarce hope of doing so. It was among friends of the military government that the plebiscite provided an alibi for supporting the regime. This alibi was particularly important in the context

[10] In a letter to Mariano Rumor written on November 8, 1973, shortly after the coup, Eduardo Frei was clearly in sympathy with the coup:

> The armed forces, we are convinced, did not act out of ambition. In fact, they long resisted doing so. If they fail now it would be a failure for the country, precipitating us into a large dead end. So, the great majority of Chileans, beyond all partisan political considerations (facing a reality from which there is no turning back) want to help, because they believe that this is the way to reestablish peace and freedom in Chile. The faster hatreds are buried and the country's economy recovers, the faster will be the exit.
>
> (De la Barra 1982)

of Chile's long tradition of legalistic government. Members of the armed forces could point to it as a justification for their participation in the government, while the general public, when considering whether to resist the regime, weighed the costs of resistance against the promise that if they were patient a timetable had already been set up for eventual elections.

Shortly after the 1980 Constitution was adopted, Latin America was rocked by the debt crisis. Dollar-denominated loans taken out during the late 1970's, when many expected double-digit inflation to become a permanent feature of the U. S. economy, suddenly became crushing burdens as double-digit *nominal* rates of interest suddenly became double-digit *real* rates. The shock was particularly heavy in Chile, where much of the debt was owed by businesses (Frieden 1991). Pinochet's weak legitimacy gave him scant leeway in dealing with foreign investors. A loss of support in the international lending community combined with his image as the dictator who brought down Chilean democracy would have left him with few allies. At the same time the business community's fear of the left was so intense that even a spate of bankruptcies would not undermine their basic support for Pinochet's government (Frieden 1991). The military government took the extraordinary step of agreeing to repay foreign investors for a large fraction of the *private* debt that had been incurred by Chileans, a measure that kept it in the good graces of the international financial community (Frieden 1991), but at a very high price.

In September 1982 the Chilean Committee on Human Rights expanded its membership (Comisión Chilena de Derechos Humanos 1982) to include more people with sympathies on the left, such as Jorge Molina and Laura Soto. From the right of the Christian Democratic Party, Patricio Aylwin, who had been the Christian Democrats' representative during the failed final round of negotiations with Allende in 1973, also joined the committee. The human rights issue served as an important initial point of contact between the Christian Democrats and the left.

As noted earlier, the Communist Party embraced violent opposition to the military government, but reactions among the Socialists were varied: some responded to the calls from the party's exiled Secretary General Clodomiro Almeyda for armed resistance. Others, including Carlos Briones, took a different lesson from the experiences of the UP government and its aftermath. This "renewed" wing of the party sought alliances with more moderate political parties to bring a nonviolent return to democracy (Constable and Valenzuela 1991). Those on the left who observed that participation in the framework of the 1980 Constitution conferred legitimacy on both the constitution and, at least by implication, on the government that had written it were certainly correct. By drawing even opponents into participating in the process the Constitution lent some legitimacy to Pinochet's rule. But as matters transpired, the Constitution was more successful at legitimizing Pinochet's rule than it was at extending it.

Opposition to continued military rule emerged more slowly on the political right. Many of the substantive policies adopted by the military government were more to the liking of Chileans on right, while the memory of the UP government and the militant opposition to military rule by some on the left sharpened suspicions that the real objective of the opposition was not democracy but a totalitarian government on the left. Thus the right remained largely dormant during the initial decade of military rule, with some politicians participating in the government, for example as part of the committee to draft the constitution.

During the early 1980s, civilian political leaders, crossing the spectrum from the Socialists such as Luis Maira to prominent figures on the political right such as Fransisco Bulnes and Andrés Allamand, began serious discussions among themselves about how to bring about a return to civilian politics (Otano 1995). While some saw the 1980 Constitution as irreparably illegitimate, Bulnes propounded the view that it was better to work within the Constitution of 1980, modifying it where necessary, rather than scrapping it entirely. As he put it, "it isn't that we should recognize the Constitution for being legitimate, but that we recognize it for being" (Otano 1995). Patricio Aylwin shared a similar perspective, contending that "put to the task of looking for a solution, the first thing is to leave aside the famous dispute over the legitimacy of the regime and its constitution" (Otano 1995). Instead Aylwin, who considered the constitution to be illegitimate, favored using its framework to supplant the military regime (Otano 1995).

1988

One of the most important developments of this period was the emergence of an important element of the socialist party interested in dialog and compromise. The socialists were divided over whether to participate in the coming plebiscite, set for 1988, which would decide whether Pinochet would remain in office for an additional eight years, or to stand aloof from procedures approved in the questionable 1980 plebiscite on the constitution. The idea of starting another party, a "Party for Democracy" which socialists could join in order to campaign for a "no" vote against the regime's candidate in the plebiscite, was floated. The proposal met with support from an unexpected corner: Jorge Arrate, political heir to Carlos Altimarano and a representative of the more strident and uncompromising wing of the Socialist Party, endorsed the idea, and so the "Partido Por la Democracia" (PPD) was formed, with Ricardo Lagos, a more moderate socialist, as its leader (Otano 1995).

Accident and Force

In one of the most effective and surprising political campaigns in Chilean history, dubbed the "Campaign for the No," Pinochet's opponents managed to unite and to portray themselves as sober centrists who sought an end to the economic suffering of the debt crisis and a return to normality. Human rights violations by the military government also served as an important weapon for the opposition. In the words of one supporter of the "No" option, "if you vote Yes, you are approving all the murders they have committed since 1973" (Constable and Valenzuela 1991). Pinochet's campaign drew on fears of a return of the UP government and of the political and economic turmoil of the Allende years.

The election itself was heavily monitored, both by outside observers and by the Campaign for the No, and it was surprisingly free from fraud. Pinochet's bid for a second term failed, earning only 43% of the vote cast. As the returns began to come in the government embargoed further reports on the official ballot count, and Pinochet summoned the heads of the armed forces to the president's palace; La Moneda. It appears that he was surprised by the outcome and was tempted to overturn the result. If so, he did not meet with enthusiasm among the heads of the armed forces. On his way to meet with Pinochet, Air Force General Fernando Matthei remarked to reporters that the "No" had won, later claiming to have done this to prevent the government from fraudulently nullifying Pinochet's electoral defeat (Sigmund 1993). Perhaps this willingness to see Pinochet go came from the Air Force's hunger for access to recent vintage U. S. military hardware. As the most technology intensive of the armed services, the Air Force was particularly sensitive to the likely embargo of U. S. weapons technology if Pinochet attempted to overturn the election. Perhaps Matthei remembered the humiliation the Air Force had suffered a decade earlier when Pinochet had his opponent in the internal politics of the Junta, Air Force General Leigh, declared unfit for command. Maybe Matthei had calculated the costliness to the country in general and the armed forces in particular of the repression that would be needed to reverse the election result, or perhaps he had simply voted for the "No" and wanted to see it win.

Early in the evening, as the government seemed to be embargoing election returns, Patricio Aylwin, leader of the Campaign for the No, and Sergio Jarpa, once a minister in Pinochet's cabinet, and at the time of the plebiscite head of the largest political party on the Chilean right, Renovación Nacional, made a joint television appearance in which they announced the victory of the "No" (Otano 1995).

Many would contend that the 1980 Constitution was in fact Pinochet's downfall. Yet his sixteen and a half years in power made him the longest ruling head of state in the postindependence history of Chile. Had he not offered guarantees and a binding timetable for his eventual exit, remaining in power might have proven much more difficult. While he lost the 1988

79

plebiscite, he only lacked the votes of 7% of the electorate to have changed the outcome. Had the opposition been a bit less skillful at portraying themselves as nonthreatening, the outcome would have been different. The 1980 Constitution probably served its primary purpose of keeping Pinochet in power more effectively than the available alternatives would have, and it very nearly kept him in power for yet an additional eight years.

After the Plebiscite

With the victory of the "No," Chile prepared itself for elections for Congress, and for a new president. At this stage many of the details of the Constitutional framework needed to be worked out. For example, the Central Bank independence promised by article 97 of the Constitution had to be translated into specific rules for the selection of the governing board and the provision of the bank's budget. Likewise, the electoral rules for selecting the Deputies and the elected Senators had to be set up, and decisions had to be made about which regions would be divided into two Senate districts and which would have only one.

An important part of this process came in the form of a "national accord" negotiated among the Concertación, Renovación Nacional, and Pinochet's government. This accord set forth a series of constitutional reforms, reforms which the Concertaciòn viewed as mostly favorable to themselves (Viera-Gallo 1989). However, the package also included two important technical details that were very useful to the outgoing military government and the political parties allied with it: a weakening of the president's powers to "insist" on legislation rejected in one chamber of Congress (Blanc et al. 1990) and preservation of a supermajority clause required to amend what are called "Organic Constitutional Laws." The Constitution of 1980 set the threshold at three-fifths of the Senate, and the Concertación and Renovación Nacional had sought to reduce the threshold to an absolute majority; a compromise threshold of four-sevenths was adopted as part of the constitutional reform (Blanc et al. 1990). This second reform was extremely important because under the transitory acts of the constitution, constitutional reforms required approval by a plebiscite (Blanc et al. 1990), whereas organic constitutional laws could be passed by the Junta without outside consultation or approval (Blanc et al. 1990). Armed with the four-sevenths supermajority threshold for amendments to organic constitutional laws, Pinochet, with the full cooperation of the Junta, was able to lock in a number of guarantees not even hinted at in the national accord.

The entire package of reforms was presented to a plebiscite as a single question; voters could either approve the entire package, or nothing at all. Most of the press discussion of the time emphasized the view that the reforms did not go far enough; very little attention was paid in the public discussion of the time to the implications of the high amendment threshold for organic constitutional laws. The plebiscite approved the package of measures with 89.7% of the voters casting ballots in favor. Among the reforms was a lifting on the injunction against union leaders holding public office, a removal of the president's up-to-then existing power under the 1980 Constitution to dissolve the Chamber of Deputies (a cheap concession for the military government in light of the likelihood the Concertación would control the presidency during the then-foreseeable future), and a repeal of some of the harshest measures taken against political opponents, such as the use of exile as a punishment for political opposition and a then-existing constitutional provision for banning political parties (Viera-Gallo 1989). Also included in the constitutional reform was an increase in the number of elected Senators from twenty-six to thirty-eight. This was achieved by specifying that six of the country's thirteen regions would be divided into two Senate districts each (Blanc et al. 1990). This division increased the number of elected members of the Senate from twenty-six to thirty-eight, thereby diluting the strength of the nine unelected Senators, some appointed by the President, some by the Supreme Court, and some by the National Security Council, but it did so by less than the Concertación and Renovación Nacional had sought (Blanc et al. 1990). While eliminating the appointed Senators entirely was among the stated goals of the Concertación, it was willing to accept the promises of Renovación Nacional to wait to negotiate that point later. Also important among the reforms negotiated was the inclusion of more civilians on the National Security Counsel (Viera-Gallo 1989).

With the constitutional reform of July 1989, and the spate of organic constitutional laws subsequently emitted by the Junta, the stage was set for elections in December 1989. The winner of the presidential election was Concertación candidate Patricio Aylwin. The congressional elections generally favored the Concertación, with 70 of the 120 seats in the Chamber of Deputies, and twenty-two of the thirty-eight seats for elected Senators going to their candidates. However, with nine Institutional Senators the Senate had a total of forty-seven members, and so the twenty-two Concertación Senators did not constitute a majority. On March 11, 1990 the presidency passed from Augusto Pinochet to Patricio Aylwin, and the newly elected Congress was also sworn in. While this was a very symbolic moment for a country that had lived under military rule for over sixteen years, the practical consequences of the change depended crucially on both the institutional details and on the objectives of the politicians Chileans had elected to run their government and make their laws. It is to the first of these considerations, the institutional details of the legislature, that our attention now turns.

81

3

Legislative Institutions in the Constitution of 1980

Of all of the institutions created by the military government, Chile's Senate is perhaps most influenced by the transition. With its provision for appointed "institutional" Senators to serve side by side with elected members of the chamber, it provides a unique window on the transition. Roll-call voting records from Senate committees make it possible to compare the issue positions of Socialists, with those of Christian Democrats, with members of the Independent Democratic Union (UDI), a party with links to the former military government, and with the positions taken by Senators appointed by Pinochet. Given the Concertación majority in the Chamber of Deputies, and their control of the presidency, the Senate, with its majority for the opposition, acts as a check on the legislative agenda of the Concertación. It is in the Senate that bills are made or broken, and it is the Senate that determines the pace at which policies change and institutions are reformed.

Opposition control of the Senate stands on two pillars: the Institutional Senators and the "binominal" electoral system. The electoral system is based on two-member districts for both the Senate and the Chamber of Deputies. The seats are apportioned according to the d'Hondt system, which has the effect of guaranteeing a seat for the party list that finishes second unless its vote share drops below half that of the first-place finisher. After the 1989 elections, this left the opposition with about 42% of the elected seats in each legislative chamber. In the Senate the nine Institutional Senators gave the opposition a twenty-five vs. twenty-two majority.

As noted in the preceding chapter, the Constitution of 1980 establishes a very strong executive. Once Pinochet realized that these powers would be wielded by one of his political opponents, the powers of the Senate to block legislation were augmented most notably with the Organic Constitutional Law of Congress, which requires a four-sevenths majority to amend. Nevertheless, much of the executive's ability to dominate the

82

legislative agenda remains: the Senate has blocking power, but it is not in a position to pass its own agenda of new legislation.

This chapter is divided into two sections. The first outlines the binominal electoral system, and the details of the process for selecting the institutional senators. The second section goes into some of the details of the legislative process in the Constitution of 1980.

3.1 SELECTING THE LEGISLATURE

The provision in article 44 of the Chilean Constitution for including appointed Senators in the upper chamber is probably the most notorious feature of Chile's legislative institutions. Nine of the forty-seven Senators in the Congress seated March 1990 in Valparaíso, the port city 70 miles west of the capital city of Santiago where the Constitution of 1980 requires the Chilean Congress to meet, were appointees. These Senators were appointed for eight-year terms under the auspices of the military government, and observers have tended to lump them together as a homogeneous group of extremists on the political right. Subsequent chapters will use the voting records of these and other Senators to assess how accurate this impression is. What is certainly true is that all nine met with at least the tacit approval of Pinochet. However, the details of the selection process differ somewhat among the Institutional Senators; while some are appointed directly by the president, others are nominated by other segments of the government: the Supreme Court, and the National Security Council. Because these Senators are appointed to terms of only eight years, the details of the appointment process have become more important over time. In 1998 the presidential appointments were made by Christian Democratic President Eduardo Frei,[1] no great friend of the former military government.

However, while nine of Chile's Senators owe their posts to appointment, thirty-eight are elected through the binominal electoral system, which is also used to elect members of the Chamber of Deputies. Like the Institutional Senators, the binominal electoral system, which favors the second-place party list relative to single-member districts, has also been widely criticized as a tactic of the former military regime to dilute the franchise of its opponents.

Not only does the binominal system favor the party list finishing second; serious questions have also been raised about the manner in which the boundaries for Chamber of Deputies districts were drawn. These districts differ in population, with districts that voted for Pinochet during the

---

[1] Eduardo Frei Ruiz-Tagle is the son of Eduardo Frei Montealba, also a Christian Democrat. Eduardo Frei Montealba served as president in the 1960s and became one of the few spokesmen within Chile against the 1980 Constitution.

plebiscite tending to be smaller, while opponents tend to be packed into relatively fewer and larger districts. While this certainly seems to suggest a gerrymander, the design of an optimal gerrymander within the binominal electoral system differs from that of a gerrymander in a first-past-the-post electoral system such as that prevailing in the U. S., and the analysis here indicates that if there was an attempted gerrymander it was not entirely successful.

The Institutional Senators

In addition to direct election, article 45 of the Constitution allows for several other avenues into the Senate. All former presidents of the Republic who have served at least six years are allocated automatic membership in the Senate. However, there are also restrictions on holding multiple offices, restrictions that forced Pinochet to choose between remaining Commander in Chief of the Armed Forces or becoming Senator for life. During the Aylwin period, from 1990 to 1994, Pinochet resolved this choice in favor of remaining Commander in Chief, though he has since resigned and taken up a seat in the Senate.

In addition to appointed former presidents, article 45 of the Constitution calls for nine Senators to be appointed to eight-year terms. The Supreme Court appoints three of these. Of the three, two must be retired members of the Supreme Court, each with at least two years of service on the Court. The third must be a former Controller General of the Republic, again with at least two years of service. The president of the Republic appoints two of the nine. One of the president's appointments must be a former university president (with at least two years of service), and the other a former cabinet minister who served for two consecutive years in an administration prior to the current president's own. Finally, four Senators are chosen by the National Security Council; of these, one must have been head of the army for at least two years, likewise another must have spent two years as head of the Air Force, another in command of the Navy, and the fourth must be a former leader of the Carbineers.[2] The Supreme Court and the National Security Council have proved to be resistant to political control by the president. Thus, even though the presidency has fallen into the hands of the Concertación, this has transferred the right to reappoint only two of the nine Institutional Senators. This has placed the Supreme Court and the military under intense political pressure, and increased the stakes in the struggle to control appointments to the court and promotions within the armed forces (interview with Sergio Diez, May 27, 1997).

[2] Chile's National Police Force.

There are loopholes permitting the appointment of individuals whose backgrounds do not exactly match those set forth in the Constitution. This is permitted when there are fewer than three individuals meeting the required conditions; for example, when there are not enough former Controllers General of the Republic. One of the Institutionals, Sergio Fernández, was subsequently elected to the Senate,[3] while none were reappointed when their terms expired in 1998.

The Institutional Senators see themselves as wise pragmatists who stand outside politics if not necessarily above it, and at least publically consider themselves as beholden to no one. Institutional Senator William Thayer laughed at the notion that he would lobby the Christian Democratic president for reappointment (Interview with William Thayer, May 22, 1997), while Institutional Senator Olga Feliú prided herself on remaining independent of even the Supreme Court that appointed her (Interview with Olga Feliú May 26, 1997). In their self-descriptions the two Institutional Senators with whom I have spoken certainly did not portray themselves as representing the corporatist interests of the organizations from which they had been chosen. Instead, they seemed to view their non elected status in much the same way as U. S. Supreme Court Justices do, as a license to promote good public policy. Of course, their views on what constitutes "good" public policy cannot have come as much surprise to those who selected them. Nevertheless, while the voting records analyzed in the subsequent chapters indicate that the Institutionals are anything but apolitical, they do not describe themselves as representing anyone.

Elected Members of Congress

Each of Chile's thirteen administrative regions is entitled in the Constitution to elect at least two Senators. These Senators are elected to staggered terms of eight years. This leads to two cohorts of Senators, one consisting of Senators from the six odd-numbered regions, and the other of those from the six even-numbered regions and Santiago. Every four years one group comes up for election. When the system started up in 1989, all thirteen regions held Senatorial elections, but the Senators from odd-numbered regions were elected to initial terms of only four years to start the cycle; in 1993 those regions held new elections for eight-year terms. The Senators from the even-numbered regions were elected to initial terms of eight years. The Constitution allows some regions to be divided. This is done in the organic constitutional electoral law, which divides six regions[4]

---

[3] In 1998 from the tenth region.

[4] Regions five, seven, eight, nine, ten, and the metropolitan region consisting of the national capital, Santiago.

into two Senate districts, so that a total of thirty-eight Senators are elected from nineteen Senate districts. Because the Constitution only allows regions to be divided once, it guarantees that people living in sparsely populated regions will be disproportionately represented. For example, the eighth Senate district, which encompasses the eastern half of metropolitan Santiago, has more than thirty-six times as many inhabitants as the eighteenth Senate district, which corresponds to the eleventh region in remote southern Chile.

The organic constitutional electoral law sets up sixty two-member districts to elect members of the Chamber of Deputies. These districts are somewhat more proportional to population, but there are still large discrepancies; for example, the twentieth district, which consists of the urban communes[5] of Cerrillos, Estación Central, and Maipú, all part of metropolitan Santiago, has over five times the population of the fifty-ninth district, which, like the eighteenth Senate district, corresponds to the relatively unpopulated eleventh region. The elected members of both the Senate and the Chamber of Deputies compete in two-member districts. Competition in these districts is by party list, and no list may include more than two candidates. The selection rule set out in article 109 of the organic constitutional electoral law grants both seats to the party list receiving the most votes if it outpolls the second-place list by at least a two-to-one margin. If the most popular list receives less than twice as many votes as the second-place list, then the first-place and second-place lists each receive one seat. If a list receives one seat it goes to the candidate on the list who received the most votes. This system was perceived at the time it was introduced as a means of creating a supermajority hurdle impeding the party gaining a majority of the votes from gaining a majority of the seats in the legislature (Martinez 1989).

The binominal system is algebraically guaranteed to give a seat to the candidate receiving the most votes. However, there are several cases in which the candidate receiving the *second* highest number of votes was nevertheless not elected to either of the seats for the district. For example, Ricardo Lagos, of the PPD, was one of two candidates on the Concertación list in the seventh Senate district, corresponding to the western half of metropolitan Santiago; sharing the list was Christian Democrat Andrés Zaldívar, who outpolled Lagos. The top vote getter on the second most popular list, consisting of an alliance of parties on the right, was Jaime Guzmán. While Guzmán earned fewer votes than Lagos, the combined total for his list, which also included Miguel Otero of the National

[5] The basic administrative unit in Chile is the commune, of which there are 335. Every square meter of Chilean soil is part of one of these communes. The number of communes per administrative region varies from nine in the second region to fifty-one in the metropolitan region of Santiago.

Renovation Party, was more than half as great as the votes received by the list for the Concertación candidates Lagos and Zaldivar, and so the second seat went to Guzmán.

There are significant discrepancies between the populations of the legislative districts: the districts that voted most enthusiastically for Pinochet in the 1988 plebiscite tend to be less populated (Martinez 1989). The scope for gerrymander is greatest in the Chamber of Deputies, because the Senate boundaries can only be adjusted in the regions with two Circunscripciones, as the Senate districts are called. Among the 60 districts for the Chamber of Deputies, the correlation between the "No" vote share in the 1988 plebiscite and the voting-age population is 0.493, indicating a strong positive association between opposition to Pinochet in the 1988 plebiscite and the number of voters per Deputy. Packed together in heavily populated districts, Pinochet's opponents live in districts with relatively few Deputies per voter, while Pinochet's supporters find themselves in sparsely populated districts with more Deputies per voter.

There is considerable variation among the sixty districts in the intensity with which they supported the "No" option in the 1988 plebiscite, ranging from only 35.6% support in the rural fortieth district to 65.4% in the forty-fifth district, which consists of working-class communities ringing the port city of Concepción. The twelve districts that gave their second Deputies seat to the Concertación in the 1989 elections tended to have larger vote shares for the "No."[6] Estimating the relationship between the "No" vote in a district, and whether it gave its second seat to the Concertación by using a probit model,[7] one sees that the vote share for the "No" earns a significant[8] positive coefficient, confirming the apparent regularity that districts with heavy votes for the "No" were more likely to elect a second Deputy from the Concertación. The relationship between the estimated probability the Concertación "duplicated" in 1989, capturing both Deputies seats, and the district's "No" vote in the 1988 plebiscite is shown as the solid curve in Figure 3.1.

The figure shows that the estimated probability of Concertación's taking the second seat does not respond linearly to the "No" vote share. Districts such as the twenty-sixth, corresponding to La Florida, a working-class suburb of Santiago, and the thirty-second, the industrial city of

[6] In the elections held in 1989, every district gave at least one of its seats to the Concertación.

[7] There are sixty observations, with the dependent variable equal to 1 if the second seat goes to the Concertación, and 0 otherwise. Estimating a probit model with the percentage vote for the "No," which equals the voteshare times 100, as the sole explanatory variable, one obtains a log likelihood of -22.685, while the estimated coefficient for % vote for the "No" is 0.191, with an estimated standard error of 0.061.

[8] The estimated t ratio equals 3.689.

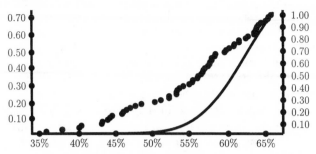

Solid Line: Probability Concertación "Duplicates" (scale on left-hand axis)

Dotted Line: Fraction of Districts with a Lower "No" Vote (scale on right-hand axis)

Horizontal Axis: "No" Vote

Figure 3.1. "No" Vote vs. Probability Concertación Duplicates.

Rancagua, each of which gave the "No" about 63% support in the plebiscite, have about an even chance of electing two deputies from the Concertación, while districts like the twenty-third, which contains of the affluent Santiago suburb of Las Condes,[9] or the rural forty-ninth district in Chile's ninth region, which gave about 40% of their votes to the "No," about two-thirds as much as in the toss-up districts, have negligible probabilities of sending two Concertación Deputies to the Congress.

The dotted curve in Figure 3.1 shows the cumulative density function for the "No" vote. For a given threshold percentage for the "No" the cumulative density function tells what fraction, shown on the right-hand scale of the graph, voted for the "No" at a lower rate. Glancing at the figure, one sees immediately that about 30% of the districts gave less than 50% of their vote to the "No" and had negligible probabilities of duplicating for the Concertación. In contrast, another 30% or so of districts gave margins of over 60% to the "No" and, according to the parameter estimates, had better than even chances of duplicating.

While the details of the Chilean electoral system are special to Chile, the nonlinear relationship between vote shares and results is observed across many electoral systems, and it is the key reason for gerrymandering. In the U. S., where members of Congress are elected in single-member districts, the basic logic of gerrymandering involves sculpting districts that contain small but safe margins of supporters, such as the Chilean Deputies districts' giving less than half of their votes to the "No," while isolating opponents into districts that contain lopsided majorities for their candidates,

[9] While the Concertación and the opposition parties split the twenty-third district in 1989, in the 1993 the twenty-third became the only district in Chile in which the parties of the right duplicated.

such as the Deputies districts giving more than 60% of their votes to the "No". To the extent that this can be achieved, the marginal votes of opponents are "wasted" on candidates who would have won anyway, while the marginal votes of supporters are used to secure extra seats. Of course, settlement patterns and the laws of topography place some constraint on a party's ability to achieve such results, but the basic principal of adjusting district boundaries to create small-but-comfortable majorities for one's own party, and lopsided majorities for one's opponents, remains the gerrymanderer's touchstone in systems with single-member districts.

But the Chilean system is different! The two-member districts create two pivotal voters, one for the one-third margin required to win the first seat, and a second at the two-thirds margin required for a second seat. This makes the tactic of concentrating opponents into districts with lopsided margins exactly the wrong thing to do, for it is in just such districts that they can hope to duplicate, capturing the second seat. Moreover, the population of "Yes" voters from the plebiscite more favorably disposed to the parties on the right is geographically diffuse. Even in the rural fortieth district in the Southern part of the seventh region, which gave only 35.6% of its vote to the "No" in the 1988 plebiscite, Christian Democrat Manual Matta was able to win a seat in the 1989 Elections. An evaluation of the district boundaries should probably take as given that in May 1989, as the military government amended the Organic Law for the Popular Vote and Voter Registration, with the sole exception of the affluent Santiago suburb of Las Condes, which gave two seats to the opposition in the 1993 Congressional elections, but not in 1989, districts with enough "No" voters to make the opposition's capturing the second seat a likely outcome could not be drawn.

As can be seen from Figure 3.1, an optimal gerrymander for the right would not isolate so many of their supporters in districts giving less than 50% to the "No" but would instead seek to combine these districts with those where the probability of the Concertación duplicating was high. If district boundaries could be drawn with complete flexibility and in utter disregard to the laws of topology, then by allocating all of the voters evenly so that each district gave 54.625% for the Concertación, the parameter estimates indicate the Concertación would have received about eight fewer seats in the Chamber of Deputies. In fact, the existing boundaries tend to favor the Concertación, with opposition voters packed into a formidable but easily bypassed electoral Maginot Line in districts such as the thirty-sixth, corresponding to Curicó Province in the eighth region, and the fourteenth district, which contains Viña Del Mar on the coast of the fifth region, where there is almost no risk of the Concertación's electing a second Deputy, rather in districts such as the thirty-second, the industrial city of Rancagua, or the twentieth, the working-class Santiago suburb of La Florida, where the marginal impact of opposition voters on the probability of second seats for Concertación would be much greater.

Of course, the laws of topography do apply, and there were limits on the degree to which the districts could have been redrawn. Nevertheless there are examples where a more cynical gerrymander by the military government as it drafted the organic electoral law could have produced a more favorable result for the parties of the right. One such example is provided by the adjoining forty-sixth and forty-seventh districts in Chile's eighth region; see Figure 3.2. The forty-sixth district gave 61.2% of its vote to the "No" in the 1988 plebiscite, and in the December 1989 general elections the Concertación list gained both seats,[10] while the adjacent forty-seventh district gave the "No" only 42.9% of its vote but nevertheless sent a split delegation to the Chamber of Deputies, consisting of Octavio Jara Wolff of the PPD, a member of the Concertación, and opposition candidate Victor Perez Varela of the UDI party. The districts are of comparable sizes; the population of the forty-sixth district, whose voters embraced the "No," was 190, 425 (Martinez 1989), while the population of the adjoining forty-seventh district, which favored Pinochet, was 266, 598 (Martinez 1989). The parameter estimates indicate that the probability of a second seat for the Concertación in the forty-sixth district was over one in three,[11] while the estimated probability of a "double win" for the Concertación in the forty-seventh district was negligible.[12]

Suppose that instead the two districts had been drawn differently, to create a pair of districts, each with the average "No" vote of 50.46% for the two actual districts.[13] In this case each district would have had a probability of a "double win" for Concertación of only 0.023, making it very unlikely that the Concertación would gain more than one seat from either of the districts. Reshaping the forty-sixth and forty-seventh districts to come up with two new districts with exactly the same support for the "No" was not possible. However, the right could have reduced the Concertación's probability of duplicating in either district with a gerrymander that moved the communes of Nacimiento, Negrete, and Mulchén from the forty-seventh to the forty-sixth, and the communes of Lota and Arauco from the forty-sixth to the forty-seventh. To keep the forty-seventh

---

[10] The district elected Claudio Huepe Garcia, a Christian Democratic economist who between 1969 and 1973 had represented Lebu in the Chamber of Deputies, and Jaime Rocha Manrique, a lawyer from the Radical Party.

[11] The estimated probability is 0.382.

[12] The estimated probability is 0.0000768.

[13] This calculation of the average uses the voting-age populations of the two actual districts as weights. Using registered voters or total district populations would lead to similar results.

Figure 3.2. Actual Boundaries of the Forty-sixth and Forty-seventh Legislative Districts.

Figure 3.3. Hypothetical Pro-Pinochet Gerrymander of the Forty-sixth and Forty-seventh Legislative Districts.

district geographically contiguous, this hypothetical gerrymander would need to be slightly modified, transferring the commune of Santa Juana from the forty-fifth district to the forty-seventh, resulting in the new districts illustrated in Figure 3.3.

Given that the electoral system was going to be denounced anyway for the heavy bias created by the binominal rule in favor of the opposition, it is interesting that the military government did not draw the district boundaries somewhat more cynically in order to maximize the seat share of the opposition parties. Of course those close to the military government would probably aver that the military government did not seek to manipulate future election outcomes and drew district boundaries with the sole intention of producing a representative legislature. But this seems inconsistent with the many other features of the Constitution of 1980, notably the institutional Senators and the binominal electoral system, that appear to have been put in place to bolster the representation of the parties on the right.

An alternative interpretation is that the military government lacked the political expertise to adapt the gerrymander to their own unique electoral system. Perhaps the military government believed that by creating a positive correlation between district populations and the vote for the "No" they guaranteed an electoral bias in favor of parties sympathetic to their interests, a belief held by many of their opponents (Martinez 1989). As they stand, the district boundaries allow a substantial number of duplications for the Concertación, largely nullifying the biases of the electoral system relative to proportional representation with a single national district: the opposition's 40% share of seats in the Chamber of Deputies differs little from their share of the overall vote.

The possibility that the military government botched the gerrymander of the electoral districts serves as a reminder that while the armed forces are professional military strategists, electoral strategy is outside the realm of their expertise. This can be an unexpected source of advantage to civilian opponents of a military regime who must choose between armed resistance and opposition within an electoral framework, even when it is designed by the regime that they oppose.

3.2 THE LEGISLATIVE PROCESS IN THE 1980 CONSTITUTION

In its broad outlines the legislative process in Chile could be thought of as a mixture of its U. S. and French counterparts. As in the U. S. the system is purely presidential; there is no prime minister. However, the Chilean president enjoys many of the legislative powers reserved for the government in France. It is almost as if the Constitution of 1980 had been written

Legislative Institutions in the Constitution of 1980

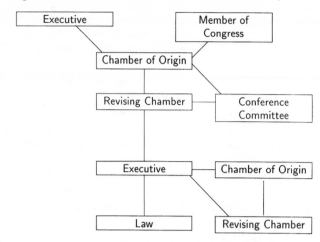

Figure 3.4. Highlights of the Legislative Process in the Constitution of 1980.

to match academics' initial (i.e., 1960s) characterization of the legislative process in the French Fifth Republic, with many of the qualifying features noted by Huber (1996) in his more recent analysis of periods of *cohabitation* edited out or replaced.

Bills can begin as either motions, proposed by a member of Congress, or as messages, proposed by the president, as shown in Figure 3.4. Bills must deal with matters of law, which are spelled out under twenty broad categories in article 60 of the 1980 Constitution. While this restriction to legislate only on matters of law somewhat limits the scope of legislation, the precise demarcation of the boundaries is nevertheless open to interpretation. Less ambiguous are the exclusive proposal rights reserved for the president in several important policy areas. These include laws that would affect the administrative and political division of the country, the budget, the size and disposition of the armed forces, laws affecting collective bargaining, and those that would change salaries, entitlements, or taxes. During its deliberations, Congress can amend proposed spending downward, but not upward. One can think of this as resolving the doubt about policy in the gray area between matters of law, which are the province of legislation, and matters of regulation, which are in the exclusive domain of the executive, in favor of the executive. These exclusive proposal powers significantly constrain the ability of the Congress to initiate proposals. The president also enjoys monopoly proposal-making power over the budget.

There are some restrictions on where legislation can originate; bills affecting the budget or the military draft must originate in the Chamber of Deputies, while those dealing with amnesties or pardons must start in the

94

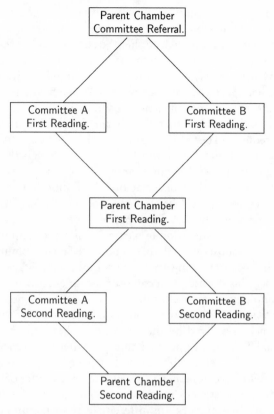

Figure 3.5. The Two Readings of a Bill.

Senate. With these exceptions, the process treats the two chambers symmetrically. The bill is considered in the chamber in which it is proposed, called the chamber of origin, where it is given two readings, called general consideration and particular consideration. At each stage the president of the chamber of origin can first direct the bill to one or more relevant committees; see Figure 3.5. While the organic constitutional law of Congress only mandates that each chamber establish one standing committee, on finance, both chambers have many more than this. In the Senate there are twenty-two.

The committee, or committees, to which the bill is referred at the first reading make reports to the parent chamber and may amend the bill at this stage, subject to not poaching on the areas of legislation reserved for the president. When the committee has made its report the bill comes up for consideration in general by the chamber of origin, with the committee's bill serving as the basis of discussion. If the bill is approved in general it then returns to the committee or committees that considered it for a second reading in particular, where all amendments are considered.

If a bill is rejected in general by either the chamber of origin or at a later stage by the revising chamber, then the president may not reintroduce it for at least one year. There is an exception to this, should the president decide to use his or her special "insistence powers," which enable the president to combine a supermajority of two-thirds in one chamber and a minority of at least one-third of the other chamber to force acceptance of the bill. This would require a special vote, and President Aylwin was reluctant to use this provision during the period 1990–1994, which is the focus of the empirical analysis in the following chapters. Given the partisan balance of the two chambers, with the Concertación falling short of two-thirds of the Chamber of Deputies, presidential "insistence" could only have succeeded with support from a substantial number of opposition Deputies.

The next stage, consideration in particular, is a very important one for the analysis in the subsequent chapters, because Senate committees' deliberations at the second reading are very porous. At this stage any member of the chamber plus the president can propose amendments. However, using the terminology developed by Shepsle (1979), amendments are subject to a *proposal germaneness restriction*. This is enforced by the committee chair and can be reviewed by the parent chamber and appealed to the Constitutional Tribunal. In practice this germaneness restriction is taken very seriously and is reasonably scrupulously enforced, though there are occasional debates over whether an amendment is a matter of law, whether it poaches on the president's reserved proposal areas, or whether it is in fact germane. While matters are different in the Chamber of Deputies, Senate rules require that every amendment be put to a publicly recorded roll-call vote, so that each committee member's vote is made public. When the committee that considered the bill has finished its deliberations, the bill, including any amendments approved by the committee, returns to the parent chamber. Any parts of the bill which were not subject to amendments are at this point considered approved. If a segment of the bill was amended by the committee then the whole floor votes on whether to approve the committee's amendment. In practice this means that if the committee was unanimous in approving an amendment the parent chamber simply adopts it by acclaim, with only amendments approved by the committee on divided votes being revisited on the floor. In addition, amendments rejected by the committee can be renewed in the Senate with the signatures of ten Senators. This means that any amendment that enjoys serious support in the forty-seven-member chamber can be brought to a floor vote despite the committee's opposition. New amendments are not permitted on the floor during consideration in particular without the unanimous approval of the chamber.

The practical effect of these rules is to deprive committees of gatekeeping power; they do not have what is known in the U. S. Congress as a closed rule. Although all amendments during the second reading must pass through the committee, the floor can revisit all of the committee's decisions. At the same time, the public roll-call votes force committee members to take positions on every amendment. These votes become part of the public record and have to be defended on the floor and explained to constituents. As is discussed more extensively in the appendix, the spotlight of public roll-call votes acts as a kind of truth serum, severely limiting the returns to strategic voting. This means that the roll-call votes from Senate committees provide important information to the Senate about the political content of amendments in a concise and easy to interpret form. At the same time, these Senate committee roll calls serendipitously provide important and useful information about the political agendas of the Senators on the committee and those making proposals, and several of the subsequent chapters will be devoted to studying this information.

Once the bill has been approved in particular, it is sent to the other chamber, called the revising chamber, where it is given two further readings, again with the committees and the floor able to amend the legislation. If, when the revising chamber has finished its deliberations, the bill approved by the revising chamber matches that approved in the chamber of origin, the bill is considered approved by Congress, and it goes to the president for his or her signature or veto. However, it is unusual for both chambers to approve major bills in identical form at this stage. Much more commonly, the bill approved by the revising chamber will differ from the bill approved in the chamber of origin on at least a few points. In this case it returns to the chamber of origin, which has the opportunity to approve the bill as rewritten by the revising chamber. If it does not do so, then the bill can shuttle back and forth between the chambers, but more commonly, the chamber of origin recommends referring the bill to a conference committee, made up of five Senators and five Deputies. In contrast with the unit rule applied by conference committees in the U. S. Congress,[14] each conference committee member has one vote, and decisions are made by a majority vote among the members. The conference committees are always chaired by a Senator. The conference committee is almost always composed of members of the committees that considered the original bill. While the standing committees of the Senate all have five members, those in the Chamber of Deputies have thirteen, so that Senators on a committee are almost guaranteed to be on the conference committee (unless there are multiple referrals, so that more than one

[14] In the U. S. Congress the entire House delegation casts one vote and the entire Senate delegation casts one vote, with the majority of each delegation determining how its vote will be cast.

Senate committee was involved in considering the bill) while their counterparts in the Deputies, where only five of thirteen members go to the conference committee, have no such assurance. If the conference committee can agree on a bill it is considered first by the chamber of origin, and then by the revising chamber, and it is debated under a closed rule: the conference committee bill must be voted up or down, with no possibility of amendment.

If at any point during the legislative process a presidential bill gets "stuck" waiting to be debated on the floor, or waiting for a committee report, the president may apply a deadline. He or she can choose among deadlines of 3, 10, and 30 days, within which the chamber currently considering the legislation must provide a decision (which of course could be to reject the bill). This means that the time-honored tactic of committee chairs and floor leaders in the U. S. Congress of bottling bills up in committee, and refusing to bring them to the floor for a vote, is not available in Chile where presidential bills are concerned. This ability to force a vote gives the president enormous leverage over Congress. Members who propose bills do not enjoy similar powers of insistence. This means as a practical matter that the best way for a member to get legislation enacted is to attach it to a presidential bill as an amendment, subject to not violating the germaneness restrictions, and not trespassing on the content areas reserved for the president.

Once a bill is approved by both houses of Congress, it goes to the president; see Figure 3.4. At this stage the president can promulgate the bill as it is written, or he or she can try to change it. The president is given the option of vetoing all or part of the bill, with the unvetoed part being enacted, while the vetoed portion returns to Congress. Thus, the Chilean president has what amounts to a line-item veto. In addition, he or she is allowed to introduce amendments at this stage, called observations. The vetoed portion of the bill, along with any presidential observations, returns to the chamber of origin. There the presidential observations are discussed under a closed rule. The president has the option of grouping the observations together, so that they must all be voted in one block, or separating them, allowing different votes. If the observations are accepted by a majority in both chambers, then the bill is considered approved in its amended form. At this stage Congress can introduce no amendments of its own. Only if the observations have been rejected does Congress proceed to attempt a veto override. If the vetoed portions of the bill meet with the support of two-thirds of the members present in each chamber, then the vetoed portions of the bill become law; otherwise, they do not, and only the elements that met with presidential approval are enacted.

Subject only to the proposal germaneness constraint, the president's veto powers enable him or her to present proposals in the form of

98

"observations" which must be considered under a closed rule. Thus, even in policy areas not reserved by the constitution for presidential initiatives, the president can make take it or leave it offers to Congress, provided he or she can count on the unflinching support of at least one-third plus one of the members in at least one of the Chambers. Of course, the political costs of doing this on a regular basis could be quite high. However, on any detail of a particular bill, the prospect of a partial presidential veto combined with a strategically chosen observation provides the president with considerable bargaining power in dealing with Congress. The Constitution essentially gives the president the last word on the legislative agenda, when he or she wants it.

4

Roll-Call Votes and Senate Committees

Now that we have taken a somewhat closer look at the legislative institutions set up by the Constitution of 1980, we require a more detailed map of the ideological terrain. The impact of institutions such as the president's insistence powers, and his "constructive" veto powers, which enable him or her to offer amendments along with his or her vetos, depends on how cohesive the president's legislative coalition is. Can we treat the president's opponents in the Senate as a single unitary actor, or do they differ in their degree of opposition? Likewise, will the Concertación Senators rubber stamp all presidential initiatives, or does the president have to adjust his or her proposals to secure their support? The same institutional structure that permits a president supported by pliant majorities in both chambers to dominate the legislative process can leave that president frustrated when faced by determined and unified opposition in even one chamber.[1] This means that we must be very careful when making broad statements about "executive dominance" and autocratic tendencies written into a constitution. This dominance can be very sensitive to the composition of the legislature and the objectives of the executive.

Measuring the ideological positions taken by competing political parties is difficult. Party manifestos and campaign literature typically reveal that all of the political parties favor prosperity, efficient government, safe streets, good schools, and high ethical standards, while all are opposed to crime, unemployment, and corruption. Moreover, even when the parties differ they typically employ asymmetric rhetoric: the party that has a majority on its side of an issue will emphasize this even while it remains quiet about issues on which its position does not meet with majority approval. This effective strategy helps the parties win votes, but it does little to clarify the differences among them. A party that favors an unpopular tax to reduce the government debt will emphasize the fiscal responsibility

---

[1] For a discussion of this issue in the context of the French Fifth Republic, see Huber (1996).

100

of reducing the debt and say very little about the tax increase; its opponents will harangue against higher taxes but without going into details about which services they plan to cut, or how high they plan to let the government debt soar. Devising objective criteria for untangling the true policy differences between the parties from the rhetorical thicket is not a trivial task.

Serendipitously the rules of the Senate require publicly recorded votes on all amendments offered at second readings of bills. These public votes offer a useful window on legislators' issue positions, and they enjoy a number of advantages over campaign rhetoric. First of all, recorded votes force legislators to take positions on the same question, while the requirement that one vote "aye," "nay," or "abstain" limits the room for rhetorical maneuver. This is especially helpful when legislators cast a large number of votes, allowing us to evaluate their consistency across a wide range of issues. The public record of roll-call votes from Senate committees provides the foundation for the analysis of Senators' issue positions in the subsequent three chapters.

This chapter provides an overview of the statistical methods that permit us to recover information about legislators' preferences, and the characteristics of the agenda on which they vote. The methods used here thrive when legislators vote "sincerely" for the issue alternatives closest to their most preferred outcomes, and when there are no gatekeepers to intercept proposals before they come to a vote. This requirement of sincerity can be relaxed somewhat; it is enough for legislators to consistently support the alternative closest to their public issue position, whether they "sincerely" prefer their public position or not. As will be discussed in this chapter, these conditions are approximated on roll calls taken at committees' second readings of bills.

Offsetting the advantages of the committee voting data is one great shortcoming: the small size of the committees, which have but five members each. This small size creates two sets of problems. The first of these is substantive: even with some turnover in committee memberships, we only observe a small fraction of the Senate's membership voting on a given committee. This means that the committee votes do not provide direct evidence about the preferences of the many Senators who do not vote. The second problem is technical; the statistical estimators used by specialists on the U. S. Congress to estimate preferences from legislative voting records fail when the number of voters is small, as it is in this application.

The first of these shortcomings is substantially alleviated by the tight control exercised by the parties over committee assignments. Because committee assignments belong to the parties rather than to individual Senators, renegades without substantial support within their parties could be removed quickly and easily, although this power rarely has to be used for its effect to be felt. Asked about the influence Senators exercise over their own committee assignments, one Christian Democratic senator summarized the process as "the senator asks, the party decides."[2] Senators on committees are very much representatives of their Senate delegations, and if they are to remain on a committee for any length of time the ideological positions they take must meet with substantial support within their own parties.

The second complication arising from the small number of Senators voting on each amendment is a special case of the so-called parameter proliferation problem. This arises because we cannot add more data, in the form of votes, without also adding more parameters, for example those that pertain to the ideological content of proposals. This essentially prevents estimators such as the one developed by Poole and Rosenthal (1985) from providing reliable estimates when the number of voters on a given proposal is as few as five. To overcome this problem, I developed a statistical estimator that incorporates a structural model of the agenda, and in the process fixes the number of parameters to be estimated (Londregan 2000).This avoids the proliferation problem. The estimator works well when, as in Senate Committees, the agenda is not controlled by a gatekeeper, and proposal making is cheap.

This chapter begins with a discussion of the institutional details of Senate committees and their role in the legislative process. The second section presents an overview of the statistical technique used to analyze the data, while the final section of the chapter provides some background detail on the data themselves, and on how they were gathered.

4.1 PREFERENCES AND VOTES IN SENATE COMMITTEES

As with most legislative chambers, the Chilean Senate delegates a good deal of important work to committees. The opposition, who control the Senate, face a well-informed political adversary in the president, who has the entire executive branch of the government at his or her disposal when formulating proposals, amendments, and vetos. In contrast, Senate staffs are tiny; a Senator typically has an administrative secretary, a political aide in his or her district, and sometimes a single legislative assistant. Committee staffs are also sparse; a secretary and assistant who are responsible for taking and transcribing the minutes of committee meetings and providing whatever research assistance members request will typically have a workload consisting of several committees: staff resources are measured in committees per secretary rather than secretaries per committee (interview with Carlos Hoffmann, May 1994). This

---

[2] "El senador pide, el partido decide."(Interview with Juan Hamiltón Santiago, May 1992).

leaves the president with an enormous informational advantage over the Congress.

There are several mechanisms for monitoring and controlling the standing committees of the Senate. The assignment of committee places is done, when possible, by unanimous accord of the legislative caucuses (Senado de Chile 1994). If such an accord is not possible, committee members are elected by using cumulative voting (Senado de Chile 1994). Once assigned, the committee memberships essentially belong to the party caucuses, which can, should they choose, substitute another Senator for the current committee member (Senado de Chile 1994), though if the replacement belongs to a different caucus then both caucuses must approve (Senado de Chile 1994). The consent of the departing committee member is not required. While this practice is almost exclusively used to deal with schedule conflicts, so that a member who must be absent from Valparaíso on the day of a committee meeting can be replaced by another member of the same caucus, it could be used to remove a recalcitrant committee member as well. Even temporary substitutions of committee members are formally treated as permanent reassignments. Some Senators appear only briefly in the records of a committee, sitting in for a fellow party member for a day or two of hearings, while a core membership of experts rotates much more slowly through the committee, with some remaining permanently active, while others will rotate to other assignments after a year or two. One expects that special expertise resides mainly with the core members of the committee.

As noted in the preceding chapter, standing committees in the Senate have little formal agenda-setting power. At the second reading of a bill any Senator, whether a member of the committee or not, is entitled to offer amendments to the bill (Senado de Chile 1994). Moreover, amendments rejected by the committee may be reconsidered by the Senate as a whole, should as few as ten Senators or the President of the Republic (Senado de Chile 1994) petition for reconsideration. Such a "renewed" amendment is then put to a vote before the bill. This means that any amendment rejected by the committee that could receive majority support on the floor of the Senate (with twenty-four votes constituting an absolute majority of the entire membership during the period under study) would easily encounter the ten signatures needed to bring it to a vote. This is just what happened to a tax reform bill approved in 1990 by the Finance Committee (Biblioteca del Congreso Nacional 1990a). This committee had a majority of three members of the Concertación, and two members of the opposition Renovación Nacional party. In the committee's second reading of the bill, Senator Piñera, one of the Renovación Nacional Senators, proposed an amendment that would limit the period during which a tax increase proposed in the bill would apply. Senator Piñera's amendment would have

103

made the increase expire just before Chile's 1993 presidential election, a difficult time to renew a tax. This amendment was rejected by a three-to-two party-line vote, with the three Concertación members voting against it. When the bill arrived in the Senate chamber, where the opposition form a majority, ten members of the opposition quickly signed their names to a petition to "renew" the amendment, which then passed the Senate on a party-line vote. Likewise, the chamber can vote whether to approve each amendment adopted by the committee, although in practice they usually agree to approve all amendments that received unanimous support in the committee, only revisiting those that were approved on divided votes or rejected but subsequently renewed on the floor. While most amendments rejected by the committees are not renewed, and most amendments the committees adopt are subsequently approved by the chamber, this is not the result of any formal committee "gatekeeping power."

Sincere Voting in Senate Committees

Another measure which enables the Senate to control its standing committees is the requirement that, at its second reading of a bill, a committee must take roll-call votes on every amendment it considers (Senado de Chile 1994). As the preceding discussion has indicated, the fact that a second reading has taken place at all virtually guarantees the Senate will approve a different bill than the Chamber of Deputies, with the most likely result being referral to a conference committee that will include the members of the Senate's standing committee. The publicly reported roll-call votes at the second reading force the Senators most likely to be on the conference committee to take public positions for or against every amendment sent to them.

Will these public votes reveal the Senators' information? Will committee members vote sincerely? Given the high information content of votes that are believed to be sincere, such votes may influence the beliefs and votes of other legislators, thereby creating a temptation to cast misleading votes. Will legislators be swayed by these temptations, or will the public nature of the committee votes induce information revelation?

There are two elements of the legislator's calculation. First there is the cost of taking a position that can later be shown to stand at variance with the legislator's announced policy goals. For example, being revealed to have taken an antilabor position in a committee roll call could prove very expensive for a legislator on the left. The public nature of roll-call votes makes it costly to cast misleading votes.

The second element in the legislator's calculation is the benefit from influencing the votes of others through a deceptive vote. Such legislative behavior is hard to take credit for with constituents. Not only does it make one look sneaky to brag about casting an insincere vote, the message is a fairly complicated one, and it would be hard to communicate credibly to constituents. A legislator trying to take subsequent credit for a disingenuous vote will probably succeed in convincing only his or her legislative colleagues. Offsetting this, a legislator who casts an insincere vote will expect a benefit only if he or she is confident of changing a policy outcome about which he or she personally cares. The costs of a misleading vote are not worth incurring if the vote does not change the subsequent outcome. By reducing the expected benefits of a strategic vote, but not its expected costs, an unpredictable agenda reduces the attractiveness of strategic voting. If the legislator cannot foresee the choices he or she is attempting to sway, or if the probability of a future amendment on which his or her strategic vote could sway the outcome is small, then the benefit against which the legislator weighs the cost of having to be ready to explain his or her vote to constituents falls. The importance of a predictable agenda on a legislator's decision of whether to vote strategically or sincerely is highlighted in the analysis of the Powell Amendment in the U. S. House of Representatives by Denzau, Riker, and Shepsle (Denzau et al. 1985). The Powell Amendment was considered under a rule that guaranteed that the vote on the amendment would be followed immediately and without further opportunity to consider additional modifications to the bill by a vote on final passage. This minimized uncertainty about the impact of strategic votes and helped to facilitate strategic voting by Republicans intent on stopping a bill to provide federal subsidies for education.

The Chilean Senate, with its porous process for legislative amendments, and the multiple stages through which bills must pass, stands in sharp contrast with the predictable agenda that included the vote on the Powell Amendment. A typical bill, such as the labor law reforms (Biblioteca del Congreso Nacional 1993a) considered in 1993, will contain a host of margins on which policy can be adjusted. Just as the concentration of a medication in a patient's bloodstream can be increased by administering doses through injection, or by pill, or perhaps by use of an inhaler, so too the pro-labor content of a bill can be increased (or reduced) to the desired level by adjusting policy on any of multiple margins: by extending coverage of the maximum workweek, by expanding the liability of contractors for workplace injuries to cover more industries, by increasing the number of mandatory vacation days, and in many other ways.

A legislator seeking to move the bill moderately in a pro-labor direction, but not as far as the unions might like, could achieve this by shortening the workweek to 48 hours, but leaving the status quo liability of employers intact, or by increasing employers' liability for injuries sustained by employees of subcontractors, but leaving the workweek untouched, or there could be requirements about the provision of workday meals, or workplace medical care, or more formalized grievance procedures. In order to move the bill moderately in the pro-labor direction, the law could be modified in just one or two of the ways suggested above. However, substantial modifications made simultaneously on all margins would lead to a much larger pro-labor shift in policy.

The multiplicity of margins in the ambit of labor law reform is shared by other issue areas as well; the role of the state in providing telecommunications services may be reduced via partial privatization and little regulation, or complete privatization and extensive regulation. The level of deregulation can be adjusted by changes in the rate base companies can use in calculating their fees, or in the form of increasing or removing explicit price caps, or by compelling local phone service to be extended to remote and unprofitable rural customers. Antiterrorism policy can be made less severe by removing some crimes from the jurisdiction of the military courts, or by reducing the budget for enforcement, or through an adjustment of the penalties for those convicted. Across the policy spectrum, leftward or rightward shifts in policy positions can be achieved through adjustments on a variety of margins. When legislators reach the conference committee they will choose only some arrows from their quiver of potential amendments. A conference committee that decides to move labor policy moderately in favor of labor will, for example, reduce the workweek but not for farmworkers, nor perhaps will it increase the number of mandatory holidays. The precise choice of instruments used to achieve the desired policy shift is something to which the committee is not committed ex ante. Moreover, given some bargaining and heterogeneity within the conference committee, we may expect that even future conference committee members will not be able to forecast accurately the set of instruments upon which the bargaining will finally settle.

The unpredictability of the agenda means the benefits of an insincere committee vote are uncertain, while the public nature of such a vote guarantees that casting such a vote will be costly. There are powerful incentives at work to induce sincere voting in Senate committees at the second reading of the bill.[3]

Measuring Legislators' Preferences

There are various ways of measuring legislators' ideological leanings, and their competence. At one extreme one can rely on the impressions

---

[3] Interested readers will find a formal model that helps to illuminate the issues involved in a legislator's decision of whether to vote sincerely presented in the Appendix.

of experts. Political scientists, journalists, and politicians themselves are asked to place political parties or individual legislators on a continuum running from left to right, or from pro-labor to pro-business, or from pro-environment to pro-user. Then there are the sometimes tongue-in-cheek surveys of legislators' competence, such as a straw poll taken among U. S. Senate staffers a few decades ago in which the Senator the survey identified as "dumbest" had set his staff to work cleaning the rust from paper clips as an austerity measure. At the opposite extreme, one can use statistical analysis to evaluate data and assign ideological locations and competence levels according to some goodness-of-fit criterion. All of these approaches are best viewed as approximations. All begin with a model, which is sometimes implicit, of a meaningful continuum of issue positions from left to right or from authoritarian to democratic. The notion here, as discussed in the first chapter, is that individuals' belief systems differ along such a continuum. All approaches to measurement then filter data through the analyst's model, whether this is done explicitly, by using quantitative data and statistical formulas, or implicitly, as substantive scholars weigh legislators' speeches, votes, the identities of their political supporters and enemies, and their behind-the-scenes activities in order to identify their ideological positions. When this is done well a better understanding of legislators' ideological positions and their competence emerges. Of course, all of the models we use are approximations. Real policies have thousands of attributes about which legislators can disagree, and each of which can potentially become the subject of a political debate. The useful classification of legislators along an ideological continuum is a constructive simplification of a more complicated reality, whether this is done intuitively or systematically. None of this is unique to the use of formal models and quantitative analysis.

Up to now the analysis here has used formal models to help clarify some of the key issues involved in the discussion about ideology, constitution writing, and political transitions toward democracy. Each of the models is an abstraction that omits some details inessential to the argument in order to illustrate and better delineate the underlying political structure. At this stage the basic model developed in Chapter 1 will be used to go somewhat further. Rather than merely using the model to clarify the logic of the arguments, I will now use it to help structure the information contained in Senators' roll-call voting records. This involves first setting out the model in careful detail and then asking the question: "Which parameters of the model, which preferred outcomes, and which locations for the proposals and status quo about which the Senators are voting are most consistent with the observed roll-call voting records?" Of course, the analytical model is only an approximation. Nevertheless, the parameter estimates provide useful guidance about Senators' ideological leanings and legislative competence. Moreover, there is a large body of statistical literature that deals with the accuracy of parameter estimates chosen in this way when the model is literally correct. It is this literature that shows us how to construct standard errors and to evaluate statistical tests.

This approach provides a nicely self-contained assessment of legislators' ideological leanings and their effectiveness. It also calibrates the accuracy of our measures. However, we must always bear in mind that these measurements, the standard error estimates that assess their accuracy, and the statistical tests that use them to evaluate hypotheses are all contingent on the structure of the model.[4] Of course, this is a general problem from which analysts cannot hope to escape. Intuitive and heuristic models are also prisoners of their own structure, and when that structure is left implicit, as is often the case, analysts are even more prone to false confidence in their results.

The good news for empirical analysis is that while our models are almost never literally correct, their implications are often robust to minor errors and approximations. Consider the usage by interest groups in the U. S. of legislative scorecards, such as the ADA Score constructed by the liberal lobby group Americans for Democratic Action. This measure, which totes up the number of times a legislator cast (politically) correct votes on key issues, is the best measure of the legislator's voting record only under very special circumstances (Londregan 2000), which are more restrictive than those imposed by the model from Chapter 1. Nevertheless, ADA scores are widely and correctly viewed as providing a useful measure of legislators' ideological leanings, and they have been shown to be highly correlated with other measures of ideology assembled by different interest groups, and by academics interested in calibrating legislators' ideological sympathies. Even when the restrictive assumptions that would make them optimal estimators of legislators' ideological positions fail, ADA scores, and other interest group ratings, continue to provide a very useful approximation. The estimator used here makes less restrictive assumptions than interest group scorecards (Londregan 2000), and it has the additional advantage that it can be calculated by using any subset of roll-call voting data so that one does not have to wait for interest groups to chart the ideological terrain. This is an overwhelming advantage for the committee roll-call voting data used here, which have not been explicitly rated by Chilean interest groups.

---

[4] For a useful discussion of the contingency of statistical tests of substantive hypothesis on the ancillary details of the statistical models used to test them, see Roll (1977).

Roll-Call Votes and Senate Committees

This section addresses the question, "If lawmakers vote sincerely, how much can we expect to learn about their preferences from observing how the legislators vote?" The answer to this fundamental question is not as simple as one would hope. We must pass through two layers of analysis. The first involves drawing a map between the parameters of the model and the data. The next logical step is to read this map "backward," looking at the data and inferring which settings of the parameters are most likely to have generated it. This is the fundamental principal of maximum likelihood. However, as we noted in the previous section, there is a second level of difficulty that hampers this exercise, stemming from what statisticians refer to as "the incidental parameters problem." This problem can be handled, but the solution requires some careful description. Some of the more technical details can be found in the Appendix, while Londregan (2000) provides an analysis of the parameter proliferation problem.

From Preferences to Votes

Starting with the quadratic spatial model developed in Chapter 1 and set forth in Equation (1.2), we have a set of parameters that pertain to the V legislators who cast votes, $\{x_v\}_{v=1}^{V}$, α, and parameters that characterize the proposals on which they vote, $\{p_i, v_i\}_{i=1}^{N}$. As we move to data analysis it is important to recognize that voting decisions include idiosyncratic factors that are related neither to ideology nor to valence. These might include the impact of the proposal on a legislator's district, or a personal reaction to the way an amendment is drafted, or an argument made. Starting with the utility function given in Equation (1.2), we can formulate the utility for legislator v from alternative i as

$$U(p_i, v_i, \xi_{vi}; x_v, \alpha) = -\frac{1}{2}(x_v - p_i)^2 + \alpha v_i + \xi_{vi}. \qquad (4.1)$$

The additional term, ξ_{vi}, represents the influence of idiosyncratic factors, and I will treat it as a random variable. Using this notation, a legislator with a preferred outcome of x_v will prefer a proposal with a valence of v_i and an ideological position of p_i to a status quo policy with valence v_{sq} and position p_{sq} provided

$$U(p_i, v_i, \xi_{vi}; x_v, \alpha) > U(p_{sq}, v_{sq}, \xi_{vsq}; x_v, \alpha). \qquad (4.2)$$

If we are confident that legislators vote sincerely then we can use their observed votes to estimate some of the parameters from this spatial model set forth in Chapter 1. With a bit of algebra, which can be found in the Appendix, it emerges that the probability that legislator v votes in favor

109

of proposal i is

$$c_i + b_v + g_i x_v > \eta_{vi}. \tag{4.3}$$

Discussion of the substantive interpretation of the c_i, b_v, and g_i parameters follows equation (4.4).

We can complete the model by positing a probability distribution over the idiosyncratic preference shocks, the η_{vi}. This gives us the probability that legislator v votes in favor of proposal i as a function of the underlying parameters.

While we would like to be able to estimate the voting model given in Equation (4.3), this turns out not to be possible. The problem stems from what statisticians call "parameter proliferation." As we add more data, we also add more parameters to estimate; each new proposal brings with it a new pair of parameters, c_i and g_i, to estimate. When the number of voters is small, as it is in Senate committees, this problem prevents maximum likelihood estimates of the parameters from converging to the true parameter values; see Londregan (2000) for details.

One way to respond to this problem is to build a model of the proposal process. Here I recognize that the stream of proposals in a given subject area from a given author arises from that author's pursuing a consistent set of objectives. Here I treat all such proposals as having the same rightward displacement, so that $g_i = g_a$ for every proposal i written by author a. Likewise, I model the consensus appeal parameters for proposals from author i as emerging from a common probability distribution, so that $c_i = c_a - v_i^*$, where c_a is the average consensus quality of proposals from author a, and v_i^* is a proposal specific shock. Unfavorable values of v_i^* correspond to outcomes such as the proposal to require eight-hour rest periods for workers on factory ships mentioned in Chapter 1, which drew criticism from union leaders and businessmen alike. The parameter α calibrates the variance of the proposal specific shock, v_i^*, relative to the variance of η_{v_i}. It is convenient to define the random variable v_i as $v_i \equiv \frac{1}{\alpha} v_i^*$, so that v_i has unit variance.

While this simple model of proposals comes at a cost (it restricts the variation we can estimate among proposals from the same author), it has the advantage of solving the parameter proliferation problem. The parameters we must estimate are now $\{x_v, b_v\}_{v=1}^{V}$, $\{g_a, c_a\}_{a=1}^{A}$, and α. Instead of trying to estimate $2V + 2N$ parameters, as in the model given in Equation (4.4), we need only estimate $2V + 2A + 1$ parameters, where A is the number of legislators who sponsor proposals. As N grows, the number of parameters we must estimate does not.

Working with this new model, which encompasses the proposal process, the condition for voting in favor of the proposal becomes

$$c_a + b_v + g_a x_v > \eta_{vi} + \alpha v_i. \tag{4.4}$$

The terms on the left-hand side, and the α term on the right-hand side of the inequality, are parameters we can estimate. The random errors, v_i and η_{vi}, capture idiosyncratic variation in proposals' appeal, and legislators reactions. Higher values for the left-hand side of the inequality make it more probable that we will observe a "yes" vote, as they open up a wider range of random error terms that still result in an affirmative vote.

Taking the terms one at a time, x_v is the preferred outcome of legislator v, and it emerges directly from the model in Chapter 1. The g_a parameter is fairly close to the model; it represents the ideological distance between proposals made by author a and the status quo they are meant to displace. Think of this as a measure of how far rightward author a proposes policy move from the status quo. Negative values for g_a indicate an author's attempt to shift policy leftward of the status quo.

The interaction of the x_v and g_a terms means that not all legislators respond the same way to a given author's proposal. The probability of a favorable vote from a legislator on the left, with $x_v < 0$, will be higher for an amendment from a Socialist author, who proposes leftward shifts in the status quo with $g_a < 0$, so that $x_v g_a$ is positive, than for a member of the UDI party on the right, for whom $g_a > 0$ and hence $x_v g_a$ is negative. Nevertheless, there is more to the voting outcome than just ideology, and this is reflected in the remaining parameters of the model.

The c_a parameter is linked to the model in a more tenuous way; it measures the consensus appeal of proposals from author a. This is an amalgam of the proposal's valence and a measure of ideological extremism. Whereas the g_a parameter tells us how far the proposal would move policy from the status quo, it is silent on the location of the status quo. Proposals from an author seeking to move policy slightly leftward from a status quo that is well to the right of all voters could be expected to meet with high levels of approval. A proposer with the same value for g who sought to move policy a similar distance leftward from a status quo that was already on the left of the other voters would encounter stiff opposition and rarely succeed in passing an initiative. We are unable to distinguish on the basis of the voting coalitions that emerge whether an author's proposals are going down in defeat because they have low valence or whether it is because he or she makes proposals with normal valence that would shift policy to a point that most voters perceive as more extreme than the status quo.

As with the well-known probit model, the error terms on the right-hand side, η_{vi} and v_i, have standard normal probability distributions, that is, they have mean 0 and variance 1. The η_{vi} term measures the idiosyncratic disturbance to preferences for voter v on proposal i. The key factor here is that the idiosyncratic factor is independent across legislators. The model also allows for a common disturbance term, v_i. This captures peculiarities of the consensus appeal of a particular proposal. The empirical regularity is that not all proposals from the same author meet with the same degree of acceptance. Presumably a substantial part of this variation is due to some proposals being "better ideas" than others. Consider the amendment discussed in Chapter 1, in which a group of Socialist senators proposed a mandatory eight-hour rest period for workers on factory ships. Not all proposals from the Socialist senators share the low valence of this failed amendment, which would have thoroughly disrupted work schedules aboard the ships. The model recognizes this by including the v_i term. Proposals with low consensus appeal, correcting for their authorship, correspond to low values for this proposal-specific shock; those with strong consensus appeal, to high values for v_i. The larger the value for α, the greater the importance of the proposal specific shock that affects all voters.

As with the choice of the units used to calibrate a thermometer that measures temperature, we are free to choose the units we use to measure ideological locations. But once we have fixed two points on a thermometer, for example making 0 deg correspond to the freezing point of water and 100 deg to the boiling point, we are no longer free to fix any of the other temperature readings; normal human body temperature is then 37 deg. Had we fixed the freezing point of water at 32 deg and the boiling point at 212, then normal human body temperature would be 98.6 deg. Here the equivalent choice of units involves selecting a reference proposer, for whom c_a and g_a are set equal to 0, and two reference voters, neither of whom needs to be the reference proposer, whose preferred outcomes are normalized to $x_v = -1$ and $x_{v'} = 1$, respectively. As with the choice of reference points for a temperature scale, the choice of whom to use as the reference proposer and as the reference voters amounts to an arbitrary choice of units.

Given the normalizations needed to identify the model, the b_v term indicates the willingness of voter v to support amendments from the reference proposer. In the results presented in the following three chapters, the reference proposer always corresponds to the National Renovation (RN) Party. Thus voters with higher values for b_v are more likely to vote for amendments offered by members of the RN. The more polarizing the content of proposals from the RN, the greater the differences we expect to see among the estimated values for the various voters b_v's.

Analyzing Roll-Call Data: Potential Pitfalls

The analysis of roll-call voting data presents several well-known pitfalls. Notably, the set of bills that comes to the floor of a legislature for a vote is not a random selection of all of the bills that have been presented.

Some bills and amendments are stopped before they reach the floor, while the fate of others is decided without a roll-call vote. When the choice of which bills to bring to a roll-call vote is correlated with idiosyncratic factors, then naive estimation that does not take this selection rule into account will tend to produce biased parameter estimates.

This is more than an idle concern. Legislative leaders have every incentive to canvass the idiosyncratic reactions of key voters and the idiosyncratic appeal of potential initiatives before they put proposals to a vote. This way leaders avoid wasting scarce political capital trying to push though doomed amendments and bills that failed at the "trial balloon" stage. While this is a perfectly sensible strategy for politicians interested in getting results, it makes life more difficult for political scientists interested in measuring preferences. The Senate rule requiring votes on all proposed amendments at the second reading of a bill makes the committee voting data ideal from this standpoint; anything that was proposed, whether its author expected it to pass, wanted to stake out an issue position, or to force committee members into taking a public position, will become part of the record.

Another very serious concern in dealing with roll-call votes is that they may be strategic, in the sense that members do not vote for their most preferred alternative because of the effects such a vote would have on the future agenda and the ultimate decision made about a bill. A prototypical example of this was the Powell Amendment mentioned earlier. However, as the discussion in Section 4.1 indicated, the incentives to vote strategically are severely attenuated by the public nature of roll-call votes, and by the unpredictability of the agenda at the time that Senate committees cast their votes.

As noted before, the small size of Senate committees presents us with a substantive problem: only a small fraction of the Senate are sufficiently active on any one committee to permit reliable estimation of their preferred outcomes. While this leaves the remainder of the Senate chamber in the shadows, the problem is less severe than it might at first appear. The parties' control of committee assignments, and their ability to shift members' committee assignments, an ability they regularly exercise, limits the leeway of a policy maverick. A committee member's party caucus can replace him or her without his or her permission. While most such adjustments to committee assignments are temporary, and made with the full approval of the Senator being rotated off the committee, the threat of an involuntary transfer is real. A Senator could not long retain a committee assignment if his or her issue positions stood at variance with the rest of his or her Senate delegation. At the very least the issue positions taken by committee members represent the stand taken by a substantial portion of the member's party.

113

As already discussed above, the small size of Senate committees is felt in a second, and more severe way. The small size of Senate committees exacerbates a serious technical problem in statistical inference, known as the parameter proliferation problem. The problem arises because the parameter estimates for legislators' ideal points, the x_v, depend on the estimated values for the ideological content of proposals, the g, and vice versa. This same issue comes up in educational testing, where the x parameters correspond to examinees' ability while the g are known as "item discrimination" parameters that calibrate the degree to which test questions reveal subjects' abilities. The problem arises because adding extra voting data in order to get extra precision in the estimates of the x_v parameters entails adding more recorded roll-call votes. But this also means adding more g parameters to estimate as well; thus the complexity of the statistical estimation problem increases along with the amount of data. This problem, which has also been analyzed in the context of the psychological testing literature, means that as more data are added, parameter estimates will tend not to converge to the true parameters and will instead exhibit bias (Haberman 1977). This problem becomes especially severe when the number of voters is small, as is the case for the Senate committees considered in the subsequent chapters. The solution here is to build the model around authors. Rather than attempt to estimate the characteristics of each proposal separately, the model estimates the characteristics of the stream of proposals coming from a particular author. This means that as more data are added, the number of parameters does not rise, and so the complexity of the model does not increase.

Another issue has to do with the informativeness of each vote. Many interest group ratings start from the implicit premise that every vote on their scorecard is equally informative about a legislator's ideology. Thus a politically correct vote on abortion and an incorrect vote on raising the debt ceiling conveys the same information about how far to the "left" a legislator is as an "incorrect" abortion vote and a "correct" vote on the debt ceiling. Of course, it is much more likely the abortion vote is in fact more important, more salient, and so more informative than the vote about the debt ceiling. One approach to this problem is to ignore or downweight lopsided votes on the grounds that these are less informative. But this leaves open some serious questions about how to set the relative weights. The model here has the effect of giving different weights to different votes because of variations in the proposer's ideological parameters, the g_a. Proposals from authors with more extreme g_a values provide us with more information about voters' preferences, the x_v, and so the estimator here gives them more weight, as it should, even when the actual vote outcome is lopsided. In contrast, a proposal from an author with $g_a = 0$ will have no impact on the estimated x_v parameter. Thus the model set forth here already recognizes the heterogeneous level of information contained in each vote, and endogenously weights the influence of the votes on the parameter estimates accordingly.

As discussed above, modeling the proposal process is both essential to being able to estimate the model when there are only a few voters, as in Senate committees, and intrinsically important as we try better to understand proposal making. However, even more than with our models of voting, our models of proposals are still very much work in progress. Here the ideological displacement of proposals from the same author is treated as the same. This will be a reasonable approximation when authors pursue a stable set of objectives and face a status quo that only changes very slowly. In this case we may expect that all proposals from a given author will be nearly the same. In more dynamic environments, or when the status quo involves a scatter of locations across policy areas, this approximation will be less appropriate. In the application at hand it seems reasonable to expect that the status quo inherited after sixteen and a half years of military rule, in which the Pinochet government was free to change policy at will is ideologically consistent across policy areas. In any case, the policy displacements here, which can differ among proposers, are far less restrictive than the assumption that undergirds the legislative scorecards used by almost all interest groups that tally the percentage of key votes legislators cast "correctly." Not only do the scorecards often discard many potentially relevant votes, but they also impose the (implicit) assumption that all of the votes used to calculate the score have the same value for g, regardless of who proposed them.

Difficult questions are raised by so-called party whip votes. It is possible that the Senators of a given party have different preferred policies, or using the notation of the model, different values for x, but that they nevertheless obey party orders on key votes. We can imagine a disciplined party in which, on key votes, the party decides how its Senate delegation is to vote and then "whips" its members to vote the party line, while leaving them free to vote their consciences (or their constituencies) on the remaining votes. The statistical estimator will tend to misinterpret this behavior as arising from policy preferences that are more similar to one another than is actually the case. This means that if we do not take account of the possibility of party whip votes, we will tend to underestimate the heterogeneity among the x's of the party's members.

Detecting party whip votes is not trivial; individual legislators have incentives to downplay the degree to which it occurs. After all, there are few constituencies that will reward a Senator for being a puppet of his or

115

her party, while the party has incentives to exaggerate its influence, both by making ex post claims it exercised party discipline when the delegation spontaneously voted together and by denying it attempted to whip party members when there is an internal rebellion of the party's delegation. However, if there is some party whipping it will leave a telltale trace: Senators from the same party will tend to vote alike more often than the differences in their x's would indicate, that is, their votes will be more correlated with each other even after controlling for their most preferred issue positions, the x's. In Senate committees, which have only five members, not all of whom are present for every vote, it is often the case that all of the committee members participating in a particular vote are from different parties. However, there are still a substantial number of cases in which two members of the same party cast votes on the same question. To test for party whipping, we can look for correlation among the votes from Senators from the same party. The details of this procedure are explained in the Appendix. However, when the correlations were estimated, they failed to differ significantly from zero. In some cases this could very well be due to the small number of votes in which two members of the same party took part, but in some committees there are in excess of a hundred such votes, and the estimated correlation still does not differ significantly from zero. Substantively this indicates that party whipping on committee votes is either very rare or nonexistent, and that for the most part, when Senators from the same party vote alike, it is because they share the same policy preferences. There is one caveat to this conclusion. The Socialists never cast more than one vote on any of the amendments in the datasets considered in this analysis, and so it was not possible to estimate a party whip parameter for them. However, there is a pronounced tendency for members of this party to cosponsor one another's amendments, suggesting at least the strong possibility that their voting behavior may be subject to a higher level of party control than their Senate colleagues.

A second means by which party control might be observed is in deference to proposals written by members of the same party. It is straightforward to test for this by allowing for the consensus appeal parameter, b_v, to shift, say to $b_v + b_{same}$, when a Senator votes on a proposal from a member of his own party. Recall that the higher the value of b_v the higher the probability that a legislator will vote in favor of a proposal, all else held equal. If there is deference to proposals from within one's own party, we would expect that b will be higher when Senators vote on proposals from fellow party members. That is, even after correcting for a proposal's ideological content and valence, committee members will give amendments from members of their own party a more favorable reception. The estimated values for b_{same} are reported along with the other parameters and give us a second measure of deference to one's party.

116

Another issue that lives at the cusp of statistical technique and substantive political analysis and has generated a considerable amount of controversy is the question of whether to estimate a multidimensional model, so that legislators' preferred outcomes differ simultaneously on a "horizontal" dimension, such as labor relations, and on a second dimension, such as the role of religion in society. The discussion to this point has dealt with models in which legislators differed along a single dimension from left to right, but this need not be so.

One approach to this dimensionality question is to remain agnostic and to attempt to estimate locations for legislators and authors in multiple dimensions while adding no information about the actual content of the proposals. Experience with this approach is that it fails to resolve ambiguities about the number of dimensions of political controversy, even when the amount of data becomes very large. Consider the ongoing controversy between Heckman and Snyder on one hand and Poole and Rosenthal on the other about the number of ideologically important dimensions in recent sessions of the U. S. Congress. This controversy in turn hinges on differences in the technical details of the statistical models used by these analysts. Although they obtain very similar results for the first "left vs. right" ideological dimension, the Heckman–Snyder estimator finds far more additional dimensions than the Poole and Rosenthal technique. These differences stem from technical differences in the assumptions about the functional form of the utility function and the distribution of the idiosyncratic preference shocks built into the two models. These technical differences are not easy to resolve on empirical grounds.

The approach taken here is to use what we actually know about the content of proposals to identify the different ideological dimensions. Shepsle (1979) showed that amendment control rules can overcome the cycling problems that emerge when there are multiple issue dimensions. This is particularly important in the Chilean context, where there is a proposal germaneness rule that prevents amendments that are not relevant to a particular bill. This will prevent the indeterminate "cycling" identified by McKelvey (1976), provided bills only attempt to move policy on one ideological dimension at a time. The committee assignment process in the Chilean Senate further reenforces this; when bills appear to straddle the domains of multiple committees, the leadership can channel which amendments go to each committee, providing a further opportunity to prevent cycling by pruning the agenda considered by each committee. Thus, a combination of proposal germaneness and careful committee assignments can serve to limit the ideological conflicts opened up in each committee to a single dimension at a time. This does not mean that every bill considered by a particular committee will necessarily deal with the same ideological dimension, nor that ideological alliances in different committees will all line up the same way. The definitions of "left" and "right" may well be different on social issues such as divorce than they are on human rights issues or education policy.

The approach taken here is first to restrict the content of the committee's agenda on substantive grounds, and then to estimate single-dimensional ideological locations for each substantive area. Thus, in effect, the analysis includes a separate explanatory variable coding for the substantive content of the issues being voted on in the various committees. The resulting estimates can then be used to test, in a very straightforward way, whether Senators actually line up in the same way across the the different substantive issue areas. As will emerge in the subsequent chapters, the data are consistent with there being at least two dimensions to Chilean politics, one of which deals with labor relations, income redistribution, and human rights, and another which deals with social issues such as drug abuse and divorce and which seems to be related to an older cleavage (dating from the nineteenth century) over the role of religion in public policy, which today divides the opposition parties and many of the Christian Democrats, who have deep roots in Catholicism, from the very secular Radical, PPD, and Socialist parties, along with a socially liberal wing of the Christian Democratic Party.

4.3 VOTING DATA FROM SENATE COMMITTEES

The roll-call voting data from Senate committees are reported in the Senate journal, *Sesiones del Senado*. These data emerge as part of the narrative accounts given in the committee reports. These reports are written by the Senate secretaries and summarize the committees' deliberations. They are not verbatim transcripts of what was said, but they often include summaries of the arguments offered by each Senator to motivate his or her vote. An account of the votes is then woven into the narrative. Except on very rare occasions, the Senate secretaries do not report the votes in the form of a summary table. Normally one needs to read through the report to find them.

The task of transcribing the votes in the committee reports into electronically readable form is a laborious one, made more complicated by the lack of a comprehensive index for the Senate journal. The task of collecting these data was much facilitated by the generous help of the Senate secretaries, especially Carlos Hoffmann, who in March 1994 allowed me to access their card files on legislative activity. These files included information on which bills had been referred to which committees. I was thus able to put together a list of all of the bills whose career through the Senate had been charted by the Senate secretaries and which had been referred to any of the Senate's 22 standing committees. These data allowed me to access the computerized legislative histories of each bill maintained on Chile's Library of Congress mainframe computer. A close reading of the legislative history of each of these bills then made it possible to identify which bills had been given second readings by the committees, and to find the date on which the committee report had been delivered to the parent chamber. Searching the *Sesiones del Senado* for the dates between the committee's report and the date of the Senate's debate of the bill will then uncover the committee report. Reading through each report to ascertain the authorship of each proposed amendment and the votes of each of the committee members is then a time-consuming undertaking. During the first half of 1994, with the highly competent and energetic research assistance of Sybil Abarca, Jesica Fuentes, and Marcela Villegas, I assembled committee voting data for the Aylwin years.

The resulting data were sparse for some committees, and ample for others. In many cases, such as the Mining Committee, and the Public Works Committee, there were very few votes taken during the second reading of bills, too few to permit stable estimates. A similar problem arose for committees such as Government Operations, for which the rate of unanimous voting was extremely high, again making the effective number of divided votes, the votes that provide the most information about Senators' ideological leanings, small, and so hampering precise parameter estimation.

Here I have chosen to focus on several of the most important and busy committees, committees that deal with issues at the heart of Chilean politics. Three committees are considered in depth in the following chapters: (a) the Committee on Constitution Justice and Rules (hereafter, the Constitution Committee), (b) the Committee on Labor and Public Pensions (the Labor Committee), and (c) the Committee on Education and Monuments (the Education Committee).

Two committees with especially important policy jurisdictions, the Finance Committee and the Foreign Relations Committee, were excluded from the analysis. For the period of analysis, I found no reports of second readings with roll call votes from the Foreign Relations Committee, which deals mostly with foreign treaties. Likewise, the Finance Committee; despite its central importance (it is the only standing committee that the organic law of Congress requires the Senate to establish) cast relatively few roll-call votes. This is partly because a select committee is formed to consider the annual budget, which therefore does not go to the Finance Committee. Thus second readings by the Finance Committee are typically restricted to the handful of amendments to bills in other committee jurisdictions that have direct budgetary implications but are not declared unconstitutional for intruding on the reserve policy domain of the president. The number of recorded votes was too small to permit precise estimation of the parameters of the model.

For the three committees considered in the subsequent chapters, the parameter estimates are the beginning rather than the end of the analysis. The parameter estimates for each committee provide an idea of which Senators are on the "left," and which are on the "right," and whether the committee is "bipolar," with a clump of homogeneous Senators at each edge of the spectrum, or whether instead there is some heterogeneity among either the Concertación or opposition Senators. This leaves open the more profound question of how to interpret "left" and "right." In terms of the discussion in the first chapter, ideology can be viewed as a form of "bounded rationality." This has three elements. First, individuals agree, more or less, on how the ideological spectrum connects with substantive policy outcomes, such as a 5% increase in the minimum wage, or a transfer of school administration from private hands to the municipal sector, or a proposal to replace a military doctor with a civilian one on a committee that reviews the professional credentials of returning political exiles. Second, individuals form attachments to ideological world views that can be represented as locations along the same spectrum (which may run from left to right, or which may have more than one dimension), for example, identifying with the "moderate left" or the "far right." The third element is the focus of the spatial model: when individuals must choose among complex policy alternatives, they evaluate them in terms of the proximity of the ideological content of the alternative to their own most preferred ideological outcome.

The introduction of valence to the spatial model leaves this basic structure unchanged, with valence adding an element of consensus appeal. People attribute an ideological content to a particular policy, and also a valence. They identify with a particular ideological point of reference, and then evaluate policy alternatives in terms of the proximity of their attributed ideological position to their own most preferred ideological outcome, taking valence into account as well.

The empirical analysis of the subsequent three chapters traces this process in reverse. Starting with the observed policy choices of the Senators, in the form of their public committee roll-call votes, the statistical analysis constructs parameter estimates that trace the connection between individuals and the ideological terrain, attributing to each Senator a most preferred ideological outcome. Senators sharing the same outcome will share the same ideological agenda and will only differ in their voting records because of idiosyncratic differences in their perception of the issues. Senators with different estimated preferred outcomes will differ systematically in their policy choices and votes. The analysis also connects the stream of amendments coming from the president and Senators with the ideological spectrum, attributing an ideological content to the group of proposals coming from each author. Thus if the Socialist Party tends to propose

120

amendments moving policy leftward, then voters on the left of the ideological spectrum will tend to vote for proposals from the Socialists, all else held equal, while those on the right will tend to vote against. Thus the spatial model helps us to locate the proposers and the voters within a common spatial framework. However, the final link between policy alternatives and the ideological spectrum remains open. The statistical estimates do not close this link for us because of the technical problems, already discussed at further length above, that preclude estimating separate ideological content parameters for each proposed amendment.

This is not the limit of what we can learn from the parameter estimates. By reviewing the substantive content of the amendments coming from different proposers, both those that divide a committee and those that produce unanimous votes, we can learn more about the important first link in the ideological chain, the connection between concrete policy alternatives and ideological locations. Thus, each of the following three chapters that analyze the activities of the committees in detail also includes a discussion of the substantive content of the votes that generated the parameter estimates, helping to illuminate the connection between the ideological positions revealed by the statistical analysis and the substantive choices associated with those positions.

5

The Labor Committee

This is the first of three chapters that use roll-call voting records from Senate committees to chart the ideological landscape, mapping Senators' policy positions and linking substantive policy alternatives to the ideological spectrum along which they are evaluated. These details are critical to understanding the impact of the institutional framework that governs Chile's democratic transition. As we shall see, the picture of the Concertación the emerges from the Labor Committee is consistent with the view that this left-of-center coalition of parties pursues a cohesive policy agenda: the estimated ideological positions for the four Concertación Senators who served on the Committee are very similar to one another and distinct from the positions taken by most of the opposition Senators. However, a very different picture emerges on the political right, with large differences both between the institutional Senators and the members of the RN Party, and also among the Senators within each of those groups. This is at variance with the bipolar model of the government and the opposition that many take as their starting point in analyzing the Chilean transition. The opposition's heterogeneity on labor policy needs to be built into theoretical analyses. However, these empirical assertions are not uncontroversial, and it is to the evidence supporting them that our attention now turns.

The jurisdiction of the Senate Labor and Social Provision Committee lies at the heart of the substantive issues that divide the left from the right throughout the industrialized world. The committee has jurisdiction over laws affecting the labor market, such as the setting of minimum wages, the rules regulating union activities, and the length of the workweek. While Chile's innovative pension system is also within the ambit of the committee, during the period under study, the Aylwin administration, which lasted from March 1990 until March 1994, no major bills affecting the pension system were considered. Nevertheless, the committee did not remain idle, considering a stream of labor market reforms, mostly proposed by the president.

The Labor Committee

The analysis of the Labor Committee begins with an overview of the legislative agenda and then proceeds to the parameter estimates returned by the statistical model, with their surprising findings about the opposition Senators. After presenting the parameter estimates, and exploring their implications for the voting coalitions that emerge in the Senate Labor Committee, the chapter goes on to discuss the links between the substantive agenda of the committee, from minimum wages to contract reporting requirements, and the parameter estimates of the model. This discussion of the details provides evidence that the parameter estimates from the statistical model have in fact identified real differences among the Senators of the right.

The Setting

During the Aylwin administration, from March 1990 until March 1994, the legislative agenda in the Labor Committee[1] was dominated by the executive. This committee held second readings of six presidential bills, each of which has since become law. The only initiative originating from within the Congress that received a second reading was a bill to extend vacation days for citizens in their districts introduced by Senators Fernández,[2] Papi, and Ruiz De Giorgio, which grew out of a defeated amendment to one of the presidential bills and has yet to be ratified by the Chamber of Deputies. Of the six presidential bills, one dealt with the treatment of workers exonerated of crimes related to their opposition to the military regime. The remaining five bills dealt directly with the traditional labor issues that divide the left from the right in virtually every industrialized democracy. Two of these bills sought to favor unions, one dealt directly with working conditions, one with disability compensation for educators, and one provided more generous pensions for public employees.

Given that the subject matter of the bills considered by the Labor Committee lies at the heart of longstanding controversies between right and left, it is noteworthy that the amendments considered by the committee produced as little division among its members as they did. Of the 244 amendments subject to votes at the second readings of the seven bills considered by the committee, 182, or 74.59%, produced a unanimous response.

The membership of the committee consisted of a Socialist, two Christian Democrats, one member of the National Renovation Party, and one of the Institutional Senators. As discussed earlier, committee memberships

---

[1] The Committee on Labor and Social Provision.

[2] At the time he cosponsored this bill, Sergio Fernández was an Institutional Senators, appointed by Pinochet. However, he subsequently won election in one of the regions targeted by the bill.

belong to legislative caucuses and not to individuals. The party caucuses differ in the degree to which they shared their committee seats. At one extreme, Socialist Senator Rolando Calderón was the sole member of his party to occupy the Socialists' seat on the committee. The Christian Democrats and Institutional Senators shared their seats more frequently. At one time or another the two committee slots belonging to the Christian Democrats were occupied by three Senators, Ricardo Hormazábal, Humberto Palza, and José Ruiz De Giorgio. Of these three, Senators Palza and Hormazábal cast the greatest number of votes, with each voting on about three-fifths of the amendments considered by the Committee, about twice the participation rate for Senator Ruiz. Likewise the Institutional Senators Feliú and Thayer shared the Institutionals' committee seat, with Senator Thayer participating more than three times as often as his colleague Olga Feliú. The National Renovation Party had the highest rate of sharing. Its seat was occupied at one time or another by seven of its thirteen Senators, though Ignacio Pérez, Miguel Otero, and Sergio Romero participated much more frequently than the others.

5.1 PARAMETER ESTIMATES

As noted earlier, four normalizations are required to identify the model. These amount to the choice of a reference proposer for whom the proposal parameters g and c are normalized to equal 0, and two reference voters used to anchor the scale on which preferred outcomes are measured. Here the National Renovation party is chosen as the reference proposer, and so sponsors with $g < 0$ propose to the left of National Renovation; those with $g > 0$ propose farther to the right. In addition, two voter locations must be pinned down. Many ideological ratings groups normalize their best friends at a location of 100 and their worst enemies at a location of 0. Here I adopt a normalization with more neutral connotations, placing Socialist Rolando Calderón on the left, with a location of -1, and Institutional Senator Olga Feliú on the right, with a location of 1.

Senators' Ideological Positions

Parameter estimates appear in Table 2. The first column, headed by x, reports estimates of Senators' most preferred policy outcomes, which are illustrated in Figure 5.1. As noted above, the preferred policy outcome of Socialist Rolando Calderón was normalized to equal -1, while the most preferred policy outcome of Institutional Senators Olga Feliú was normalized to equal 1. The remaining Senators estimates are all taken with reference to these two. On the left we encounter Senator Ruiz De Giorgio, a trade unionist, with an estimated preferred policy outcome of -0.997,

Table 2. *Parameter estimates for the labor committee*

Participant	Parameter[a]			
	x	b	g	c
PS/PPD			−12.173	−9.608
			(4.832)	(4.822)
Rolando Calderón A.	−1.000	0.222		
		(0.501)		
Partido Democrata Cristiano			−8.939	−8.973
			(4.297)	(4.188)
Ricardo Hormazábal S.	−0.895	1.302		
	(0.084)	(0.567)		
Humberto Palza C.	−0.982	0.975		
	(0.075)	(0.595)		
José Ruiz De Giorgio	−0.997	0.672		
	(0.094)	(0.618)		
Union Democrata Independiente			2.205	−4.225
			(3.225)	(2.974)
Institutional Senators			3.458	−3.376
			(4.020)	(3.463)
Olga Feliú S.	1.000	18.401		
		(8.808)		
William Thayer A.	−0.797	2.530	−8.685	−8.073
	(0.116)	(0.662)	(4.453)	(4.353)
Renovación Nacional	−0.595	3.869	0.000	0.000
	(0.184)	(0.806)		
Miguel Otero L.	−0.012	8.956		
	(0.434)	(2.308)		
Executive Proposals			−9.692	−5.687
			(4.557)	(4.473)
Own Party Proposals		0.334		
		(0.463)		

[a] Estimated standard errors are show in parentheses.

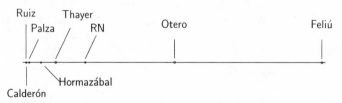

Figure 5.1. Estimated Preferred Outcomes.

virtually identical to the preferred outcome for the Senator Calderón. Also on the left, and virtually indistinguishable from Senators Calderón and Ruiz, is Christian Democrat Humberto Palza, with an estimated preferred outcome of −0.982. Senator Hormazábal, a Christian Democrat and the remaining member of the Concertación on the Labor Committee, has an estimated preferred outcome of −0.895, somewhat to the right of the other three members of his coalition, but nevertheless considerably closer to them than to the positions of any of the opposition senators.

Unlike the very homogeneous preferences of the Concertación Senators on the Labor Committee, there is considerable heterogeneity among their counterparts in the opposition. Most striking is the gap between Senator Thayer, with an estimated preferred outcome of −0.797, and his fellow Institutional Senators Olga Feliú, whose preferred outcome is normalized to equal 1. These two Institutional Senators bracket the remaining opposition Senators. Because most of the National Renovation Senators who served on the Labor Committee did so only briefly, they must be grouped to permit individual estimation. This means that a common ideal point is estimated for the National Renovation Senators, less Senator Otero. While Senator Pérez cast slightly more votes than Senator Otero, I estimate Senator Otero's preferred outcome separately from the other members of his party to permit a subsequent comparison with his estimated ideal point on the Constitution Committee, where he also served. As with the Institutional Senators the members of the National Renovation Party do not take identical positions on Labor policy, with Senator Otero's preferred policy position of −0.012 considerably to the right of the remaining members of his party, who are estimated to take a position of −0.595.

The relatively extreme locations for Senators Feliú and Otero stem from the ideological purity of these two legislators' voting records. Each often cast the only dissenting vote on amendments shifting policy leftward. To get a clearer sense of the meaning of the estimated gaps among the Senators' ideological positions, there are several questions we need to answer. First, are the estimated differences in the ideological parameters for these Senators statistically significant? That is, do the gaps we are looking at represent systematic differences among the Senators' voting behavior, or are the observed differences simply the result of "fitting noise," differences that do not reach the threshold of statistical significance? Second, we can ask what the differences that we have estimated imply about the voting coalitions that will emerge on amendments considered by the committee. Third, and perhaps most importantly, if our answers to the first questions indicate that the parameter estimates have in fact uncovered differences among the Senators' ideological positions, we want to ask what Senators' positions imply about the substantive policy alternatives they will prefer. Concretely, what does the difference between the estimated preferred issue position of a National Renovation Senator like Ignacio Peréz, at −0.595, and a Christian Democrat like Ricardo Hormazábal, with an estimated issue position of −0.895, say about their preferred setting of the minimum wage for domestic workers, or their stand on paid leave for the parents of newborn children?

Turning to the first of these questions, recall that to estimate Senators' preferred issue positions four normalizations were needed; we need to normalize the units in which we measure ideology, using two reference voters, in this case Senators Calderón and Feliú, and we also need to select a "reference proposer," in this case RN, for whom the proposal parameters, g and c, are normalized to equal 0. Given the idiosyncratic preference shocks are drawn from a standard normal distribution, as in a probit model, Equation (4.4) tells us that the probability Senator v votes for an amendment from the reference proposer, RN, for whom $g_{RN} = 0$ and $c_{RN} = 0$, is[3] $\Phi(b_v + \alpha\epsilon_j)$. Here $\Phi()$, denotes the standard normal cummulative density function. This says that the probability that Socialist Senator Rolando Calderón votes for an amendment proposed by a member of the conservative RN Party does not depend on the Socialist Senator's value for x. Instead Senator Calderón's ideological antipathy for amendments from the opposition RN Party is captured by his estimated value for b of $b_{Calderon} = 0.222$, the lowest value for any member of the Committee. This means that both the x and the b parameters reflect Senators' ideological leanings, and any test of whether Senators have the same ideological outlook must check for equality for both the Senators' estimated values for x and the estimates for b.

It is perhaps not surprising that the estimated values for the b parameters are very similar to the estimates for x. In fact, for the Labor Committee both parameters give the same relative ranking of the Senators moving from left to right; Senators Calderón, Palza, and Ruiz all have fairly low values for b, and that for Senator Hormazábal is only slightly higher, while at the other end of the spectrum, Senators Otero and Feliú have estimated values for b of 8.956 and 18.401, respectively, indicating that they are almost sure to vote for proposals from the opposition RN Party.

While the parameter estimates suggest that Senator Hormazábal is slightly to the right of the Committee's other three Concertación Senators, the data do not allow rejection of the hypothesis that all four Concertación Senators share the same values of x and b. Even subjecting the hypothesis of Concertación solidarity to sterner jeopardy, by testing whether the Senators with the least similar voting records, Senators Calderón and

---

[3] Substituting $g_{RN} = 0$ and $c_{RN} = 0$ into Equation (4.4) and letting $\Phi(x)$ denote the standard normal cumulative density function evaluated at x, we find that the probability that Senator v votes "yes" will be:

$$\Phi(0 + b_v + \alpha\epsilon_j + 0x_v) = \Phi(b_v + \alpha\epsilon_j).$$

Hormazábal, share the same values for x and b, leads to acceptance at all conventional significance levels.[4] In contrast, the gap between the RN Senators, omitting Miguel Otero, and even the rightmost of the estimated positions for the Concertación legislators, that of Senator Hormazábal, is statistically significant.[5]

The contrast between the united ideological position of the Concertación Senators and the sharp differences in the positions of the opposition Senators is marked. The large estimated gap between Institutional Senators Thayer and Feliú is highly statistically significant,[6] as is the difference between Senator Otero and the remaining members of his party.[7] Similar tests reveal significant differences between Senators Otero and Thayer.[8]

While the estimated position of Senator Thayer, to the left of all of the other opposition Senators on the Labor Committee, is surprising, it is nevertheless the case that his position as the leftmost of the opposition Senators is still to the right of the rightmost of the estimated preferred policies of the Concertación Senators, that of Senator Hormazábal. Likewise, while Senator Thayer's estimated value for b indicates that he is less likely than any other member of the opposition to vote for an amendment from the reference proposer, the National Renovation Party, he is nonetheless more likely to do so than any member of the Concertación.

In contrast to the unambiguously significant gap between the estimated ideology parameters for Senator Hormazábal and the RN Senators,[9] the differences between the intermediate preference parameters of Senator Thayer and those of the more moderate RN Senators is just at the threshold of significance,[10] while a similar comparison with the estimated

---

[4] Under the null hypothesis that both Senators share the same ideology parameters, x and b, the test statistic will be asymptotically distributed as χ_2^2. The realized value for the test statistic of 3.8318 corresponds to a p value of 0.1472.

[5] Under the null hypothesis that $x_{RN} = x_{Hormazábal}$ and $b_{RN} = b_{Hormazábal}$, the test statistic will be asymptotically distributed as χ_2^2. The realized value for the test statistic of 10.074 corresponds to a p value of 0.0064, leading to rejection of the null hypothesis at all standard significance levels.

[6] A test of the null hypothesis that these two Senators have the same values for x and b leads to a χ_2^2 test statistic of 414.6028, literally leading to off-the-chart rejection, corresponding to a p value of 9.335×10^{-91}.

[7] Under the null hypothesis that Senator Otero and the remaining RN Senators on the Committee have the same values for x and b, the test statistic is asymptotically distributed as χ_2^2. The realized value of 8.0725 corresponds to a p value of 0.0177, indicating rejection at $\alpha = 0.10$ and $\alpha = 0.05$, though not at the more stringent $\alpha = 0.01$ significance level.

[8] The χ_2^2 statistic takes on a value of 10.058, corresponding to a p value of 0.0064.

[9] The χ_2^2 statistic takes on a value of 14.324, corresponding to a p value of 0.0008.

[10] A test of the null hypothesis that Senator Thayer and the National Renovation Senators (less Senator Otero) share the same x and b parameters generates a χ_2^2 statistic of 4.779, corresponding to a p value of 0.0917, indicating rejection at $\alpha = 0.10$ but not at either $\alpha = 0.05$ or $\alpha = 0.01$.

128

preferences of the rightmost member of the Concertación delegation to the Labor Committee, Senator Hormazábal, falls just a shade below statistical significance.[11] Similar tests lead to borderline evidence of a difference between the preferences of Senator Thayer and each of the remaining Christian Democrats on the Committee,[12] and more decisive evidence of a difference between Senator Thayer and Socialist Senator Rolando Calderón.[13] These results are consistent with the hypothesis that Senator Thayer occupies an intermediate position, between the left of the National Renovation Party and the right of the Christian Democrats.

The statistical picture of a united Concertación delegation on the Labor Committee confronting an ideologically heterogeneous opposition delegation is no mere statistical artifact: the differences between Concertación Senators and the opposition, and the differences among the opposition Senators, are statistically significant. This brings us to the second basic question about the results: what do the differences in the estimated preference parameters signify about the voting coalitions in the committee? To deal with this question we first need to know something about the agenda on which the Senators vote. A sufficiently extreme agenda can lead ideologically very distinct legislators to vote alike; imagine U. S. Democrats and Republicans voting on a policy agenda consisting of the Communist Party manifesto, while a tepid agenda of small changes can make an ideologically bland and homogeneous legislature appear polarized. The roll-call record also contains information about the agenda on which the Labor Committee voted, and it is to this that our attention now turns.

The Agenda Parameters

The proposal parameters provide important evidence about the agenda on which the Labor Committee voted, and also about the types of amendments proposed by the various Senators. Again an important difference emerges between Senator Thayer and the remaining members of the opposition, with Senator Thayer's proposal parameters resembling those made by the Christian Democrats more closely than they do those of the other

[11] A test of the null hypothesis that Senators Hormazábal and Thayer share the same x and b parameters generates a χ_2^2 statistic of 4.274, corresponding to a p value of 0.1180, indicating acceptance even at $\alpha = 0.10$.

[12] The χ_2^2 statistic corresponding to the null hypothesis that Senators Thayer and Palza share the same values for x and b of 5.164 corresponds to a p value of 0.0756; the χ_2^2 statistic for the hypothesis of identical preferences for Senators Ruiz and Thayer is 5.491, with a p value of 0.0642.

[13] The χ_2^2 statistic is 10.058, corresponding to a p value of 0.0065 and leading to rejection even at $\alpha = 0.01$.

opposition Senators.[14] A test of the hypothesis that Senator Thayer and the remaining Institutionals make ideologically identical proposals leads to similar results.[15] In contrast there is virtually no difference between the estimated value of g for Senator Thayer of -8.685 and the corresponding value of -8.938 for the Christian Democrats: the p value for the null hypothesis that Thayer and the Christian Democrats have the same value for g is 0.7553. The estimated value for g is significantly rightward of the Socialists. However, these parameter estimates do not tell the whole story: when Senator Thayer coproposed amendments he did so with other members of the opposition, not with the Concertación. Thus the estimated leftward tendency of his proposals represents at least in part a tendency to moderate amendments he coproposed with senators of the right.

Estimates for the ideological content of proposals, g, appear in column 3 of Table 2. Recall that the value of g for the National Renovation Party has been normalized to equal 0. The estimated values of g for the Institutional Senators (less Senator Thayer) and the UDI Senators are statistically insignificantly to the right of the normalized value for the National Renovation Senators. Because of the relatively small numbers of proposals coming from each individual, it was not practical to estimate different values of the proposal parameters for each Senator; hence the partywide parameter estimates for National Renovation and UDI. Because of the surprising evidence about Senator Thayer's preference parameters, an individual set of proposal parameters has been estimated for this Senator.

The proposal parameters for the Christian Democrats and for President Aylwin, also a Christian Democrat, are very similar, and significantly to the left of the normalized value for the National Renovation Senators.[16] The Socialist/PPD Senators who frequently cosponsor amendments tend to propose somewhat leftward of the other members of the Concertación. The estimated gap of 3.217 between the PS/PPD and the Christian Democrats is on the border of statistical significance.[17]

The consensus appeal parameters for proposals, c, discussed in the preceding chapter, appear in column 4 of Table 2. These proposal quality

---

[14] The t ratio for the difference between estimated value of g for Senator Thayer and the value of $g_{RN} = 0$ for the National Renovation Senators is -1.950, corresponding to a p value of 0.0511, so that we can reject the null hypothesis that he and the National Renovation Senators make proposals with the same ideological content at $\alpha = 0.10$ but not at $\alpha = 0.05$.

[15] The χ_1^2 statistic of 3.541 corresponds to a p value of 0.0598, significant at $\alpha = 0.10$ but not $\alpha = 0.05$.

[16] The t ratios for these proposal parameters of -2.080 and -2.127, respectively, permit rejection of the null hypothesis of no difference between the ideological content of their proposals and those of RN at $\alpha = 0.05$.

[17] The χ_1^2 statistic of 5.9604 corresponds to a p value of 0.0146, leading to acceptance of the null hypothesis of no difference at $\alpha = 0.01$ but not at $\alpha = 0.05$.

parameters are mostly similar, though the Christian Democrats, and the PPD have values that are just above the threshold of being statistically significantly lower than those of the National Renovation Party.[18] The consensus appeal for presidential proposals is not precisely estimated, and while its estimated value is below that for proposals from the RN Party the estimated gap is not statistically significant.

The high and statistically significant estimate for α of 4.866 indicates that variations in the consensus value of proposals swamp idiosyncratic preference shocks, whose variance has been normalized to equal 1. To put this another way, the correlation between the voting "errors," $\alpha v_i + \eta_{vi}$ for two Senators on the same amendment, is estimated[19] to equal 0.959. Even this high value for α, while it is sufficient to produce a large number of unanimous votes, does not render the ideological content of proposals irrelevant. Socialist Senator Rolando Calderón will be approximately indifferent between a proposal from another Socialist Senator with an average consensus shock and a proposal from a National Renovation Senator with a consensus value drawn from the top half-percent of the distribution. While consensus quality matters, it takes a lot of it to overcome Senators' ideological leanings.

Parameter Estimates and Voting Coalitions

We can now turn to our second question: what do the parameter estimates gleaned from Labor Committee voting records tell us about the voting coalitions that are likely to emerge, and when they are likely to do so? The membership of Senate Committees is somewhat fluid, with the identities of the five members of most changing at least occasionally. Although the Labor Committee is no exception to this regularity, some voters participated more frequently than others. Let's consider what would happen to various hypothetical proposals with votes being cast by five of the most frequently participating Senators: Rolando Calderón, Humberto Palza, José Ruiz, William Thayer, and Miguel Otero.

It is straightforward to calculate what the parameter estimates from Table 2 imply about proposals written by various authors. Excluding the possibility of abstention, there are thirty-two possible voting outcomes that can emerge when a committee consisting of these five Senators considers a proposal. The first column of Table 3 displays the probability

---

[18] The t ratios are -2.142 and -1.993, respectively.

[19] Straightforward calculations reveal that this correlation satisfies

$$\rho = \frac{\alpha^2}{1+\alpha^2}$$

and substituting $\hat{\alpha} = 4.866$ into this formula yields an estimated correlation of $\hat{\rho} = 0.959$.

Table 3. *Hypothetical labor committee votes*

Committee voting outcome					Probability by proposer[a]		
Ruiz	Calderón	Palza	Thayer	Otero	Exec.	PDC	RN
yes	yes	yes	yes	yes	0.690	0.400	0.453
no	yes	yes	yes	yes	0.008	0.012	0.043
yes	no	yes	yes	yes	0.015	0.035	0.071
yes	yes	no	yes	yes	0.006	0.019	0.028
yes	yes	yes	no	yes	0.008	0.016	0.001
yes	yes	yes	yes	no	0.060	0.041	–
no	no	yes	yes	yes	0.003	0.019	0.030
no	yes	no	yes	yes	–	–	–
no	yes	yes	no	yes	0.002	0.004	–
no	yes	yes	yes	no	0.012	0.010	–
yes	yes	yes	no	no	0.012	0.014	–
yes	yes	no	yes	no	0.009	0.008	–
yes	yes	no	no	yes	0.001	0.003	–
yes	no	no	yes	yes	0.002	0.007	0.020
yes	no	yes	no	yes	0.003	0.012	–
yes	no	yes	yes	no	0.021	0.031	–
yes	yes	no	no	no	0.001	0.003	–
yes	no	yes	no	no	0.004	0.010	–
yes	no	no	yes	no	0.003	0.006	–
yes	no	no	no	yes	–	0.002	–
no	yes	yes	no	no	0.002	0.003	–
no	yes	no	yes	no	–	–	–
no	yes	no	no	yes	–	–	–
no	no	no	yes	yes	–	–	0.032
no	no	yes	no	yes	0.001	0.003	0.00
no	no	yes	yes	no	0.004	0.008	–
yes	no	no	no	no	0.001	0.003	–
no	yes	no	no	no	–	–	–
no	no	yes	no	no	0.002	0.004	–
no	no	no	yes	no	0.001	–	–
no	no	no	no	yes	–	–	0.289
no	no	no	no	no	0.127	0.350	0.030

[a] A dash indicates a probability of less than 0.0005.

the parameter estimates imply for each of these thirty-two possible responses to an executive proposal. As previously noted, the high value for α of 4.866 implies that the most probable outcomes are unanimous votes, with a probability of 0.690 that the proposal will be accepted unanimously and a probability of 0.127 of unanimous rejection. There is a probability of 0.098 of but a single dissenting vote, and that most likely to come from Senator Otero, and a probability of 0.064 of two dissenting votes, with Senators Otero and Calderón the most likely pair of dissenters. This odd-looking alliance between a Socialist Senator and a Senator from the right emerges because of the Senator Calderón's generally jaundiced view of any proposals not moving policy far to the left.

As noted earlier, the estimated consensus appeal of executive proposals is higher than it is for the other Concertación proposers. This almost certainly stems from the president's exclusive proposal powers in certain issue areas, which gives him or her added bargaining leverage, which shows up in the model as a higher value of c. The president's advantage may also stem in part from the added staff resources available to the president to research and draft amendments. A Christian Democratic proposer not among the voters on the Committee, someone like Nicolas Diaz or Maximo Pacheco, is revealed by the parameter estimates to make proposals with virtually the same ideological content as those coming from the executive; compare the estimated g_{PDC} of -8.939 for the Christian Democrats with the g_{exec} estimate of -9.692 for the Executive reported in Table 2. However, as a quick look at the second column of Table 3 reveals, the probability a proposed amendment from one of the Christian Democratic Senators meets with unanimous approval by the committee is considerably lower than it is for a proposal from the executive, only 0.400, as opposed to 0.690 for a presidential proposal. Correspondingly, there is a much higher probability of unanimous rejection: 0.350, almost three times the 0.127 probability an executive proposal is unanimously rejected. Conditional on a split vote, with at least some committee members dissenting from the majority, the differences between proposals from the executive and members of the Christian Democratic Senate delegation is much less pronounced. The conditional probability that an executive proposal is approved given that at least one Senator casts a dissenting vote is 0.890, while for one of the Christian Democratic Senators the corresponding probability of winning a split vote is 0.833. This similarity of fortunes arises because we only observe divided votes when the proposal's consensus quality is sufficiently near that of the alternative that will be adopted if the proposal is rejected, and so does not overwhelm ideological considerations, considerations which the estimates reveal are much the same for the president as they are for members of his party's Senate delegation.

Next let's consider the consequences of a proposal from a member of the National Renovation party, such as Sergio Diez, or Ignacio Peréz. These proposals are much more likely to split the Committee than either proposals from the president or from the Christian Democratic Senators, with a probability of 0.517 that at least one Committee member dissents from the majority's position. When they do not, so that the committee votes unanimously, it is almost always to approve the National Renovation Senator's proposal; the probability of unanimous approval, shown in the fourth column of Table 3 is 0.453, fifteen times the probability such a proposal meets with unanimous rejection, but only slightly higher than the 0.400 probability that a proposal from one of the Christian Democratic Senators is unanimously approved. The elevated probability of a divided vote comes entirely from the tendency for Senator Otero to support proposals on the ideological right, with over half the divided votes involving a single dissent from this Senator. While the probability that a proposal from a National Renovation Senator is unanimously rejected is quite low, the probability that it is rejected by a margin of four against one is correspondingly higher than it is for the Christian Democratic Senators, so that if we compare the likelihood proposals are either unanimously rejected or rejected by margins of four to one, we find that for the National Renovation Senators this probability is 0.319, while for the Christian Democrats it is 0.357, only slightly higher. Remarkable among the results for proposals from the National Renovation Senators is the low probability that Senator Thayer joins Senator Otero on the same side of a divided vote, something the estimates indicate will only happen on 43.5% of the proposals from the RN Senators that divide the Committee.

Because of the remarkable parameter estimates for William Thayer, it is worthwhile calculating hypothetical outcomes for amendments proposed by this Institutional Senator. Because he is also hypothesisized to be a member of the Committee, this requires us to take a position on how Senators vote on their own proposals. Senators vote on their own proposals with some frequency, and not surprisingly they almost always vote favorably. Because the exceptions to this behavior are so unusual, Senators' votes on their own proposals were omitted from the calculation of the parameters. Here Senator Thayer will be treated as a certain vote in favor of his own proposal. While Table 3 provides considerable information, it is perhaps more convenient to work with a more concise summary of hypothetical outcomes. Accordingly, Table 4 reports just the vote totals for and against a hypothetical proposal from Senator Thayer. In contrast with the Senators of the National Renovation Party, Institutional Senator Thayer is much more likely to propose amendments that produce a unanimous response from the other members of the Committee, and he is much more likely to win on votes that divide the Committee. The probability that a proposal from Senator Thayer meets with unanimous acceptance is 0.514, somewhat higher than for the Christian Democratic Senators. While Senator Thayer's proposals will always meet with his own favorable vote, the probability that no other Senator joins William Thayer in support of his proposal is 0.345, about the same as the probability that a noncommittee Christian Democrat's proposal is unanimously rejected.

The Labor Committee

Table 4. *Hypothetical labor committee vote margins*[a]

Votes		
In favor	Against	Prob. of margin
0	5	0.000
1	4	0.345
2	3	0.009
3	2	0.024
4	1	0.107
5	0	0.514

[a] Committee consists of Senators Ruiz, Calderón, Palza, Thayer, and Otero; hypothetical proposal is by William Thayer.

The probability that Senator Thayer loses on a vote conditional on the remaining members of the committee being split, 0.065, is a bit less than the probability the president fails to win a vote that splits the committee. This similarity results from the similar values for both the ideology and consensus quality parameters. The Senator most likely to cast the lone dissenting vote on a proposal from Senator Thayer is Socialist Senator Calderón, but the second most likely dissenter is National Renovation Senator Otero! This stems from the ideology of Senator Thayer's proposals, which is very similar to that of proposals from the Christian Democrats.

One of the most striking features of the parameter estimates is the large gap between the preferred points of Institutional Senators Feliú and Thayer. The model permits us to address the question of how the committee's votes would differ if Senator Feliú occupied the Institutional's Committee seat instead of Senator Thayer. Table 5 reports the vote totals for and against various hypothetical proposals, this time with Senator Thayer replaced on the Committee by Senator Feliú. Consulting the third column of Table 5, we see that as with Senator Feliú on the committee, the most likely outcome for an amendment proposed by President Aylwin is unanimity, with a 0.662 probability of unanimous acceptance and a 0.128 probability of unanimous rejection. However, the probability of two negative votes is higher than the probability of only one when Senator Feliú replaces Senator Thayer on the committee, rising from 0.064 to 0.092, with Feliú and Otero by far the most likely pair of dissenters. The probability the committee rejects the proposal rises little with Feliú replacing Thayer, increasing from 0.147 to 0.178. The increase is small because none of the Concertación Senators Palza, Calderón, and Ruiz De Giorgio is likely to oppose an executive-sponsored amendment. Hence on

Table 5. *Hypothetical labor committee vote margins*[a]

Votes		Prob. by proposer			
In favor	Against	Exec.	PDC	Thayer	RN
0	5	0.128	0.350	0.334	_[b]
1	4	0.008	0.008	0.019	0.030
2	3	0.042	0.039	0.003	0.321
3	2	0.092	0.097	0.026	0.052
4	1	0.068	0.109	0.109	0.143
5	0	0.662	0.396	0.510	0.454

[a] Committee consists of Senators Ruiz, Calderón, Palza, Feliú, and Otero.
[b] A dash indicates a probability of less than 0.0005.

most divided votes Feliú's presence on the committee simply increases the number of dissenting votes from one to two.

The fate of proposals from the Christian Democrats is very similar with either Senator Thayer or Senator Feliú on the committee (see Table 5, column 4), while proposals by Senator Thayer receive less support mainly because they can no longer count on the vote of their author. In the case of a proposal from one of the National Renovation Senators, the presence of Senator Feliú on the committee means that National Renovation proposals meet with two virtually guaranteed votes instead of one, although the probability that the committee endorses such a proposal, 0.649, is virtually the same as it would have been, 0.643, with Senator Thayer on the Committee. Given that the Committee's decisions can be easily overturned on the floor, the substantive difference made by having Senator Feliú serve in lieu of Senator Thayer is fairly small. Once Senator Otero has voiced his dissent on an amendment approved by the committee, it is already identified as a candidate for renewal by the opposition and new debate on the floor. Senator Feliú's vote is seldom enough to change the committee's majority, while it contains mostly the same information as the vote of Senator Otero.

The parameter estimates derived from roll-call votes cast on the Labor Committee reveal a unified Concertación delegation. These Senators have a strong tendency to vote together and pursue nearly the same ideological vision of labor relations. In contrast, the parameter estimates reveal a divided opposition. While Institutional Senators William Thayer, a former Christian Democrat and later supporter of the Pinochet government, pursues a labor policy agenda just a bit to the right of the Christian Democrats, his fellow Institutional Senator, Olga Feliú, has a labor relations ideology so far to the right that it dwarfs the distances among the positions of the Committee's remaining members. Nor are the differences confined to the Institutional Senators. The National Renovation Senators differ among themselves and from the Institutionals. These differences are both statistically significant and substantively important. They affect the voting coalitions that emerge on the committee. Now it is time to place these ideological differences in the context of concrete choices about labor policy.

5.2 PUTTING THE ESTIMATES IN CONTEXT

We now turn to the third, and perhaps the most important, of the basic questions raised by the parameter estimates extracted from the roll-call voting data: What do Senators' ideological positions imply about the substantive policy alternatives they will prefer? What do they tell us about how the Senators will stand on concrete questions such as whether maternity leave should apply to household workers, what fines employers should pay for violating the labor laws, whether bankrupt firms' obligations to their workers should have precedence over other debts, how soon new contracts must be put into writing, and which workers should be allowed to serve as longshoremen? How do the estimates of legislators' ideological preferences and proposal-making tendencies presented in the preceding section connect with these policy choices? To address this question our attention now turns to the content of the proposals over which the Labor Committee voted. The model allowed for the possibility that we would encounter variation even among proposals from the same author, an effect captured by the αv_i term in Equation (4.4) of Chapter 4. The large and statistically significant estimate for α reported in Table 2 confirms this expectation and means that the set of proposals from a given author, or group of authors, should be viewed as draws from a distribution which includes both high- and low-valence ideas. For each proposer it is thus useful to consider several proposed amendments, bearing in mind that these are draws from a distribution which vary in their appeal. A major presidential bill which sought to overhaul Books I, II, and V of the Chilean Labor Code serves as a useful setting for this enterprise, and all of the proposed amendments discussed in the following subsections were offered to this bill, and are included in the dataset that gave rise to the parameter estimates presented in the preceding section.

Distributional Questions

A proposal that epitomizes the nature of the ideological conflict on the labor committee was offered by PPD Senator Soto, and Socialist Senators Calderón, Gazmuri, Nuñez, and Vodanovic. The amendment "would add an article 5 *bis.* to the Labor Code to establish that in case of doubt or ambiguity labor legislation should be interpreted in the way that results most favorably to the worker." Senator Calderón argued the importance of establishing a pro-worker principal in the labor law to counterbalance the inequality between employer and employee. Senator Otero countered that the law should be written so clearly that there remained no ambiguity to interpret. He added that the amendment was both unnecessary and harmful, because judgments about doubts and unclarity are fundamentally subjective, whereas the law needs to be objectively based. Senator Hormazábal responded to Senator Otero, defending the proposal by noting that there was ample precedent for seeking to respect the spirit of the law in cases of ambiguity, for example by consulting the legislative history. Senator Feliú opposed the amendment, arguing that legal interpretation needed to recognize the specifics of a case, and that a blanket injunction to resolve doubt in favor of workers swept aside consideration of specifics. The Minister of Labor defended the amendment, contending that it would reenforce rather than replace existing rules, adding that resolving doubt in favor of workers was in keeping with the existing principals of labor law. Sensing defeat, Senator Otero said he would accept an amendment that contained a general statement of principal, but objected to what he characterized as the dangerous wording of the amendment being offered. The committee split along party lines, with Senator Calderón being joined in support of the amendment he had coauthored by Senators Hormazábal and Palza, while Senators Feliú and Otero voted to reject the proposal (Biblioteca del Congreso Nacional 1993a). However, victory proved short lived. When the Senate as a whole took up the debate, it rejected the amendment by seventeen votes against fourteen, with four Senators paired and so unable to vote (Biblioteca del Congreso Nacional 1993a).

The treatment of obligations to workers in the case that a firm goes bankrupt also divided committee members on ideological lines. A series of four unsuccessful proposed amendments by Senator Feliú would have denied precedence to debts owed by bankrupt firms to their workers (Biblioteca del Congreso Nacional 1993a). Defending the first of these, which would have suppressed a newly written article Senator Feliú argued that giving precedence to worker debt increased the risk premium businesses would have to pay in capital markets, and so reduced their access to credit. Moreover, she contended that for this reason the new article, which she sought to suppress, was more properly in the ambit of the Economics Committee, and should be referred there for study. Senator Hormazábal disagreed, contending that the subject was part of Labor Law, and so within the Committee's jurisdiction, notwithstanding the economic effects it might produce for businesses, just as in the cases of remuneration, and vacations, and numerous other employer obligations. The Minister of

Labor also objected, observing that the proposal would make the distribution of income less equal, as the largest volume of preferential credits are concentrated among the oldest and least well paid workers. The proposal was rejected by the negative votes of Senators Calderón, Hormazábal, and Palza, while Senator Romero joined the author in supporting it. While siding with Institutional Senator Feliú on this vote, it is noteworthy that Senator Romero who had to contend with an electoral constituency sought some cover for taking such a tough stance, justifying his vote on the procedural grounds that he had been persuaded by Senator Feliú's argument that the proposal should be studied by the Economics Committee (Biblioteca del Congreso Nacional 1993a).

Another issue that divided right and left on the committee was the extent of employers' obligations to provide worksite amenities. Senators on the right offered amendments to partially excempt night watchmen from the 48 hour work week, to penalize absentee workers by denying them vacation days, and to limit agricultural employers' obligations to provide food, lodging and transportation for their temporary workers. Senator Thayer joined the Concertación Senators in opposing many of these amendments. (Biblioteca del Congreso Nacional 1993a).

Divisions among the Concertación Senators emerged in this issue area. Senators Soto, Calderón, Gazmuri, Nuñez, and Vodanovic sought to modify "The Law of the Chair" that required employers to provide a chair or a cot for every worker. They proposed eliminating qualifying language in the status quo law that this requirement need only be fulfilled when the workers jobs "permitted." The amendment went on to specify the fine that would be levied on an employer who failed to meet this condition. The Committee Chairman, Humberto Palza, declared that the part of the proposal setting fines was inadmissible, contending that setting fines was part of the subject matter reserved under article 62 of the constitution for executive proposals. Surely the Socialists anticipated this, and merely sought to highlight the seriousness they attached to the legislation by proposing the fines which they knew would be eliminated as unconstitutional. The initial part of the proposal was unanimously accepted, but only after being rewritten along lines recommended by Senator Hormazábal substantially limited its content, requiring that the form and timing with which workers could avail themselves of the chairs and cots be specified in the internal rules of each firm (Biblioteca del Congreso Nacional 1993a), e.g. when the workers' jobs "permitted."

The impact of the executive's proposal monopoly can be seen clearly in two executive proposals to adjust the minimum wage. In Part 4 of article 62, the constitution reserves proposed changes in minimum wages for the executive. Sometimes this involves simple housekeeping, as with an executive amendment to adjust references in the Labor Code to the minimum wage for workers over 65. This had recently been adjusted upwards from 28, 400 pesos per month to 32, 219 monthly,[20] and the executive suggested changing the references in the law under consideration to comport with the change, a suggestion meeting with the unanimous approval of Senators Calderón, Hormazábal, Palza, Romero, and Thayer (Biblioteca del Congreso Nacional 1993a).

Another executive proposal added text to article 147 of the Labor Code, setting the minimum wage for household employees in private homes at 75% of the monthly minimum wage, and prevented employers from counting the value of benefits in kind, such as food and shelter, toward this minimum. With respect to benefits in kind, this proposal placed household employees on the same footing as other workers, for whom such benefits could not be counted toward the monthly minimum (Biblioteca del Congreso Nacional 1993a). This measure also met with unanimous approval from Senators Calderón, Hormazábal, Larre, Palza, and Thayer.

While the Constitution does not permit legislators to initiate legislation to change minimum wages, proposing such a change is a very effective way to stake out an issue position. This is just what Senators Soto, Calderón, Gazmuri, Nuñez, and Vodanovic did, sponsoring an amendment to alter article 147 of the Labor Code to require that domestic workers living outside the homes of their employers receive a money wage no less than 100% of the minimum monthly wage, while those living in their employers homes would have a minimum money wage equal to 75% of the monthly minimum. The amendment received a favorable vote only from its cosponsor Senator Calderón, while Senators Hormazábal, Larre, Palza, and Thayer all voted to reject it (Biblioteca del Congreso Nacional 1993a). It is interesting that Committee Chairman Palza allowed the question to come to a vote, as he could certainly have ruled it unconstitutional and avoided a vote on the substance. However, the vote permitted him and Senator Hormazábal to take a public position distinct from their Socialist and PPD colleagues.

As discussed in Chapter 1, the Concertación and opposition also clashed over the schedules of transportation workers. While all agreed on the importance of keeping tired drivers off the road, the Concertación Senators favored expanding coverage to include interurban truck drivers, and imposing weekly and monthly limits on hours at the wheel. (Biblioteca del Congreso Nacional 1993a). The position of the Concertación Senators was self-conciously close to that of the unions. For example, Christian Democratic Senator Palza supported including truck drivers among those

---

[20] In U. S. dollars this represented an increase in the monthly minimum from about $71 to about $80.

covered by time limits at the wheel noting that the measure had the express support of the truck drivers (Biblioteca del Congreso Nacional 1993a).

In a similar vein National Renovation Senator Miguel Otero proposed an injunction against urban bus-drivers also acting as fare collectors, except when the bus was equipped with an automated collection box and a system of mirrors to monitor all of the doors. The Labor Minister expressed concerns about the consequences the measure might have for the earnings of drivers, whom he conjectured would be harmed by the change. He thus counciled canvassing the opinion of those involved in urban transit, especially the bus drivers (Biblioteca del Congreso Nacional 1993a).

Corporate Shells

A loophole in the status quo labor law permitted unscrupulous employers to evade their responsibilities to provide employee benefits and evade legal judgments, for example in the case of workplace accidents. Under the status quo law a firm could escape liability by letting workers sue bankrupt subcontractors. If the firm's identity were not uncovered before the statute of limitations expired, the suit could not be subsequently expanded to include the firm. The executive proposed imposing fines on those who "hide, disguise, or change their identity or involvement in a business" to avoid complying with their legal obligations to employees; the executive's proposal also allowed the time limit with which which legal action had to be expanded to include a firm to be extended once action had been initiated against a subcontractor.

The ability of Institutional Senator Thayer to divide the Concertación is illustrated by an amendment to this executive proposal which he co-authored with RN Senator Romero. This amendment required that the fines for hiding one's identity would only apply if its effects were "harmful."[21] Senator Romero argued that if this change were not made it might be interpreted as making any contract or subcontract a violation of workers' rights, while Senator Thayer echoed that as it had been written the amendment proposed by the president could cover any good faith subcontract, while the fines should only be applied when there was a harmful dissimulation of ownership.

The Labor Minister observed that the word "harmful" had been withdrawn from the article at the first reading of the bill because its inclusion

---

[21] It should be kept in mind that because the proposal was cosponsored by Senators with different proposal characteristics, it should be viewed as occupying a middle position, with an ideological proposal parameter of g midway between those of the two proposers ($g = g_{\text{Thayer}}/2 + g_{\text{RN}}/2 = 1.265$) and likewise for the consensus parameter c ($c = g_{\text{Thayer}}/2 + g_{\text{RN}}/2 = -4.037$).

141

was unnecessary, but he was not opposed to reincorporating it into the text to avoid any doubt about the interpretation of the law. Nevertheless, controversy over technicalities ensued. Christian Democratic Senator Hormazábal complained that the law called for different responses to dissimulations about subcontractors, which would be dealt with by labor tribunals, and attempts within a firm to hide or avoid completing responsibilities to workers, which would be heard by the judiciary. He added that in the latter case limiting the law to instances in which the dissimulation could be shown to be "harmful" would impose such a burden of proof as to render the prohibition inoperative in practice.

However, the proposed modification in the wording of the amendment passed with the favorable votes of its authors, Romero and Thayer, and the support of Senator Palza. It was opposed by Senators Calderón and Hormazábal (Biblioteca del Congreso Nacional 1993a). However, the Chamber of Deputies balked at the new wording of the amendment, and the issue was reopened in the Conference Committee. As did Senator Hormazábal, the Deputies objected to the separate treatment of employers who sought to occlude their ownership by using third parties, and for employers who used whatever other means to hide their identities in order to avoid having to fulfill their responsibilities to their workers. However, just as the Conference Committee was meeting to resolve the differences between the Senate and Deputies versions of the bill, the executive endorsed the Senate's version, and the Conference Committee unanimously chose to do the same. Senator Thayer's amendment divided the Concertación and was carried into law (Biblioteca del Congreso Nacional 1993b).

Written Contracts

Another issue area that evoked ideological responses from committee members was the extent and seriousness of employers obligations to have written contracts with their employees, and to report them to the government. Senators Soto, Calderón, Gazmuri, Nuñez, and Vodanovic would have expanded the requirements in article 91-B of the Labor Code, requiring firms to have a written contract with any newly hired employee, and that within five days of having written the contract, a copy would have to be filed with the Government's Labor Inspection office. This stipulation was to apply regardless of the length of the employment period, while the version of article 91-B approved in the Chamber of Deputies required contracts to be reported only when the employment period exceeded twenty-eight days. National Renovation Deputy Angel Fantuzzi, a member of that chamber's Labor Committee who was sitting in on the Senate Labor

Committee debate, contended that by requiring that even contracts of short duration be filed with the Labor Inspection Office the main result would be to impede the function of that office, and that it would be more efficient simply to require firms to have the contracts on hand when a Labor Inspector arrived. Senator Hormazábal indicated sympathy for the difficulties the measure would cause employers, especially fruit producers and exporters, who frequently contract with harvest workers on a short-term basis. However, he also expressed concern that the status quo laws did not prevent abuses, noting cases in which employees had signed blank contracts. Senator Thayer responded, contending that far from solving the problems to which Senator Hormazábal alluded, the proposal might actually make them more acute. The Labor Minister agreed, observing that the same issue had been considered in the Chamber of Deputies, and arguing that the Deputies had balanced the need for compliance against the amount of paperwork involved in reporting every contract. This amendment divided the Christian Democrats with Senator Hormazábal joining Senators Prat, and Thayer in opposition, while it received supporting votes from its coauthor, Senator Calderón, and from Christian Democratic Senator Palza (Biblioteca del Congreso Nacional 1993a).

Senator Thayer sought to remove language that would subject changes in contracts to the same system of reporting deadlines that applied to newly drawn contracts. This proposed amendment was unanimously defeated, with the opposition of Senators Calderón, Feliú, Hormazábal, Otero, and Palza (Biblioteca del Congreso Nacional 1993a). Nevertheless, by the time the bill arrived on the floor, Senator Otero had changed his mind and wanted to renew the amendment. The petition to renew was signed by Senators Feliú, Cooper, Cantuarias, Jarpa, Lagos, Otero, Pérez, Rios, Romero, and Thayer (Biblioteca del Congreso Nacional 1993a). During the debate on the Senate floor Senator Thayer spoke for his proposal: "the labor contract, being consensual, is often seen in practice to be subject to minor modifications demanded by the very development of the activity," while "demanding that every change, no matter how minimal, be treated with the very same protocol as the making of a labor contract, under pain of a fine, we will create legal rigidity or incite widespread violation of the law…" (Biblioteca del Congreso Nacional 1993c).

Senator Hormazábal was adamant in his opposition, noting how difficult it would be for workers to prove their cases without a written contract. He foresaw employers abusing the lack of a written contract to excuse any change of treatment, from insisting that the employee work at a different jobsite to impromptu salary reductions (Biblioteca del Congreso Nacional 1993c). He emphasized the difficulties workers would encounter in practice trying to bring legal action, asserting that for many workers toiling in isolated regions of the country distant from branches of the Office of Labor Inspection, access to labor tribunals was a "summer night's dream."

The renewed amendment of Senator Thayer passed in a voice vote, with fifteen votes in favor and thirteen votes against, and three Senators paired with members absent from the Chamber and so unable to vote (Biblioteca del Congreso Nacional 1993c). Again Senator Thayer had won a narrow victory.

Conclusion

Roll-call votes cast in the Senate Labor Committee provide a useful window on the ideological divisions among Senators' positions on issues that divide the right from the left throughout the industrialized world. The Concertación Senators exhibit a high degree of cohesion in the Labor Committee, where it is the opposition who are not united. The Christian Democrats and the Socialists share a pro-union position on the left of the labor spectrum, with only statistically insignificant differences among their estimated preferred outcomes. Likewise, both groups of Senators propose leftward changes in the status quo of very similar magnitudes. Executive-sponsored proposals likewise shift policy leftward.

In this highly contested, ideologically charged area, the consensus appeal of proposals from the Concertación Senators is statistically significantly lower than for the opposition National Renovation Party, while instead of being very high, the consensus appeal of executive proposals differs insignificantly from that of the National Renovation Party. This is probably due in part to these proposals having "cutpoints" on the left, rather than to endemically low valence.[22]

On the right the National Renovation Party displays a lack of unity, with the estimated preferred policy outcome for Senator Otero significantly to the right of the remaining National Renovation voters. But this gap pales in comparison with the breach between the estimated preferred outcomes of Institutional Senators Feliú and Thayer. While Senator Thayer's preferred outcome is between the preferred outcome for the leftmost voters among the opposition and the rightmost among the Concertación, the position of Senator Feliú is far to the right of even Senator Otero. The estimated gap between Senators Feliú and Thayer is both highly statistically significant and larger than even the estimated distance between National Renovation Senator Otero and Socialist Senator Calderón. Moreover, the estimated characteristics of proposals sponsored

---

[22] Recalling the discussion in Chapter 1, the consensus appeal parameter for the proposer labeled p is a combination of the proposer's valence advantage, va_p, and ideological characteristics of the proposals, $c_p = va_p - g_p m_p$.

by Institutional Senator Thayer closely resemble those of the Christian Democrats, moving policy a similar distance leftward. Among the Senators of the opposition, Thayer is the most successful at formulating proposals that divide the Concertación Senators.

An analysis of the substance of the debates in the Labor Committee supports the picture revealed by the parameter estimates, with a united Concertación delegation and a divided opposition. The debates also provide insights about the substance of the Senators' issue positions. The left and right of the ideological spectrum on the Labor Committee resemble the ideological spectrum in Western Europe and North America. Positions on the left correspond to a "pro-labor" and "pro-union" outlook, concerned with protecting the interests of workers, providing more workplace amenities, more tolerable workering conditions, higher guaranteed salaries, a right to unionize, and more opportunities to appeal employers' decisions and to air grievances. Senators on the right advocate employers' interests in minimizing costs, and maximizing the flexibility with which businesses can adapt to the vagaries of the marketplace. The right believe workers' best guarantee of a comfortable income and decent working conditions is a competitive and expanding market in which the government intervenes as little as possible.

6

The Education Committee

The Education Committee deals with an issue area emphasized in the political campaigns of both the Concertación and its opponents. The disagreements about education are not simply about the level of spending, but about the most desirable type of spending. From the left, teachers' unions exert significant influence. Banned and harassed during the Pinochet years, the major teachers' union has emerged since 1990 as one of the most important in Chile, staging various national strikes. From the right there is pressure to provide more funds to subsidized private schools, and to allow them more flexibility.

Labor relations issues constitute a significant part of the committee's agenda. This happens because in Chile public education is administered by the national government. Thus, details about working conditions and compensation that in many other places are resolved by school boards and local unions are worked out at the national-level in Chile. Moreover, the teachers' union is probably the most powerful national-level union in Chile. In contrast with the labor committee, on which the policy agenda mostly applies to settings in which the government acts as a referee, in education policy the government constitutes the employer half of a bargaining dyad.

A second important part of the committee's policy agenda deals with public subsidies for students in private schools. During the Pinochet years the educational system was the subject of a major and controversial reform. With the objective of promoting school choice and competitive pressures, the Pinochet government established a system of educational subsidies for private schools that acted like a voucher system: under this system parents could, in theory, choose whether to send their children to one of the subsidized schools, or instead to their local municipal public school. The subsidized schools found themselves with large classes and long queues of applicants, while class sizes fell

146

in the municipal schools. The traditional private schools for the elite, where tuition levels were much higher than the subsidies being offered, were essentially unaffected by the program; however, these only account for a small fraction of Chilean students. Just as the new system began operating, the debt crisis of the early 1980s forced heavy budget cuts, creating pressures to increase class sizes and reduce teachers' salaries.

Because it promotes competition with the municipal schools, the right are very supportive of the subsidized sector, while because of the low wages paid in the subsidized sector, and the difficulties it poses for collective bargaining, the unions prefer to have resources channeled to the municipal sector. An added wrinkle in education policy is that the municipal governments consisted largely of appointees left over from the Pinochet regime, sparking "turf battles" between the Ministry of Education and the municipal school systems.

In contrast with the Labor Committee, where the status quo after sixteen and a half years of military rule was far to the right, the status quo education policy was more mixed when civilian government resumed in March 1990. While the status quo labor policy regarding teachers was more closely aligned with the preferences of Senators on the right, the budget for the subsidized sector was closer to the preferred outcome for the government, which favored the municipal public schools, and lower than most on the right would have liked. While the right were largely successful in using their Senate majority to blunt the labor reforms that the government wanted to implement, this legislative veto did not give them much leverage over the budget for the subsidized sector, a policy area in which the right sought to move away from the status quo.

The estimated preference parameters for Education Committee members on the right exhibit considerably more homogeneity than those of their counterparts on the Labor Committee. The voting Senators on the left also emerge as a homogeneous group, though there are greater differences among parties in the ideological content of amendments they formulate to education legislation than observed for labor legislation. However, direct comparisons with the Labor Committee are thwarted by the paucity of overlapping members. Only two Senators, Feliú and Palza, cast sufficient votes on both committees to permit estimation of individual preference parameters, but the statistical tests require at least three overlapping members. Yet the evidence does suggest that Senator Feliú takes a more moderate position on education policy than she does on labor policy, hinting that the labor and education policy debates may tap somewhat different ideological axes.

147

The Education Committee

The Setting

As with the Labor Committee, the Education Committee of the Chilean Senate considered a homogeneous agenda during the Aylwin years, with ten bills receiving second readings, all of them executive initiatives. Eight of these were squarely within the ambit of education policy; dealing with such questions as the administration of the government's school voucher program, and the working conditions of teachers. In contrast with the U. S. and many other countries with federal systems, public education in Chile is administered directly by the national government, so that many of the practical issues of class sizes and the working hours of teachers resolved by local school boards in the U. S. are part of the Congressional debate in Chile. Two bills were somewhat further afield; one dealt with how to certify foreign educational credentials obtained during the period of military rule by political exiles, while another dealt with copyright laws.

The Christian Democrats held two of the Committee seats, which they shared among themselves, and with fellow Concertación Senator Laura Soto. At one time or another six Christian Democrats cast votes in the committee. The National Renovation Party held one of the committee seats as well, but this was shared less frequently. The main participant for the National Renovation party was Senator Enrique Larre, while Senator Fransisco Prat occasionally substituted. The UDI party also had a seat on the committee, occupied by the committee's Chairman Eugenio Cantuarias. The fifth seat belonged to the Institutional Senators, with Senator Feliú as the most frequent occupant, while Senators McIntyre, Ruiz Danyau, and Thayer acted as infrequent substitutes. In addition the opposition parties occasionally shared their slots on the Committee with Arturo Alessandri, who, while nominally independent, has close ties to the parties of the right.[1]

6.1 PARAMETER ESTIMATES

As discussed in Chapter 1, in order to estimate the parameters of the voting model in Equation (4.4), several normalizations are required. This is done here by setting the preferred outcome for Senator Soto at -1.000. This will facilitate comparisons with the Constitution Committee, on which this PPD Senator also served. The preferred outcome for Senator Feliú is normalized to equal 1.000, again facilitating comparison with the Constitution Committee on which that Institutional Senator was also a frequent participant. As for the Labor Committee, The National Renovation

---

[1] As noted earlier, Arturo Alessandri was the presidential candidate of the right in 1993.

Party is the reference proposer, whose g and c parameters are normalized to equal 0.

Senators' Ideological Positions

The parameter estimates reported in Column 1 of Table 6 indicate greater cohesion among the Education Committee's voters on both the left and the right than we encountered on the Labor Committee. The Senators' estimated preferred positions, the x's, are illustrated in Figure 6.1. This especially true for the Senators on the right, where even for the opposition legislators with the least similar voting records, the National Renovation Senators[2] and Arturo Alessandri, no statistically significant difference in the preference parameters is observed.[3] This should be compared with the estimated gap between the preferred outcome of the National Renovation Senators at 0.830 and the infrequent voters among the Christian Democrats, whose preferred outcomes are estimated jointly[4] with a common estimated preferred outcome of -0.545. The gap between the leftmost of the opposition senators and the rightmost of the Concertación Senators is over two and a half times the gap between the leftmost and rightmost members of the opposition, and moreover it is highly statistically significant.[5] In contrast with the Labor Committee, where Senator Feliú's preferred policy was far to the right of the other opposition senators, her estimated preferred outcome is in the middle of the estimated preferred outcomes for the opposition Senators on the Education Committee, somewhat to the left of UDI Senator Eugenio Cantuarias and Institutional Senator Alessandri, somewhat to the right of the National Renovation Party and the remaining Institutional Senators. A formal test for equality among all five pairs of estimated preference parameters for the opposition Senators voting on the Education Committee[6] leads to acceptance at all standard levels of significance.

---

[2] These were Senators Larre and Prat; because the latter voted infrequently a common position is estimated for the pair.

[3] A formal test of the hypothesis that the voting parameters for National Renovation (x_{RN}, b_{RN}) equal those for Senator Alessandri $(x_{Alessandri}, b_{Alessandri})$ leads to a test statistic of 1.9062. Compared with its asymptotic distribution under the null hypothesis of χ_2^2, this corresponds to a p value of 0.3855, indicating acceptance at all standard significance levels.

[4] These were Senators Diaz, Lavandero, Ruiz Esquide, and Ruiz de Giorgio.

[5] A test of the null hypotheses that these two groups of Senators, the infrequently voting Christian Democrats and the National Renovation Senators, have the same preference parameters gives rise to a χ_2^2 test statistic of 11.573, corresponding to a p value of 0.0031 and leading to rejection at all standard significance levels.

[6] The resulting test statistic is 4.873. Compared with the asymptotic χ_8^2 distribution for this test statistic under the null hypothesis of no differences, this corresponds to a p value of 0.7710.

Table 6. *Parameter estimates for the education committee*

Participant	Parameter[a]			
	x	b	g	c
PS			−1.507	0.442
			(0.630)	(0.672)
PPD				
Laura Soto G.	−1.000	0.930	−0.607	0.293
		(0.760)	(0.878)	(0.850)
Partido Democrata Cristiano	−0.545	−0.152	−3.154	1.444
	(0.462)	(0.455)	(0.993)	(0.941)
Maximo Pacheco G.	−0.664	−0.262		
	(0.453)	(0.450)		
Humberto Palza C.	−0.781	0.087		
	(0.505)	(0.503)		
Executive Proposals			−1.568	9.588
			(0.824)	(1.189)
Radical/Socialdemocrata			0.007	−2.044
			(0.549)	(0.564)
Renovación Nacional	0.830	−0.642	0.000	0.000
	(0.203)	(0.506)		
Institutional Senators	0.870	−0.847	1.773	4.144
	(0.392)	(0.725)	(0.886)	(0.941)
Olga Feliú S.	1.000	−0.799		
		(0.461)		
Union Democrata Independiente				
Eugenio Cantuarias L.	1.134	−0.165	3.212	6.162
	(0.306)	(0.450)	(1.383)	(1.655)
Arturo Alessandri B.	1.237	0.697	0.000	0.000
	(0.562)	(1.181)		
Own Party Proposals		1.081		
		(0.543)		

[a] Estimated standard errors are show in parentheses; $\hat{\alpha} = 5.417$, $\hat{S}d(\hat{\alpha}) = 0.560$, $\log(\text{lik}) = -354.259$, $n = 328$ amendments.

Figure 6.1. Estimated Preferred Outcomes.

The Education Committee

The picture of homogeneity is little different on the left, though this is less of a contrast with the Labor Committee, where the Senators of the left are also highly unified. On the Education Committee the largest estimated gap is that between the infrequently voting Christian Democrats,[7] at -0.545, and Senator Soto of the PPD, whose preferred outcome is normalized to equal -1. Not only are the gaps among the Senators on the left small; they are statistically insignificant.[8]

Thus we see the Senators of the left spread across a narrow-band with Senator Soto on the left at -1.000, Christian Democrats Palza and Pacheco a bit to her right, at -0.781 and -0.664, respectively, and the infrequently voting Christian Democrats (marked "DC" in Figure 6.1) at -0.545. Then we encounter a wide gulf, with the Senators of the right again spread across a narrow range, from National Renovation Senators Larre and Prat[9] at 0.830, followed by the infrequently voting Institutional Senators[10] (marked "S. I." in Figure 6.1) at 0.870, to Senator Feliú, with a preferred outcome normalized to equal 1.000, Senator Cantuarias of the UDI party with an estimated preferred outcome of 1.134, and on the right Senator Arturo Alessandri, with an estimated preferred outcome of 1.237. A test of the null hypothesis that all of the Senators on the left share one set of preference parameters, which implies that all four pairs of estimated preference parameters for the Concertación senators are equal, and that at the same time all of the Senators on the right have the same preference parameters, so that all five pairs of estimated parameters for the opposition are equal to one another (but not to the preferences of the Concertación Senators), leads to acceptance at all standard significance levels.[11] In sharp contrast to the Labor Committee, the data from the Education Committee do not permit us to reject the hypothesis of a bipolar system, in which all of the Senators on the left share one set of preferences, and all of the Senators on the right share another.

[7] These were Nicolas Diaz, Jorge Lavandero, Mariano Ruiz Esquide, and José Ruiz De Giorgio.

[8] A test of the null hypothesis that all four of the estimated pairs of preference parameters for the Concertación are identical leads to a χ_6^2 statistic of 5.7677, corresponding to a p value of 0.4497, which corresponds to acceptance at all standard significance levels. A more stringent test, and one "loaded" against the null hypothesis, is to compare the most distant pair of ideal point estimates among the Concertación, those of Senator Soto and the infrequently voting Christian Democrats. A test of the null hypothesis that these ideal points are in fact identical leads to a χ_2^2 test statistic of 3.8362, corresponding to a p value of 0.1469 and leading to acceptance at all standard significance levels.

[9] The vast majority of these votes were cast by Senator Larre. Senator Prat's infrequent voting precluding estimating a separate pair of parameters.

[10] These were Senators Danyau, McIntyre, and Thayer.

[11] The χ_{14}^2 test statistic of 10.5110 corresponds to a p value of 0.7239.

The Agenda Parameters

The homogeneity among the voting parameters for the Education Committee does not carry over to the proposal-making side. There are noticeable differences in the partisan content of proposals made by Senators within the opposition, and among the Concertación Senators, as captured by the estimated values for g reported in Column 3 of Table 6. Given the findings on the voting Senators' preference parameters, these differences probably emerge from differences in proposal-making capacity rather than from differences in preferred outcomes. In addition there are important differences among proposers in the consensus appeal of the amendments they offer, as measured by the c parameters reported in Column 4 of Table 6.

Turning first to the ideological parameters, we see that both the UDI and Institutional Senators propose to the right of the National Renovation Party. The estimated value of $g = 3.212$ for UDI Senator Cantuarias is well to the right of the 0 value for National Renovation, the reference proposer. A test of the null hypothesis that UDI and National Renovation have the same value for g leads to borderline rejection.[12] Likewise, the Institutional Senators, with an estimated displacement of $g = 1.773$, are also to the right of the National Renovation Party by a marginally statistically significant gap.[13]

Significant differences also emerge on the left; there the Christian Democrats make proposals moving policy farther to the left, with $g_{PDC} = -3.154$, than the Socialists, whose proposals are estimated to move policy by $g_{PS} = -1.507$. Nor is this estimated difference a mere statistical anomaly.[14] In contrast, the displacement of executive proposals is very similar to that of proposals from the Socialists, with an estimated value of $g_{exec} = -1.568$. Moving further toward the National Renovation Party, we encounter PPD Senator Soto, with an estimated displacement of $g_{Soto} = -0.607$, and the Senators of the Radical/Social Democratic caucus, whose estimated value for g of 0.007 is actually to the right of the displacement for the National Renovation Party, though that gap is both minute and statistically insignificant. Somewhat surprisingly the odd estimate for the Radical/SD Senators cannot be brushed off entirely as the byproduct of imprecise estimation. The parameter estimate for $g_{Rad/SD}$ is

---

[12] The χ_1^2 test statistic of 5.3937 corresponds to a p value of 0.0202, leading to rejection at $\alpha = 0.10$ and $\alpha = 0.05$, though not at the 0.01 level.

[13] The χ_1^2 test statistic of the null hypothesis of no difference gives rise to a test-statistic of 4.0065, with a corresponding p value of 0.0453.

[14] A test of the hypothesis that both parties actually displace policy by the same amount, sharing a common value of g, leads to a χ_1^2 test statistic of 3.8567, corresponding to a p value of 0.0495 and leading to rejection at the 0.10 and (barely) at the 0.05 levels, but not at $\alpha = 0.01$.

actually more precise than the estimate for any of the other Concertación proposers, with an estimated standard error of only 0.549. Moreover, while the Radical and Social Democratic Senators proposal parameter does not differ statistically significantly from that of PPD Senator Soto, the difference between the Radical/SD proposals and those of the Socialists is on the border of statistical significance.[15]

While there is considerable heterogeneity among the proposal parameters, both among members of the Concertación and among the opposition, the gulf between the two groups is blurred. Differences between the estimated g values for the National Renovation Party and either the Radical/SD Senators or Senator Soto are statistically insignificant. However, while the National Renovation Senators propose similarly to some of the Concertación members, differences remain with the Christian Democrats and the Socialists, and probably with the executive as well.[16]

While these parameter estimates conform more or less with what one would expect, there are several surprises. The most striking finding is that the Senate's Christian Democrats make proposals that are to the left of their Socialist coalition partners, and also to the left of the president, a member of their own party. The gap between the Christian Democratic Senators and their president may in part result from the executive's need, as head of the Concertación, to accommodate the remaining members of the coalition. A second factor at work may be related to the special proposal-making powers of the president. Given the president's monopoly over making certain types of proposals, it may be that the opposition use their ability to derail legislation to bargain over the content of presidential proposals, so that the proposals finally offered by the president have been shifted rightward during the process of negotiation.

Another surprise is the moderateness of the National Renovation Senators in terms of the spectrum of proposals. Both of these findings are probably tied up with the issues of how to treat the teachers, and how to treat the subsidized sector of private schools. On the first question, the Christian Democratic executive has an interest in keeping the public sector budget small while at the same time avoiding costly strikes in the municipal public schools, while the Socialists, with closer ties to the unions, are more inclined to allow wider scope for the public sector teachers' unions. On the second issue, of how to treat the subsidized sector, which was created as part of Chile's school voucher program during the Pinochet years, the right

---

[15] The χ_1^2 test statistic of 4.1669 corresponds to a p value of 0.0412, and it leads to rejection of the null hypothesis of no difference between $g_{Rad/SD}$ and g_{PS} at either $\alpha = 0.10$ or $\alpha = 0.05$, though not at the 0.01 level.

[16] The p values corresponding to the hypothesis that $g_{RN} = g_{exec}$ is 0.0570, while the hypotheses that $g_{RN} = g_{PDC}$ and $g_{RN} = g_{PS}$ generate p values of 0.0.0015 and 0.0168, respectively.

want more generous subsidies for these competitors of the public schools, while the government would like to keep subsidies low. Thus the left end of the policy spectrum for the Education Committee probably signifies not only a larger role for the public schools, but also austerity measures, some of which cut against the interests of the unions, and the Socialists who represent them, while others come at the expense of the subsidized private schools, and the oppositions parties that represent their interests. If this is the case pro-union reforms would not be at the extreme left end of the spectrum of proposals placed before the Education Committee.

Grouped by the consensus quality of their proposals, the Education Committee participants break into four ranges. At the topmost level, with an estimated value of c equal to 9.588, is the executive. The next rung down contains the UDI and Institutional Senators, with estimated consensus parameters of 6.162 and 4.144, respectively. The Christian Democrats, the Socialists, PPD Senator Soto, and the reference proposer, the National Renovation Party, form a third group, with values of c of $c_{PDC} = 1.444$, $c_{PS} = 0.442$, and $c_{Soto} = 0.293$, while c_{RN} is normalized to equal 0. The Radicals and Social Democrats form a forth cohort with minimal acceptance. The estimated differences among members of each of these four cohorts are statistically insignificant at all standard levels; the differences between members of different cohorts are significant at at least $\alpha = 0.10$.

The high estimated consensus appeal for presidential proposals may stem from the president's added bargaining power. With the president's monopoly, proposal rights within the domains reserved by article 62 of the Constitution combined with the threat of a constructive veto as set forth in article 70 mean that the president is essentially able to act as agenda setter when he or she is determined enough to do so. A little care in setting the agenda will result in a high approval rate for executive proposals in the reserved issue domains. Even in areas that are not off limits to legislative amendments, the president enjoys the advantage of the extra administrative resources available to the executive. As noted before, while Senators will typically have a single assistant, and perhaps some small additional administrative support from their party or from committee staffs, the president has entire agencies of the government at his or her disposal to assist in formulating proposals. It would be a surprise indeed if all these extra resources did not result in somewhat higher-valence proposals.

Likewise, the participation of committee chairman and UDI party member Eugenio Cantuarias in the UDI's proposals may at least partially account for the ready acceptance received by that party's proposals. With the power to rule on the constitutionality of proposals, albeit subject to reversal by the president of the Senate should the decision be revisited on the floor, the committee chairman enjoys some bargaining power relative to the other members of the committee. While this bargaining power, if indeed that is what lies at the root of the high consensus acceptance of UDI proposals, did not result in high consensus quality of proposals from Labor Committee chairman Humberto Palza, we are not able to observe what Senator Palza's consensus quality would have been had he been stripped of his chair. Perhaps in that case his proposals would have enjoyed even less acceptance.

The low consensus appeal for the Radicals and the Social Democrats may stem from their weak position within the Concertación. The dominant center party in Chile until the early 1960s, the Radicals lost many supporters to the Christian Democrats and the Socialists during the period from 1964 to 1973. While the Radical Party became part of the Concertación, in the 1989 election it drew mostly on its preexisting base of support; it has had limited success attracting younger voters. Once this weakness was revealed it is likely the remaining parties came to view the Radicals as moribund, leaving them with little bargaining power either within or outside the Concertación.

The importance of consensus issues on the Education Committee is very similar to that encountered on the Labor Committee. The estimated value of α, 5.417, with an estimated standard deviation of 0.560, is very similar to the estimate obtained for the Labor Committee.[17] For both committees the consensus element of policy is important, and both exhibit high rates of unanimous voting, though not so high as to neutralize partisan differences.

Parameter Estimates and Voting Coalitions

To better understand the implications of the parameter estimates, it is useful to calculate the voting outcomes they imply for amendments offered by various proposers. This is done in Table 7, which reports the probability distribution implied by the model for vote margins on various hypothetical proposals in a session of the committee attended by Senators Cantuarias, Feliú, Larre, Palza, and Pacheco. The probabilities shown in this table are built up from the probabilities implied by the model for each of the thirty-two possible voting outcomes that could emerge. The earlier discussion of the Labor Committee included a table, Table 3, that displayed the probabilities associated with each of the thirty-two possible voting coalitions that could emerge with all of that committee's members participating in the vote. To save space here, Table 7 only reports the totals for and against.

Consulting the first column of Table 7, we see that proposals from the executive are likely to encounter unanimous support, because of their high consensus appeal. However, the second most likely outcome, and it

---

[17] The correlation this implies between Senators' voting errors, the $\alpha v_i + \eta_{vi}$, is 0.967.

Table 7. *Hypothetical education committee vote margins*[a]

Votes		Probability by proposer						
In favor	Against	Exec.	PDC	PS	Soto	Rad./SD	UDI	Instit.
0	5	0.048	0.160	0.361	0.381	0.634	0.028	0.123
1	4	0.017	0.049	0.022	0.043	0.010	0.014	0.008
2	3	0.063	0.423	0.220	0.119	0.004	0.044	0.037
3	2	0.005	0.016	0.042	0.083	0.009	0.175	0.159
4	1	0.043	0.027	0.009	0.020	0.050	0.004	0.009
5	0	0.824	0.325	0.347	0.353	0.292	0.736	0.664

[a] Committee consisting of Senators Cantuarias, Feliú, Palza, Pacheco, and Larre.

is a distant second with a probability of only 0.063, is that the proposal is defeated with three votes against two and in favor. This is the split that arises when the Concertación Senators vote in favor and the opposition Senators vote for defeat. Because of their ideological content, executive proposals must overcome a higher threshold of consensus quality (measured in the model by ϵ_p) to receive support from the Senators on the right than is needed to secure the votes of the Senators of the Concertación. A similar pattern is observed for the high consensus quality proposals of the UDI and Institutional Senators (see the last two columns of the table), though the probability of unanimous support is somewhat lower for these proposers on the right; the most likely split vote involves approval by three votes against two. This is the approval margin for proposals that enjoy the support of the three opposition Senators and resistance from the Committee's two Concertación Senators.

The remaining proposers tend to produce more symmetrical outcomes, with more equal probabilities of unanimous acceptance and unanimous rejection. However, proposals from the Christian Democrats are the most polarizing, because of the large leftward ideological impact implied by the estimated value of $g_{PDC} = -3.154$, leading to three against two margins for rejection in over two-fifths of all cases. Proposals from PPD Senator Soto and from the Socialist Senators are predicted to produce unanimous rejection and unanimous acceptance about equally often, with an estimated probability of about three-eighths for each type of unanimous outcome. However, among the divided outcomes the Socialists, with an estimated value of $g_{PS} = -1.507$, are much more likely to produce a three to two rejection along ideological lines, while Soto's proposals are more likely to produce idiosyncratic splits. Proposals from the Radicals and Social Democrats are predicted to meet with unanimous rejection almost two times out of three.

The Education Committee

To better understand the linkage between the parameter estimates presented in the previous section and the concrete policy choices to which they correspond, it is useful to examine some of the proposals in detail. The most complicated piece of legislation considered by the committee during the Aylwin period was the "Teacher's Statute," a major overhaul of the legislation affecting the teaching profession. This bill gave rise to over two hundred amendments, a few of which help to illustrate the issue positions corresponding to the parameter estimates reported in Table 6.

Credentials Committees

One important area of contention was the procedure for hiring new teaching staff. The executive's proposal sought to establish credentials committees that would evaluate job applicants for the municipal schools. (Biblioteca del Congreso Nacional 1991a). Controversy emerged over the composition of these committees, and about the powers accorded to them.

In the executive's proposal the mayor of the respective municipality would be obliged to appoint the candidate chosen by the committee. However, at the first reading of the bill the Education Committee modified this proposal to have the committees designate the three best qualified applicants for the job, leaving the choice among these three at the mayor's discretion. Since the current government and its supporters would be well represented on the credentials committees, while the mayors at that time were almost all appointees left over from the military government, this shifted control over appointments away from the government and toward friends of the opposition. Osvaldo Verdugo, president of the major teachers' union the Colegio de Profesores (CP), denounced this change (La Epoca, May 15, 1991), while Christian Democratic Senators Diaz and Pacheco proposed renewing the requirement that the job go to the candidate who received top ranking from the credentials committee. However there is a tradition in Chilean government practice of "concursos publicos," or credentials committees, selecting lists of candidates from which administrators are given the discretion of choosing the top three. Thus, the proposal may have coupled a large leftward change in educational policy with a reduction in consensus quality. The Education Committee unanimously rejected this proposal, with PPD Senator Soto joining opposition Senators Cantuarias, Feliú, and Larre in opposing it. The majority justified their rejection, asserting that the credentials committees were consultative in nature, and should not be permitted to encroach on the mayors' decision-making powers (Biblioteca del Congreso Nacional 1991a) Given the PPD Senator's reputation as an advocate of the left, it seems likely she joined her colleagues on the right in voting against this proposal because of its low consensus quality.[18]

Another of Verdugo's demands, that school administrators be included among those chosen by the credentials committees (La Tercera, May 16, 1991b), was proposed as an amendment cosponsored by Socialist Senators Calderón and Gazmuri, and by PPD Senator Soto. Their proposal would have included the director of the the Municipal Department of Education to the list if jobs the credentials committees would be charged with filling. The model predicts that a proposal by this coalition of two Socialists and their PPD colleague will have a leftward impact on the content of policy of $\bar{g} = -1.207$.[19] Unlike the proposal to remove mayors from the hiring process for teachers, the intermediate consensus appeal of this leftward proposal meant that Senators chose their positions on ideological grounds. Senators Cantuarias and Larre voted with Senator Feliú against the amendment, while Senators Pacheco and Soto voted for the defeated amendment (Biblioteca del Congreso Nacional 1991a). This proposed amendment adhered to the pattern of bipolar voting observed on the Education Committee, with most divided votes pitting the Concertación Senators, with preferred outcomes estimated close together on the left, against the opposition, with estimated preferred policies clumped on the right.

Mr. Verdugo was also displeased with an amendment introduced at the Education Committee's first reading of the bill which restricted the scope of the credentials committees to vacant jobs (La Epoca 1991). This reaction was shared by Christian Democratic Senators Diaz and Pacheco, who proposed renewing the executive's "mechanism for normalizing the jobs of such teaching supervisors as may have entered by paths distinct from public competition" (Biblioteca del Congreso Nacional 1991a). This was essentially a measure that would allow the removal of administrators appointed by the Pinochet government. The number of jobs this proposal would have affected was somewhat difficult to determine, as the records were maintained by the various municipalities, but Education Minister Ricardo Lagos noted that it might affect the principals of as many as 3,200

---

[18] Asked several years later why she had opposed this proposal, the Senator was unable to recall the vote. Interview with the author, Valparaíso, June 1994.

[19] This is a weighted average of the estimated Socialist displacement of $g_{PS} = -1.507$ and the corresponding PPD parameter of $g_{PPD} = -0.607$:

$$\hat{g} = \tfrac{2}{3}g_{PS} + \tfrac{1}{3}g_{PPD}$$
$$= \tfrac{2}{3}(-1.507) + \tfrac{1}{3}(-0.607)$$
$$= -1.207$$

schools (Biblioteca del Congreso Nacional 1991b). In any event, the proposal was rejected by a three to two margin, with Senators Cantuarias, Feliú, and Larre constituting the majority, while Senators Pacheco and Palza voted unsuccessfully in favor of the executive's initial wording (Biblioteca del Congreso Nacional 1991a).

This was not the end of the matter. Unlike the proposal to take mayors out of the hiring process for teachers, the consensus quality of this proposal was neither so high nor so low as to neutralize its polarizing ideological displacement, which for a proposal coauthored by two Christian Democrats on the Education Committee is $g_{PDC} = -3.154$. The amendment was renewed when the bill reached the Senate floor, where, after a lengthy legal debate about whether it was properly worded as an amendment, it was put to a vote. It was narrowly defeated, with eighteen votes against, sixteen in favor, and two Senators paired and so unable to vote (Biblioteca del Congreso Nacional 1991b). During the voting several Senators[20] spoke against the amendment. Senator Thayer objected that language in the amendment promising directors fired as a result of the amendment "full protection of their rights as workers" without specifying the severance pay to which they were entitled was dangerously vague, and could give rise to "every class of problems and conflicts"(Biblioteca del Congreso Nacional 1991b). Essentially he was arguing against the proposal on the valence grounds that it would be hard to administer. Senator Urenda argued that the proposal would compromise the professional dignity of the affected administrators, and further objected that it acted retroactively, imposing a posteriori conditions on rights already granted (Biblioteca del Congreso Nacional 1991b). Senators Diaz and Hormazábal spoke in favor of the proposal, with Senator Hormazábal arguing in ideological terms that it would constitute some much needed housecleaning:

> Moreover, in the time of democratic reconstruction that we are living, the fewer unpleasant reminders of the unjust authoritarian past that remain, the better will be the quality of education and coexistence.
>
> (Biblioteca del Congreso Nacional 1991b)

At the basis of the disagreement between Senator Urenda, who argued against the injustice of imposing retroactive conditions on employment, and Senator Hormazábal, who argued in favor of reviewing the teaching supervisors appointments, was the question that recurred throughout many debates during the Aylwin years: which policy initiatives undertaken by the military government were illegitimate?

[20] They were Senators Alessandri, Feliú, Larre, Thayer, and Urenda.

159

A proposal, by Senators Gazmuri and Soto, with an estimated ideological displacement[21] of $\hat{g} = -1.057$, called for adding two representatives of the regional leadership of the main teacher's union, the CP, to the credentials committees. Senator Feliú objected that the proposal presupposed collaboration of all teachers' unions with the CP. Senator Larre opined that teachers' participation was already guaranteed with the inclusion on the credentials committees of two teachers chosen by lot. The executive proposed rewording the amendment to include two representatives of the regional leadership of whatever union should have the most members in the area. This suggestion failed to avert an ideologically polarized vote, with Senators Cantuarias, Feliú, and Larre opposing the proposal, while Senators Pacheco and Soto voted for acceptance (Biblioteca del Congreso Nacional 1991a). As with the executive's proposal to replace one of the teachers selected at random with a representative of the Education Ministry, this proposal was neither spectacularly high in valence, nor abysmally low, so that ideological considerations determined Senators votes.

More guidance about the substantive content of the ideological considerations that motivated Senators' votes can be had from the debate that resulted when it was renewed on the floor. Senator Palza's opening remarks indicate considerable influence by the teachers' associations: "Following the criteria that we have proposed, in the sense of taking the suggestions that have been made to us – I would say almost unanimously – by the country's teachers, we have renewed this proposed amendment because we think that when we speak of real participation by educators, we must follow through by acting concretely" (Biblioteca del Congreso Nacional 1991a). While the floor vote was by "votación economica" so that the identities of those voting in favor and against is not part of the record, several Senators gave brief speechs justifying their positions as they voted. The Concertación Senators equated representation of the teachers' union with teacher participation in decision making. Senator Palza argued

"...that when we speak about participation we do well to mean it, in a way that if it is possible to permit it, one has to do so."

(Biblioteca del Congreso Nacional 1991a)

The opposition Senators characterized the teacher's union as a special interest, noting that the existing text allowed for the inclusion of

---

[21] This is a weighted average of the estimated Socialist displacement of $g_{PS} = -1.507$ and the corresponding PPD parameter of $g_{PPD} = -0.607$:

$$\hat{g} = \tfrac{1}{2}g_{PS} + \tfrac{1}{2}g_{PPD}$$
$$= \tfrac{1}{2}(-1.507) + \tfrac{1}{2}(-0.607)$$
$$= -1.057$$

two teachers on the credentials committees chosen by lot without given monopoly to the CP. RN Senator Otero picked upon Senator Palza's theme of participation:

"Here participation has been spoken of. And we are all in favor of that. But it means this: that all can participate, and not just one sector, to the exclusion of others." Arguing that selection by lot meant "every teacher has our recognition and respect to participate."

(Biblioteca del Congreso Nacional 1991a)

The proposed amendment was narrowly defeated by a margin of nineteen votes against,[22] and seventeen in favor,[23] while four Senators were paired, and so unable to vote (Biblioteca del Congreso Nacional 1991a).

Independent Municipal Schools

Closely related to policy toward principals appointed during the military regime was the disposition of fifty-four municipal school systems that in 1980, during the period of military rule, had been given administrative independence from their respective municipal governments. In the executive's initial bill these would have been returned to the municipal governments from which they were transferred. However, at the first reading, the committee struck this language from the bill, over the vigorous protest of the teachers' union (La Epoca 1991). The executive, joined by Socialist Senator Hernán Vodanovic,[24] promptly proposed an amendment to revive this measure.

Ideological considerations dominated, producing a bipolar split with the three opposition legislators with estimated preferred policies on the right, Senators Cantuarias, Feliú, and Larre, voting to defeat the measure, while the two Concertación members on the left, Senators Pacheco and Palza, voted in favor (Biblioteca del Congreso Nacional 1991a).

The question did not end with the committee's rejection. Discussion of the proposal resumed on the floor of the Senate, where the amendment

---

[22] The "no" voters included Senators Cantuarias, Feliú, Otero, Piñera, Rios, and Thayer, who spoke for the record to justify their votes.

[23] Senators Hormazábal, Lavandero, Pacheco, Palza, Ruiz-Esquide, and Zaldivar, all Christian Democrats, gave speeches explaining their affirmative votes.

[24] The ideological displacement for this model of $\hat{g} = -1.538$ is a weighted average of the estimated Socialist displacement of $g_{PS} = -1.507$ and the corresponding executive parameter of $g_{exec} = -1.568$:

$$g = \tfrac{1}{2}g_{PS} + \tfrac{1}{2}g_{exec}$$
$$= \tfrac{1}{2}(-1.507) + \tfrac{1}{2}(-1.568)$$
$$= -1.538$$

was renewed.[25] During the floor debate the question of the amendment's constitutionality was quickly raised, and Gabriel Valdes, Christian Democratic President of the Senate, was sufficiently unsure of the correct ruling that he allowed a debate on whether he should declare the amendment unconstitutional. During the debate the Concertación senators emphasized the schools' origins as municipal schools that had been privatized during the period of military rule, while on the other side the opposition Senators focused on their current status as "personas jurídicas," that is, as legal persons with property rights protected by the Constitution.

The real issue in question was the legitimacy of the Constitution of 1980. Consider the sardonic remarks of Senator Hormazábal about the origins of the Constitution of 1980: "I value the opinion of the distinguished Opposition Senators, who also have the comparative advantage of having participated in the drafting of the Constitution of 1980, while others of us could not intervene in the debate." Rankled by the status of the independent schools as legal persons, and recalling the military regime's tactic of claiming that victims of clandestine detention and summary execution had never existed, the same Senator commented: "It would have pleased me if the rights and attributes that turned human beings into fictitious persons during the last regime had also been in accord with general principals of law." Nor did the opposition Senators fail to understand that key to the government's position was the contention that the status quo policy was illegitimate. Seeking to counter this argument, Senator Otero responded[26] to Senator Hormazábal's remarks:

Moreover, Mr. Chairman, I was not the father of the 1980 Constitution. I would have liked to have intervened; but I believe that, on the matter of property law, it ratifies what was already set forth in this respect by the Constitution of 1925. Of course in those days other senators had not yet been born, and neither had I. But this does not mean that the document of 1925 has no value, nor that it should not be respected. Moreover, it appears to me that here we must appeal to legal arguments; and so it follows logically that speaking in an ironic manner does not contribute to a better understanding of the matter.

Even as the Senator Hormazábal busily sought to tie the independent municipal schools to the perceived illegitimacy of the military government, Senator Otero worked just as hard to untie them, framing his response in terms of legal principles from the period before military rule.

[25] Signing the petition to renew the amendment were Socialist Senators Nuñez and Vodanovic, Radicals Sule and Navarrete, Social Democratic Senator Papi, Christian Democrat Carmen Frei, PPD Senator Soto, and three others whose signatures the Senate Secretary Mr. Eyzaguirre could not make out.

[26] The Senate rules do not permit direct debates; Senators must address themselves to the chair when they speak during discussion of a bill. They respond to this rule by addressing one another in the third person.

The Education Committee

After extensive discussion in the Chamber, Senator Valdes put the question of constitutionality to the Chamber as a whole, where it was declared unconstitutional by a margin of seventeen votes to thirteen, with three Senators paired, and so unable to vote. Senator Valdes abstained (Biblioteca del Congreso Nacional 1991a).

Teachers' Councils

Another feature of the executive's initial proposal was to create teachers' councils within the schools. At the first reading of the bill, the Education Committee amended the bill to deprive these councils of decision-making power. The teachers' union responded predictably, protesting this loss of power (La Tercera 1991a). Socialist Senators Calderón, Gazmuri, and PPD Senator Soto cosponsored an amendment to restore the power of these teachers' councils to resolve technical questions about teaching, questions to be defined by the implementing regulations for the Teachers' Statute.[27] The committee rejected the proposal on a split vote, with Senators Cantuarias, Feliú, and Larre voting for rejection, while Senators Diaz and Pacheco cast affirmative votes. Not to be outdone, Christian Democratic Senators Diaz and Pacheco proposed a virtually identical measure to allow the teachers' councils established in each school to make binding decisions on questions of pedagogical technique, and met with precisely identical results, as Senators Cantuarias, Feliú, and Larre voted to reject the proposal, while its authors voted for acceptance (Biblioteca del Congreso Nacional 1991a).

The PS/PPD version of the amendment was renewed during the Senate Chamber debate, where Senator Palza spoke on its behalf. The right remained opposed, and Education Minister Lagos proposed a face-saving compromise:

> Given the preceding comments the redaction could be the following: "Nonetheless, the Teachers' Councils will be able to make binding decisions about matters of pedagogical technique in conformity with the educational objectives of the school, and its internal rules." In this way the nature of these councils as binding decision-makers with respect to technical pedagogical technique is established, and simultaneously schools' educational objectives are not affected.

---

[27] The ideological displacement for this model of $\hat{g} = -1.207$ is a weighted average of the estimated Socialist displacement of $g_{PS} = -1.507$ and the corresponding PPD parameter of $g_{PPD} = -0.607$:

$$\hat{g} = \tfrac{2}{3}g_{PS} + \tfrac{1}{3}g_{exec}$$
$$= \tfrac{2}{3}(-1.507) + \tfrac{1}{3}(-0.607)$$
$$= -1.207$$

Opposition Senators Diez and Cantuarias quickly agreed to this language about school's "educational objectives" and "internal rules" which rendered the proposal toothless, and the amended version was passed (Biblioteca del Congreso Nacional 1991a).

Nursery School Teachers

While the Concertación united to support the policies advocated by the major teachers' union, this unity broke down when workers outside the unions protective umbrella were concerned. Nursery school teachers did not belong to the CP, and not by coincidence they were excluded from the provisions of the teachers' statute. Two proposals from the left sought to remedy the latter condition. The first, cosponsored by Socialist Senator Calderón and PPD Senator Soto,[28] would have expanded the scope of the Teachers' Statute to cover nursery school teachers. The amendment met with the disapprobation of the executive, who opined that it would increase costs, and the committee agreed that the measure could result in expanding education subsidies, and the committee unanimously voted to reject the proposal, with Christian Democratic Senator Pacheco joining opposition Senators Cantuarias, Feliú, and Larre in voting "no" (Biblioteca del Congreso Nacional 1991a).

Failing in their attempt to extend the full benefits of the Teachers' Statute to nursery school teachers, Senators Calderón and Soto tried for a more limited objective, proposing an amendment to extend continuing education benefits to nursery school teachers.[29] This was still too much for the committee, where Senators Cantuarias, Feliú, Larre, and Pacheco, unanimously voted to reject the proposed amendment on the grounds that it was inconsistent with the language that had already been approved (which excluded nursery school teachers).

When the chamber as a whole took up discussion, this proposal was renewed,[30] only to be immediately declared inadmissible by the chamber's president, Christian Democrat Gabriel Valdes on the grounds that

---

[28] The ideological displacement for this model of $\hat{g} = -1.057$ is a weighted average of the estimated Socialist displacement of $g_{PS} = -1.507$ and the corresponding executive parameter of $g_{PPD} = -0.607$:

$$\hat{g} = \tfrac{1}{2}g_{PS} + \tfrac{1}{2}g_{PPD}$$
$$= \tfrac{1}{2}(-1.507) + \tfrac{1}{2}(-0.607)$$
$$= -1.057$$

[29] As with the previous proposal by the same authors, the model estimates the ideological displacement for this proposal to be $\hat{g} = -1.057$.

[30] Among those signing the petition for renewal were Socialists Rolando Calderón and Ricardo Nuñez, Christian Democrats Carmen Frei and Humberto Palza, Social Democrat Mario Papi, and PPD Senator Laura Soto.

it could imply expenditures not contemplated in the law, and so transgressed on the material reserved under article 62 of the Constitution for executive proposals. Socialist Senator Vodanovic questioned whether the proposal would in fact signify greater expenditures, and asked for a more extensive discussion of the issue. During the ensuing exchange, both Christian Democratic Senator Lavandero and Institutional Senator Feliú argued that the proposed extension of subsidies for continuing education to nursery school teachers would represent an additional expenditure. This persuaded Senator Valdes, who for a second and final time declared the proposal unconstitutional (Biblioteca del Congreso Nacional 1991a).

Labor Code vs. Municipal Employees Administrative Statute

During the second reading, the Senators of the right offered over five dozen amendments to the teaching statute, most with cosponsors from both parties on the right plus Institutional Senator Feliú. The stated objective of the National Renovation Party was to protect the interests of the professoriate, as well as educational freedom, municipal autonomy, and support for the subsidized "voucher schools"(El Mercurio 1991). One of these proposals succeeded in producing some cracks in the unity of the Concertación, but ultimately failed to gain passage. This was an amendment proposed by Senators Cantuarias, Diez, Feliú, Larre, and Otero, which specified that questions not addressed in the Teachers' Statute would be governed by the Labor Code.[31] The executive, with an eye toward limiting labor costs, favored using the Administrative Statute that applied to other municipal employees to supplement the Teachers' Statute, rather than the Labor Code. Education Minister Ricardo Lagos argued that work rules for teachers in the municipal sector should conform with the regulations covering other public employees.

Senator Larre mentioned several provisions in the Labor Code that would tend to improve conditions for teachers, for example provisions for binding arbitration in case of strikes, and favorable employee benefits in case of workplace accidents. At this Mr. Lagos became more frank, noting that municipalities, with their limited taxing authority, could not generate their own resources, so that conceding to municipal employees the benefits

---

[31] The ideological displacement for this model of $\hat{g} = 0.997$ is a weighted average of the estimated UDI displacement of $g_{\text{UDI}} = 3.212$, the corresponding parameter for the Institutional Senators of $g_{\text{Instit}} = 1.773$, and the displacement for the three members of the National Renovation party, which is the reference proposer with $g_{\text{RN}} \equiv 0$:

$$\hat{g} = \tfrac{1}{5} g_{\text{UDI}} + \tfrac{1}{5} g_{\text{Instit}} + \tfrac{3}{5} g_{\text{RN}}$$
$$= \tfrac{1}{5}(3.212) + \tfrac{1}{5}(1.773) + \tfrac{3}{5}(0)$$
$$= 0.997.$$

provided for in the Labor Code would imply either an increased subsidy from the State or compensatory cuts in other parts of municipal budgets.

The committee supported the amendment on an ideologically polarized vote pitting amendment sponsors Feliú, Larre, and Cantuarias against Christian Democrats Pacheco and Palza, with the latter uttering the refrain that the position being taken in the amendment was not what the teachers were asking for. (Biblioteca del Congreso Nacional 1991a).

However, the discussion in the Education Committee was but the opening skirmish in the battle over whether the Teachers' Statute would be supplemented by the Labor Code, or the Municipal Functionaries' Administrative Statute. Because the Teachers' Statute overlapped the jurisdiction of the Labor Committee, some amendments, among them the proposal to supplement the Teachers' Statute with the Labor Code, were multiply referred. The Labor Committee, where the Concertación had a majority of the seats, chose differently than the Education Committee, preferring to supplement the Teachers' Statute by using the Municipal Functionaries' Administrative Statute. This left it to the floor to resolve the differences between the conflicting committee reports. The question was put whether to accept the Education Committee's proposal, or that of the Labor Committee. The vote was by a show of hands, allowing many Senators to keep their positions off the record. However, Senators Cantuarias, Feliú, and Otero made speechs in favor of the amendment they had coauthored. Joining them in public declarations for the Education Committee's version were Senators Otero, Thayer, and, notably, Socialist Senator Calderón. The Socialist Senator explained his favorable vote on the grounds that the Education Committee's version of the bill would permit teachers to bargain collectively, a reform he viewed as long overdue. This view was not shared by Christian Democrats Hormazábal, Lavandero, and Palza, who spoke out in favor of supplementing the Teachers' Statute with the Municipal Functionaries' Administrative Statute. The final margin was thin, with sixteen votes against the Education Committee version, fifteen in favor, and three Senators paired, and so unable to vote. Thus the Labor Committee version of the bill, which left teachers under the Municipal Functionaries' Administrative Statute, prevailed in the Senate (Biblioteca del Congreso Nacional 1991a).

That Socialist Senator Calderón spoke in favor of this proposal, whose proposers give it an estimated ideological content of $\hat{g} = 0.997$, moving policy to the "right" on the education spectrum, suggests that the proposed use of the Labor Code had substantial consensus appeal, or in the language of the model, valence. It also provides an important insight into the meaning of "left" in the Education Committee parameter estimates. For here the administration and the teachers' union were in potential conflict, with the administrations wanting to control costs and limit the scope for union independence in the municipal schools. The Christian Democrat's proposal parameters are estimated leftward of the corresponding parameters for the very pro-union Socialist and PPD Senators.[32] This is consistent with the hypothesis that the left end of the education policy spectrum corresponds to the expansion of control by the Concertación-controlled Department of Education, rather than to a fully pro-union position.

Adjustments to Staff Levels

The sensitive area of staff-size adjustments was the subject of some pragmatic proposals by the socialists, as well as a turf battle between the government and the opposition.

An amendment offered by Socialist Senators Calderón and Gazmuri and PPD Senator Soto[33] proposed a November deadline for municipal departments of education to set the following school year's staff sizes[34] some three months before the beginning of the school year, thereby providing some warning to teachers being downsized. The proposal gained the unanimous approval of Senators Cantuarias, Feliú, Larre, and Pacheco (Biblioteca del Congreso Nacional 1991a).

A second proposal from the same Socialist and PPD Senators sought to solidify further the requirement that municipal teachers receive advance warning of downsizing, requiring that any staff-size reductions must await the beginning of the following year. According to its authors the amendment would provide an opportunity to explain the reasons for the staff reduction. RN Senator Larre and Institutional Senator McIntyre joined Senators Pacheco, and Soto in voting to approve the amendment.[35] Oddly, UDI Senator Cantuarias opposed the amendment, arguing that the Teacher's Statute should not establish means to fire personnel! (Biblioteca del Congreso Nacional 1991a).

In fact, neither the government nor the opposition seemed allergic to at least some provisions for teaching-staff size reductions, as suggested

---

[32] Recall from Section 6.1 that a test of the hypothesis that the Socialists and Christian Democrats actually displace policy by the same amount, sharing a common value of g, leads to a χ_1^2 test statistic of 3.8567, corresponding to a p value of 0.0495 and leading to rejection at the 0.10 and (barely) at the 0.05 levels, but not at $\alpha = 0.01$.

[33] As with the proposal by the same Senators to include the chief of the municipal education departments among the positions to be filled by the credentials committees, the estimated ideological displacement for this proposal is $\bar{g} = -1.207$.

[34] The Chilean school year runs from March through mid-December.

[35] The committee did make a minor change in wording, calling for any recommended reductions to await the beginning of the following academic year, rather than the following calendar year. But in Chile this is the difference between the beginning of summer vacations and the end.

by a turf battle over the role of the Department of Education provoked by a proposal by Senators Cantuarias, Diez, Feliú, Larre, and Otero[36] to remove a provision allowing the Provincial Department of Education fifteen days to challenge changes in staff sizes proposed at the municipal level. The executive objected strenuously, arguing that either through these means or some other the Provincial Department of Education must be given the faculty of objecting to proposed staff levels, and Senator Pacheco agreed, arguing that the article affirmed a proper function of the Ministry, that of supervision.

Senator Cantuarias countered that an organism outside the municipality should not fix staff sizes. Senator McIntyre joined the amendment's cosponsors Senators Cantuarias and Larre in voting to accept the proposal, while Senators Pacheco and Soto cast negative votes (Biblioteca del Congreso Nacional 1991a).

This amendment, because it had budgetary implications, was also referred to the Finance Committee, where Concertación Senators formed a majority. There it was defeated by three votes, those of Concertación Senators Arturo Frei,[37] Lavandero, and Soto, while opposition Senators Larre and Piñera voted in favor (Biblioteca del Congreso Nacional 1991a).

When the two versions of the bill, one approved by the Education Committee, the other by the Finance Committee, arrived in the Senate Chamber, there ensued an extensive debate. Finally, Senator Piñera recommended a compromise, in which the Provincial Department of Education would be permitted to review staffing levels, but could in no case recommend changes that would signify increases over the staff sizes recommended by the respective municipality, a compromise adopted by the chamber (Biblioteca del Congreso Nacional 1991a).

Working Conditions

One of the changes to the bill at the first reading that met with union opposition was the removal of a provision reducing classroom hours for the most senior teachers (La Epoca 1991). Christian Democratic Senators Diaz and Pacheco proposed reinstituting this reduction for teachers with more than thirty years of experience.[38] The committee unanimously approved the proposed twenty-four-hour ceiling on the hours these senior teachers could spend conducting classes, with their remaining weekly

---

[36] As with the proposal by the same authors to supplement the Teachers' Statute with the Labor Code, the estimated ideological displacement for this measure is $\hat{g} = 0.997$.

[37] Senator Arturo Frei Bolivar, and two of his first cousins, Carmen Frei Ruiz-Tagle and Eduardo Frei Ruiz-Tagle, all served in the Senate during the Aylwin years.

[38] As with other proposals by this pair, the estimated ideological displacement for this amendment is $\hat{g} = -3.154$.

168

hours to be spent in other activities, with UDI Senator Cantuarias adding his favorable vote to those of the authors (Biblioteca del Congreso Nacional 1991a).

Christian Democratic Senators Diaz and Pacheco proposed that teachers be entitled to appeal appraisals and evaluations which they deemed unjustified, and that they be ensured assistance from their employers should they become the subjects of third-party complaints. This proposal received unanimous support from the committee, with opposition Senators Cantuarias, Feliú, and Larre joining the authors to vote for the amendment (Biblioteca del Congreso Nacional 1991a).

Not all proposals by Senators Diaz and Pacheco were so successful. Responding to language in the bill obliging teachers to submit to evaluation of their work, the two Christian Democrats proposed that a pedagogical evaluation must be an evaluation of the school as much as of the teacher. This proposed amendment was rejected with the negative votes of Senators Cantuarias, Feliú, and Larre. The latter argued that the amendment was redundant, as the evaluation of schools was already covered in the second passage of the same article of the bill (Biblioteca del Congreso Nacional 1991a).

The Subsidized Sector

As noted in Section 6.1, the model identifies statistically significant differences among the proposals offered by Senators on the right, with both UDI and Institutional Senators making proposals to the ideological right of the National Renovation Party. While all three of these groups were active participants in the debate on the Teachers' Statute, they displayed a high degree of cooperation, with multiparty cosponsorship for almost all of their numerous proposed amendments. Information about the differences in policy content corresponding to the estimated gap between proposals from the National Renovation Party and those made by their coalition partners on the right can be found among the amendments offered to another bill, which dealt with the subsidized sector, that is, private schools subsisting on the educational voucher program initiated by the Pinochet government.

Institutional Senator Feliú, with an estimated rightward displacement of $g_{Instit} = 1.773$, proposed a guarantee of due process for those accused of infractions of the law. This high-valence proposal received unanimous approval, with the votes of Senators Cantuarias, Diaz, and Larre. (Biblioteca del Congreso Nacional 1992).

This bill also attracted several amendments from Senator Eugenio Cantuarias of the UDI party, with an estimated ideological displacement of $g_{UDI} = 3.212$. One of these sought to eliminate the special auditing role set forth for the Education Ministry, which was charged in the president's version of the bill with making certain that government funds were properly used. This proposal met with unanimous approval from the committee, gaining the support of Senator Diaz of the Christian Democratic Party as well as the votes of Senators Feliú and Larre (Biblioteca del Congreso Nacional 1992).

The rules for indexing private school subsidies were the subject of separate amendments from the UDI Senator Cantuarias, Institutional Senator Feliú, and Senator RN Senator Larre, all of which met with opposition from the Concertación. Of these three, the indexing formula of Senator Larre was the most generous (Biblioteca del Congreso Nacional 1992).

Senator Pacheco argued that all three proposed amendments should be rejected as encroachments on the subject matter reserved for the president under article 62 of the constitution, an opinion shared by the subsecretary of education.

But one thing that all three amendment sponsors could agree on was the constitutionality of their own proposals. They contended their proposed amendments did not imply increased spending, but simply conserved the real value of the subsidies. They went on to assert that maintaining the value of these subsidies was an indispensable means for preserving private schools.

At the end of the discussion, Senator Feliú combined her proposal with the almost identical amendment offered by Senator Cantuarias, and the combined proposal was approved with cosponsors Senators Cantuarias and Feliú voting in favor, against the dissenting vote of Christian Democratic Senator Diaz. Senator Larre's more generous formula for indexing met with defeat, gaining the affirmative vote of its author, while Senators Diaz and Feliú voted for rejection, and Committee Chairman Cantuarias abstained. Here we see that the more extreme proposals by Senator Feliú, with $g_{\text{Instit}} = 1.773$, and Senator Cantuarias, with $g_{\text{UDI}} = 3.212$, were more concerned with limiting government spending, even on the subsidized schools, while the proposal of Senator Larre, with its more liberal indexing, gave more weight to sustaining the subsidized schools and somewhat less to limiting government spending. The policy position of Christian Democratic Senator Diaz on the left, who opposed all three measures, was consistent with the objective of expanding the municipal schools at the expense of the subsidized sector.

Conclusion

The estimated preference parameters for Education Committee members comport with a bipolar pattern. In this issue area the Concertación behaves very much like a single political party, as the estimates reveal it does on the Labor Committee as well. The opposition Senators are also highly united on the Education Committee, which stands in contrast with the wide divisions observed among the opposition Senators on Labor. However, while committee members within each coalition, the Concertación and the opposition, exhibit very similar issue preferences, there are significant differences among parties in the ideological content of amendments they formulate to education legislation, with amendments from the UDI party moving policy farther rightward than amendments offered by the other main opposition party, National Renovation. Parameter estimates further indicate that it is proposals from the Christian Democratic Senators that attempt to move policy farthest to the left.

For education policy the position on the left was associated with the conflict between public and private education, and with the conflict between the Education Ministry, controlled by the Concertación, and the municipal governments, many of whose functionaries had been appointed during the Pinochet regime. The left end of the spectrum corresponds to the Concertación's position in favor of expanding the power of the Education Ministry and of promoting public education over the educational voucher system implemented by the military government. The issue position on the right involved defending the subsidized schools and preserving the power of the municipal governments, which at the time were being run by supporters of the right, vis a vis the Education Ministry. Labor relations issues also arose with considerable frequency on the Education Committee, which considered legislation affecting the details of working conditions for teachers. The pro-labor position tended to be associated with the left of the spectrum, although on some occasions it came into conflict with the government's interest in containing costs in the public schools.

7

The Constitution Committee

The Constitution Committee considered an agenda that included both human rights questions and other more standard legal reforms dealing with issues common to many industrialized democracies, from drug enforcement to domestic violence. Of all of the Chilean Senate's committee jurisdictions, the issue area most affected by sixteen and a half years of military rule was that of human rights. During the period of military government, a number of decree laws dramatically expanded the jurisdiction of the military courts and reduced the scope for judicial appeal. In addition, there were numerous antiterrorist measures written into decree laws which expanded the policing powers of the armed forces, including the Carbineers. Because of this, the very first legislative initiatives of the Aylwin Administration were in the ambit of human rights, with executive-sponsored bills proposed to abolish the death penalty, protect freedom of speech, and reform various statutes, such as the internal security law and the weapons control law. These were followed by later proposals from members of the legislature, mostly on the right, to restore or further strengthen the antiterrorism laws.

The committee was sufficiently active in both the human rights and social policy areas of its issue domain that separate sets of parameter estimates for each of these two issue areas can be obtained. This permits a direct test of whether both areas map into the same ideological dimension based on the estimated preferred outcomes of the four Senators who cast a substantial number of votes on both sets of issues.[1] This analysis reveals a substantial difference between the relative issue position of Senator Pacheco on human rights and the same legislator's position on the social issues. Analysis of the substantive content of the votes confirms that this Christian Democrat took a socially conservative position

---

[1] These were Senators Diez, Letelier, Pacheco, and Vodanovic.

172

on questions such as marital law, where he found himself on the same side of many debates as the political opposition, while this cofounder of the Chilean Human Rights Committee took a position on the left of the spectrum on human rights questions. Nor was he alone in this combination of issue positions. A controversial amendment to decriminalize adultery, defined by the then status quo legislation as a crime for women, though not for men, led to revealing debate on the Senate floor. The Socialists, the Radicals, and the PPD all took the position that adultery should be a civil, not criminal, matter, while the parties on the right and the Institutional Senators favored raising the criminal penalties for men to match those imposed on women. The Christian Democrats split, with many siding with Senator Pacheco, who argued forcefully against decriminalizing adultery, while others, such as Jorge Lavandero, took equally impassioned positions for decriminalization. This division among the Christian Democrats stands in sharp contrast to their unified position on human rights issues.

The parameter estimates presented in this chapter thus identify a potentially serious fault line in the political bedrock of the Christian Democratic Party. The contrast between the party's positions on human rights and social issues indicates how Chilean politics might change over the next decades, as the agenda surrounding the transition to democracy which was central during the Aylwin years recedes in importance. This agenda drew the Christian Democrats together, uniting them despite their other differences. As human rights fades from the legislative agenda these differences may reshape political competition. The Christian Democratic party is nominally secular (no credal litmus is imposed on members), but it has its roots in the Catholic Church and has historically taken a position that is closely affiliated with Catholic thinking. Given the Church's outreach to the poor, its Catholic affinities made the Christian Democratic Party attractive to many on the left of a more secular bent, who shared its sympathies for income redistribution. The position as a defender of human rights that the Church came to occupy during the period of military rule strengthened the links between the Christian Democrats and the left. But on questions such as abortion and divorce, social liberals of the secular left and the Catholic Church part company. These are issues that divide the Christian Democratic Party, and also the voters who support it. Eventually this rift may split the party, or cost it a substantial portion of its members. For the time being the factors holding the Christian Democrats together, particularly agreement about the nature of the democratic transition, have a stronger influence, but the democratic transition is likely to fade as an important issue in Chile's politics.

Table 8. *Human rights bills given second readings by the constitution committee*

Bill ID	No. of votes	Description
1-07	10	to modify the aeronautic, military, and penal codes to abolish the death penalty
2-07	37	to modify various legal texts in order to better guarantee personal rights
27-06	72	bill on freedom of expression
334-07	7	to modify the penal code and law 18.314, which determines terrorist conduct and fixes its penalty
342-07	3	motion of the honorable Senators Diez, Jarpa, Otero, Rios, and Siebert to create new sanctions against members, collaborators, and propagandists of terrorist groups
566-07	18	bill to modify diverse norms in the penal code and military justice, penal procedures, and other legal dispositions dealing with the security of persons
625-07	3	to modify the penal code and law No. 18.314, which determine terrorist conduct and fix its penalty, with the objective of improving the norms relative to the crime of kidnapping minors
819-07	4	motion of the honorable Senators Frei (don Eduardo), Pacheco, and Ruiz-Esquide to modify the penal code in relation to the crime of genocide

7.1 HUMAN RIGHTS

A subset of eight of the bills considered by the Constitution Committee dealt directly with human rights policy (Table 8). These included the bills that became the "Cumplido laws," named after Aylwin's secretary of Justice who was closely involved in writing them, and in lobbying for their passage. These eight bills gave rise to 136 amendments during their second reading. The remaining twenty bills receiving second readings from the committee were the subjects of 693 amendments. These bills included major presidential initiatives to reform the laws governing marital property, to deal with domestic violence, to reform the bureaucratic administration of the courts, and to increase penalties for narcotics trafficking, as well as a number of minor bills, such as a change in the laws governing legitimate self-defense for crime victims, and reforms dealing with nonprofit corporations.

The Constitution Committee

The Setting

The Concertación controlled two of the seats in the committee, with one belonging to the Socialist Party. This was occupied by the Committee's chairman, Hernán Vodanovic. The other Concertación seat on the committee belonged to the Christian Democratic Party and was occupied almost exclusively by Senator Máximo Pacheco. This cofounder of the Chilean Human Rights Committee cast all of the party's votes on the human rights bills considered by the Constitution Committee. The executive was an active proposal maker on the human rights agenda, sponsoring or coauthoring over half the amendments considered by the committee. However, on this highly polarized issue area, proposals by the executive enjoyed little success, winning barely a quarter of the available votes, not including the votes of cosponsors.

Three of the committee's seats belonged to the Opposition Senators; one was controlled by the National Renovation Party, and two by the Institutional Senators. One of the Institutional seats was often occupied by UDI Senator Jaime Guzmán, prior to his assassination by terrorists in April 1991. Most of the human rights bills considered by the committee came during the first year of the Aylwin period while Guzmán was still alive. He did not live to participate in the subsequent debates on social issues. His successor, Miguel Otero of the National Renovation Party, was also an active participant in the committee. However, most of the human rights votes took place before Senator Otero took office. Two Institutional Senators cast votes on the human rights bills; they were Sergio Fernández, who had worked as Pinochet's Secretary of the Interior, and Carlos Letelier, an octogenarian former Supreme Court Justice. Two Senators who did not vote on the human rights agenda but nevertheless contributed numerous amendments were Christian Democrat Jorge Lavandero, who had publicly opposed the military regime, and Institutional Senator Olga Feliú.

Parameter Estimates. As discussed in the analysis of the Labor and Education Committees, two voting Senators must be chosen to "anchor" the measured voting positions of the Senators. Here the voters chosen are Socialist Senator Hernán Vodanovic, whose position is anchored at -1, while Institutional Senator Carlos Letelier has a position normalized to equal 1. This normalization places the the Socialist Senator on the left and the Institutional Senator on the right, in keeping with the standard characterization of the ideological continuum.

Both of these Senators also cast frequent votes on the other issues considered by the committee, where they also serve to normalize the social issues scale, thereby facilitating comparisons between the two scales. Four

175

The Constitution Committee

Figure 7.1. Estimated Preferred Human Rights Outcomes.

other Senators voted on the committee's human rights agenda with sufficient frequency to permit estimation of their preferred points: Christian Democrat Máximo Pacheco, Institutional Senator Sergio Fernández, and two former members of the Ortúzar Committee that recommended an early draft of the Constitution of 1980[2]: Sergio Diez of the National Renovation Party and Jaime Guzmán of the UDI party. Of these Senators, Diez and Pacheco are of particular interest because they also voted frequently on the other bills considered by the committee, permitting us to compare their issue positions on human rights and on the remainder of the committee's agenda.

The parameter estimates appearing in Table 9 reveal a tremendous gulf between the Concertación and the opposition, and remarkable cohesion within each group. The estimated preferred human rights outcomes are illustrated in Figure 7.1. The preferred outcome of Christian Democrat Máximo Pacheco is nearly identical with the normalized location for his fellow Concertación member, Socialist Senator Hernán Vodanovic. Moreover, the point estimate of −1.002 is relatively precise, with a standard deviation of only 0.432. The b parameters, which measure the receptiveness to initiatives from the reference proposer, here the National Renovation Party, are likewise almost identical, with $b_{\text{Pacheco}} = -1.891$, while $b_{\text{Vodanovic}} = -1.882$. A formal test for equality of the preference parameters for these two Senators leads to acceptance at all significance levels.[3]

On the other side, all three of the remaining opposition Senators, Diez, Fernández, and Guzmán, have estimated preferred outcomes that are even more precisely estimated than for Senator Pacheco, and all are within half a standard deviation of Carlos Letelier's ideal point, which has been normalized to equal 1. A formal test of the hypothesis that the preferences of these four opposition Senators are identical receives ample support from

---

[2] See the discussion of that committee's activities in Chapter 2.

[3] A test of the null hypothesis that $x_{\text{Pacheco}} = -1$ and $b_{\text{Pacheco}} = b_{\text{Vodanovic}}$ leads to a test statistic of 0.00017339766. Compared with its asymptotic distribution, which is χ^2_2, this corresponds to a p value of 0.99991330, indicating acceptance at all standard significance levels.

Table 9. *Parameter estimates for the constitution committee: human rights votes*

	Parameter[a]			
Participant	x	b	g	c
PS/PPD			−12.717 (6.547)	−20.000
Hernán Vodanovic S.	−1.000	−1.882 (1.061)		
Partido Democrata Cristiano / Partido Radical			−1.606 (1.003)	2.600 (1.468)
Máximo Pacheco G.	−1.002 (0.432)	−1.891 (1.045)		
Executive Proposals			−5.325 (1.542)	3.476 (1.684)
Renovación Nacional			0.000	0.000
Sergio Diez U.	1.187 (0.332)	0.608 (1.328)		
Institutional Senators			1.327 (1.160)	11.893 (2.741)
Sergio Fernández F.	1.165 (0.367)	−0.081 (1.171)		
Carlos Letelier B.	1.000	−0.362 (1.214)		
Union Democrata Independiente			−0.142 (0.985)	3.713 (1.382)
Jaime Guzmán E.	0.854 (0.315)	−1.305 (1.069)		
Own Party Proposals		−0.520 (1.172)		

[a] Estimated standard errors are show in parentheses; $\hat{\alpha} = 6.236$, $\hat{S}d(\hat{\alpha}) = 1.230$, $\log(\text{lik}) = -114.807$, $n = 136$ amendments.

the data.[4] Even relative to the highly bipolar Education Committee, these results are striking: both among the Concertación and the among opposition there is a remarkable consensus, while each group is equally clearly in disagreement with the other. One way to check this is by making pairwise comparisons between each of the two Concertación Senators, and

[4] The hypothesis tested is $x_{\text{Guzman}} = 1$, $x_{\text{Diez}} = 1$, $x_{\text{Fernandez}} = 1$, $b_{\text{Guzman}} = b_{\text{Letelier}}$, and $b_{\text{Diez}} = b_{\text{Letelier}}$, while $b_{\text{Fernandez}} = b_{\text{Letelier}}$, the test statistic for this hypothesis, which is asymptotically distributed as χ^2_6 equals 2.2106411, corresponding to a p value of 0.89934246 and indicating acceptance at all standard significance levels.

each of the four opposition Senators. This is straightforward for seven of the eight possible pairings, while comparing the preference parameters of Senators Letelier and Vodanovic is complicated by the fact that their preferred outcomes have been normalized to equal different values, with $x_{Letelier} \equiv 1$ and $x_{Vodanovic} \equiv -1$. For each of the remaining seven pairs for which a full comparison of the preference parameters is possible, the estimates overwhelmingly reject equality between the Concertación Senator and the opposition Senator with which he is paired.[5]

Proposal Parameters. In contrast with this high degree of homogeneity in voting, the Concertación Senators seem to pursue somewhat different proposal strategies. Comparing the entries of the g column in Table 9, we see that the Socialist and PPD Senators tend to propose the largest leftward reforms, while the Christian Democrats propose the smallest. The proposal parameter for the executive is somewhere in between and may reflect a compromise among the initiatives sought by various members of the Concertación. The proposal parameters for the Christian Democratic Senators differ from those for their Socialist/PPD colleagues and from those of the executive at all standard significance levels, while the estimated gap between the executive's ideological proposal parameter and that for the Socialist/PPD Senators is on the threshold of significance.[6]

In contrast with the heterogeneous proposal parameters for the Concertación Senators, the ideological content of proposals from the opposition Senators is quite homogeneous.[7] Moreover, while the precision of the parameter estimates leaves the question at the threshold of significance,[8] the proposal parameter for the Christian Democrats of $g_{PDC} = -1.606$ is well to the left of the corresponding parameter for the Institutional Senators at $g_{Instit} = 1.305$.

Implied Voting Probabilities. More insight about the interpretation of the parameter estimates can be had by considering the probability

[5] The pairings, which all resulted in p values below 0.001, were Pacheco and Letelier, Diez and Vodanovic, Guzmán and Vodanovic, Fernández and Vodanovic, Diez and Pacheco, Fernández and Pacheco, and Guzmán and Pacheco.

[6] The p values for the hypothesis that $g_{PS/PPD} = g_{exec}$ was 0.0255, while the hypotheses that $g_{PS/PPD} = g_{exec}$ and $g_{PS/PPD} = g_{PDC/Rad}$ could each be rejected at $\alpha = 0.01$.

[7] The test statistic for equality among the g parameters for the Institutional Senators and their colleagues in the National Renovation and UDI parties is asymptotically distributed as χ_2^2, so the realized value of 1.5229, corresponding to a p value of 0.4670, leads to acceptance at all standard significance levels.

[8] The test statistic for equality between the g parameters for these two parties is asymptotically distributed as χ_1^2, so the realized value of 4.8687, corresponding to a p value of 0.0273, leads to rejection at the $\alpha = 0.10$ and $\alpha = 0.05$ significance levels, but not at $\alpha = 0.01$.

The Constitution Committee

Table 10. *Hypothetical vote margins: human rights issues*[a]

Votes		Probability by proposer[b]					
In favor	Against	PS/PPD	Exec.	PDC/Rad.	RN	UDI	Instit.
0	5	0.906	0.127	0.349	0.427	0.266	0.011
1	4	0.049	0.007	0.003	0.141	0.080	0.017
2	3	0.045	0.503	0.006	0.070	0.007	0.003
3	2	–	0.010	0.056	0.009	0.001	0.044
4	1	–	0.007	0.144	0.002	0.024	0.043
5	0	–	0.346	0.440	0.351	0.622	0.881

[a] Committee consists of Senators Diez, Guzmán, Letelier, Pacheco, and Vodanovic.
[b] A dash indicates a probability of less than 0.0005.

distribution they imply over voting outcomes in response to amendments sponsored by various authors. Consider first a hypothetical proposal by a member of the Socialist/PPD delegation, other than committee member Hernán Vodanovic, so that he would not be voting on his own proposal. The very low value of c for Socialist/PPD proposals mean that they have very low consensus value, while the large negative estimated value of g for these Senators indicates that their human rights proposals tend to polarize the Committee. Of the two effects, the low value for c dominates, so that the parameter estimates indicate a better than 90% chance of unanimous rejection. However, conditional on a divided vote, the highly polarizing nature of these proposals means that they are almost guaranteed not to gain any votes on the right; see the third column of Table 10.

When the votes split they are almost certain to divide along partisan lines, with the two Concertación Senators voting for acceptance and the three opposition Senators voting to reject. The large leftward shift represented by executive proposals, with $g_{exec} = -5.325$, makes all but the lowest valence executive proposals attractive to the Concertación voters, Pacheco and Vodanovic, who both have preferred policy outcomes of about -1, while it dooms all but high-valence executive proposals to rejection by the Senators on the right.

In contrast with proposals by the other members of the Concertación, the ideological content of human rights related proposals from the Christian Democrats is much closer to that of proposals from the National Renovation party. The probability of a unanimous vote for a proposal from one of the Christian Democratic Senators is much higher than that for an executive proposal, with the probability of unanimous rejection just above one in three, while the probability of unanimous acceptance is about

179

four-ninths, considerably higher than for the executive. This is because the less polarizing ideological content of proposals from the Christian Democrats more than compensates for their lower attractiveness to the Committee's Concertación Senators by being more acceptable to the opposition voters on the committee. The reception for National Renovation party proposals is similar, with a slightly higher probability of unanimous rejection, and a slightly lower likelihood of unanimous acceptance; see column 6 of Table 10.

Proposals from the UDI party and from the Institutional Senators are the most likely to gain unanimous acceptance, with the probability this happens for a proposal from the Institutional Senators almost equal to the probability that a proposal from the Socialists is rejected. However, the Institutional Senators do polarize the committee, so that when the committee vote splits, the likely dissenters are Concertación Senators Pacheco and Vodanovic.

Putting the Estimates in Context

As with policy in the areas of labor and education, it is useful to examine the substantive content of the human rights initiatives considered by the committee. This is useful both because it provides a sense of how ideology on human rights questions matches up with substantive policy choices, and as a check on the qualitative implications of the parameter estimates. The estimates indicate that the human rights agenda was highly polarizing, with the Concertación and opposition Senators dividing into two blocks of voters. At the same time, the estimates indicate some divergence among proposals from members of the Concertación, with the Socialist and PPD Senators tending to make proposals characterized by both a high ideological content and low consensus appeal. To gain a better understanding of just what these proposals were, we now turn our attention to the committee debate generated by two of the Cumplido laws.

Freedom of Expression. The goals of free speech and personal privacy are often in conflict, and the Chilean left and right disagreed about how to balance these goals. Both goals enjoy the protection of the Constitution of 1980; No. 4 of article 19 allows for the free and uncensored expression of opinion, while No. 12 of the same article seeks to protect privacy and personal honor. Several decree laws from the period of military rule and a preexisting law dealing with press abuses resolved these competing aims largely in favor of privacy, even for public officials. So, for example, in 1984 when then-President Pinochet was formally accused of fraud by a prominent group of Chilean politicians, including Patricio Aylwin, Ricardo Lagos, Máximo Pacheco, Gabriel Valdés, and Andrés Zaldívar,

Law No. 18.313 was invoked to prevent press coverage, on the grounds that the accusation, which dealt with the details of a real-estate transaction that allegedly amounted to the use of the state to subsidize the purchase of some property by President Pinochet,[9] was a private matter (Biblioteca del Congreso Nacional 1990b). This affair left its scars. Senator Jorge Lavandero, then a private citizen, was badly beaten by members of the military government's secret police as he attempted to distribute copies of a dissident newspaper that defied censorship to report on the scandal (Interview with Jorge Lavandero, May 20, 1997). Senator Lavandero bore both the physical and psychic scars to the debate on how to amend the laws dealing with press censorship, as the executive sought to strike a new balance more favorable to freedom of expression by proposing the Freedom of Expression Bill, which eventually became Law No. 19.047. This bill, which passed through the Constitution Committee, repealed or amended some of the statutes restricting free speech, included extensive changes to the Press Abuse Law.

Censorship. Article 1 of the bill repealed several preexisting laws that had been written to implement press censorship and sanctions against members of subversive organizations.[10] In the original version of the bill proposed by the executive, the article would also repeal Law No. 18.662, which implemented language in article 8 of the Chilean Constitution dealing with subversive organizations declared "unconstitutional." Given that article 8 had been repealed in 1989 as part of the constitutional reforms negotiated during the transition, the executive argued that the law had become an anachronism. Nevertheless, at the first reading of the bill, the committee had changed article 1 to preserve Law No. 18.662.

During the second reading, the executive, along with Christian Democratic Senators Lavandero and Pacheco and Socialist Senator Vodanovic (Senado de Chile 1990), proposed restoring the initial language which called for the repeal of Law 18.662 (Biblioteca del Congreso Nacional 1990c). Senator Guzmán acknowledged that article 8 of the constitution had been abolished, but he argued that it would be better to rewrite Law 18.662 in recognition of the new state of the constitution. He thought it advisable to deal with the subject right away rather than waiting to do so after cases had been brought to the Constitutional Tribunal.

Mr. Cumplido, the Minister of Justice, noted that the existing laws already resolved the ambiguities Senator Guzmán was concerned with. In the case of political parties, the Organic Constitutional Law of Political

[9] A mansion named La Casa Melocotón, or "Peach House."

[10] The bill called for repeal of Laws No. 18.150 and 18.313, and articles 1 and 3 of Law No. 18.015, and for a reduction of the penalties set forth in article 2 of Law No. 18.015.

Parties (Blane et al. 1990) already regulated declarations of unconstitutionality by the Constitutional Tribunal, while the Penal Code and article 19, No. 15 of the constitution dealt with other organizations and natural persons advocating violent political change. Senator Vodanovic added that article 8 of the constitution corresponded to a political climate that had been left behind, and so considered it unlikely the issue would arise.

Senator Diez agreed that repeal of Law 18.662 was the right course, adding that it was essential to legislate a resolution of what he characterized as ambiguities in the status quo laws regarding how the Constitutional Tribunal should carry out its responsibility outlined in article 19, No. 15 of the constitution to declare unconstitutional any "parties, movements, and other organizations whose objectives, acts or conduct do not respect the basic principals of a democratic constitutional regime, seeking the establishment of a totalitarian system, as well as those that make use of violence, or advocate or incite it as a means of political action" (Blanc et al. 1990).

This proposal led to a split vote, with Senator Diez of the National Renovation Party joining the bill's Concertación cosponsors, Senators Pacheco and Vodanovic, to form a majority in support of the measure, while Senator Fernández voted against repeal of Law 18.662, and Senator Guzmán abstained (Biblioteca del Congreso Nacional 1990c).

Abuses of Publicity. The second article of the bill dealt with abuses of publicity. Senator Piñera sought to modify the language dealing with responsibility for libel. The bill proposed that if a broadcast or press organization was found guilty of libel, the author of the libel, as well as the organization's proprietors, concessioners, editors, directors, and administrators would share unified responsibility for any fines or indemnifications imposed. Senator Piñera's amendment would have removed administrators from the list, replacing them with "the administrators' legal representatives."

This proposal met with serious opposition on the Committee, with opponents noting that the authors and accomplices of crimes often used their "legal representatives" to avoid responsibility, choosing as their representatives those disposed to serve prison time (presumably in exchange for some consideration) or lacking assets to attach in the case of indemnifications and fines. Senator Guzmán joined Concertación Senators Pacheco and Vodanovic in a majority vote against the measure, while votes in favor of Senator Piñera's defeated amendment were cast by Senators Diez and Fernández (Biblioteca del Congreso Nacional 1990c).

Senator Lavandero proposed a group of three amendments that would affect the treatment of "offenses" against the Armed Forces by the Code of Military Justice. Noting that almost all of the cases brought under these laws had been against members of the press, he argued that the amendment was related to freedom of expression, therefore germane. He sought to eliminate the word "offense" from the language used in the military code, language which others had interpreted as requiring a lower standard of proof, thereby making prosecutions under the law easier. Senator Lavandero argued that this was a misinterpretation that could be avoided by replacing the word "offense" with the word "injury," and he cited public statements by the committee that drafted the Constitution of 1980 that they had intended "offense" purely as a synonym for "injury." The committee report indicates that while the Senators present sympathized with the objective pursued by Senator Lavandero's amendments, they did not believe that the amendments were germane, and so the committee's chairman, Hernán Vodanovic, ruled them inadmissible, commenting that they would be more appropriately introduced as amendments to a more general bill to improve human rights that was about to be dispatched by the Chamber of Deputies (Biblioteca del Congreso Nacional 1990c).

Taking the advice given to him when the committee ruled his amendments to the Freedom of Expression Bill were not germane, Senator Lavandero introduced a similar series of amendments to the executive's Human Rights Bill. These consisted of five amendments to alter articles 284 and 417 of the Military Code. At the second reading of the Human Rights Bill, much to the Senator's chagrin, the committee unanimously decided to reject all but one of the five amendments. The accepted amendment required that in order for someone to be charged with making a threat against the armed forces, the threat had to be serious and credible and to consist of an announced intention to take criminal action against the armed forces (Biblioteca del Congreso Nacional 1990d). When the Human Rights Bill came up for a vote on the floor, Senator Lavandero expressed his anger at the committee for not having approved his amendment, and his reasons for having proposed it. After quoting from the committee's report on its second reading of the Freedom of Expression Bill, the Senator added: "And all manifested to me that in the bill that now occupies us they would be unanimously in favor of repealing the allusion to 'offense' in articles 284 and 417 of the Military Code of Justice." The Senator went on to reassert his contention that the word "offense" was just a synonym for "injury" and that its inclusion in the bill simply invited inappropriate interpretations (Biblioteca del Congreso Nacional 1990d).

Senator Guzmán claimed to the contrary that "offense" did not mean the same thing as "injury," with the difference being the standard of proof required: to establish that a statement was injurious it would be necessary to establish that there was a will to injure, something very difficult to prove given its subjective nature. In contrast the UDI Senator argued, "offense" did not require any proof of intentions on the part of the person making the statements (Biblioteca del Congreso Nacional 1990d).

Senator Lavandero countered that this new interpretation was not only incorrect but would lead to more severe problems of subjectivity:

> "...in this way we can drag citizens before the tribunals of justice and subject them to proceedings without the crime having been properly defined. This is the serious part. There is a discriminatory and subjective interpretation, that could go so far as to say: 'Look, Mr., you are guilty of the crime of offense.' 'But how!' 'Yes, because you gave me a dirty look, you didn't say 'hello,' or for whatever thing."
> (Biblioteca del Congreso Nacional 1990d).

Notwithstanding these objections, the Human Rights Bill was passed without removing the word "offense" from the Military Code. The failure of the proposed amendments to gain passage did not surprise their author, who later characterized them as "too fundamental for the moment," saying that he had proposed them because "I wanted to make clear what were the right criteria." (Interview with Jorge Lavandero, May 20, 1997) As noted in the discussion in Chapter 1, there is political value in publicly sponsoring amendments even when they are not expected to win.

An amendment to the Freedom of Expression Bill proposed by the executive and cosponsored by Senators Lavandero and Pacheco would change the obligatory award of compensation for psychic and pecuniary damages stemming from psychological depression caused by libelous statements made in the press. Instead of being mandatory, the amendment would leave compensation for such damages at the discretion of the judge before whom the case had been brought. Noting the difficulties inherent in proving damages of this type, the majority of the committee, consisting of Concertación Senators Pacheco and Vodanovic, joined by Institutional Senator Sergio Fernández, found that leaving the award of damages at the discretion of judges was a reasonable measure. Senators Diez and Guzmán were not persuaded, and voted against the amendment. Senator Guzmán responded with a counterproposal that would preserve mandatory indemnification of the psychic costs of depression, while conceding the award of pecuniary damages to the discretion of the judge. This measure was defeated, with the supporters of the executive amendment, Senators Fernández, Pacheco, and Vodanovic, voting in contra, while Senator Guzmán was joined in voting favorably on his own amendment by Senator Diez, who who had also opposed the executive amendment to allow discretion (Biblioteca del Congreso Nacional 1990c).

Another amendment proposed by the executive and Senators Lavandero and Pacheco sought to reinstate language removed at the committee's first reading of the bill which would reduce the time limit for filing civil and criminal charges arising from press abuses to thirty days. As rewritten by the Committee at the first reading, this time period had been extended to three months. Opponents of the bill, Senators Diez, Fernández, and Guzmán, argued that the thirty day limit was extreme and did not allow victims of press abuses to become aware of the damage that had been done. Senator Vodanovic joined the bill's cosponsor Máximo Pacheco in voting in favor of the amendment (Biblioteca del Congreso Nacional 1990c).

Not all executive-sponsored amendments were controversial. Some were recognized by Senators across the political spectrum as improvements in the effectiveness of the law, for example, a change in the wording to cover not only the malicious and substantially false imputation of "news" but also the malicious and substantially false imputation of "deeds" (Biblioteca del Congreso Nacional 1990c; Senado de Chile 1990). Another consensus improvement proposed by the executive (Senado de Chile 1990) dealt with the use of the truth as a defense against libel. The bill would prevent the truth of the accusation being used as legitimate defense except when the accusations were restricted to facts and deeds, and one of several links to the public domain existed. One could use the truth as a defense if the allegations related to the performance of his or her duties by a public official, a manager of a publicly traded firm, or a priest or minister of a religion recognized by the state. Also defensible were allegations related to the testimony of a witness. A final catch-all category applied when "the allegation should be made with the motive of defending a real public interest in the common good." The executive, with the cosponsorship of Senators Lavandero and Pacheco (Senado de Chile 1990), proposed eliminating the phrase "of the common good" on the grounds that the redundant phrase might be misinterpreted as creating yet another hurdle of proof that those accused of libel would have to meet to use the truth as a defense (Biblioteca del Congreso Nacional 1990c).

There were also executive proposals that failed to meet with any support on the committee, such as one that would have left the decision of whether to punish press abuses covered by articles 19, 21, and 22 of the press abuse law, No. 16.643, dealing with calumny and news about people's private lives, at the discretion of the judge (Biblioteca del Congreso Nacional 1990c; Senado de Chile 1990).

Even in this highly contentious issue area, the executive did not have a monopoly on amendments receiving consensus approval. For example, Senator Guzmán proposed language that the unified responsibility of editors and managers of news organizations facing libel charges extended not only to any indemnification that might be imposed, but to fines as well (Biblioteca del Congreso Nacional 1990c).

Executive Pardons. Senator Huerta proposed a controversial measure that would add a new article to the bill preventing the executive from granting pardons to people convicted of violating press abuse law No. 16.643. Senators Pacheco and Vodanovic, both of whom voted against the measure, argued that the measure violated article 32, No. 16 of the Constitution, which stated that presidential powers included "authorizing special pardons in the cases and ways determined by the law." These Senators contended that the norm that set the means of exercising this presidential power could not reach the extreme of restricting or eliminating it. In contrast, Senators Diez, Fernández, and Guzmán, who voted as a majority to accept the amendment, contended that it was precisely to permit such limitations that the qualifying language "...in the cases and ways determined by the law" had been included in the constitution. They added that because of the highly political nature of the press, it did not seem reasonable to allow the president to grant pardons at will, and that it might be better to require that another branch of government approve presidential pardons of this nature (Biblioteca del Congreso Nacional 1990c).

Curiously, as the bill was being debated in the full Chamber, Senator Huerta took the floor to announce that he was retiring his amendment already approved by the committee, saying that the spirit of his amendment had been misinterpreted in the debate. Minister Correa was forthcoming with praise: "In the name of the Government I want to make present a public recognition of the gesture of the Honorable Senator Huerta of retiring the amendment that he presented" (Biblioteca del Congreso Nacional 1990e). Whether there was also some private recognition of the Senator's gesture, he did not say. At this point the Senate Secretary Rafael Eyzaguirre pointed out that once the committee had approved the proposed amendment it could only be withdrawn by its author with the approval of a majority of the Senators present (Biblioteca del Congreso Nacional 1990e), tantamount to forcing a vote on the amendment, just as though the author had not attempted to withdraw it. Approval of Senator Huerta's request was a foregone conclusion: the Concertación Senators were already opposed to the amendment; while at least some of the opposition were sure to vote in deference to Senator Huerta's wishes, but the discussion gave Senators on both sides a chance to stake out their positions.

Senator Guzmán raised concerns that the executive would abuse the ability to pardon press abuses in favor of his political partisans, while he could not resist the opportunity to goad those who had once complained about the strong executive established in the Constitution of 1980: "This puts false the caricature that many made of the Constitution of 1980, titling it 'Caesarist'"(Biblioteca del Congreso Nacional 1990e). In their speeches, the Concertación Senators split on the question of whether Senator Huerta's amendment was unconstitutional, with Christian Democratic Senators Hormazábal, Lavandero, and Pacheco arguing forcefully that it was unconstitutional (Biblioteca del Congreso Nacional 1990e), while Social Democratic Senator Papi contended that it would be both constitutional and even reasonable to require that presidential pardons be subject to some form of review (Biblioteca del Congreso Nacional 1990e).

Omnibus Human Rights Bill.   One of the very first executive initiatives presented to the Congress was a broad set of reforms designed to "better guarantee the rights of persons." This bill modified provisions in many existing laws, including the State Security Law, the Weapons Control Law, the Criminal Code, the Code of Criminal Procedure, the Aeronautic Code, and the Military Code of Justice.

At the Committee's first reading of the bill, many of the reforms recommended by the president and approved by the Deputies were partially or wholly rolled back. The executive-sponsored reforms removed or blunted at the Committee's first reading involved reductions in the penalties proposed for violations of the State Security Law and the Weapons Control Law, as well as changes in the composition of Martial and Naval Courts that would tend to make them more insulated from the military chain of command, and increase civilian participation. In addition these amendments eliminated several transitory provisions allowing more lenient treatment of political prisoners left over from the period of military rule. In response the president, with the coauthorship of Senators Pacheco and Vodanovic, reintroduced many of these reforms as part of a series of jointly sponsored amendments, the vast majority of which were defeated in three to two votes, with opposition Senators Diez, Guzmán, and Letelier voting for rejection, while the amendments' coauthors Pacheco and Vodanovic voted in favor (Biblioteca del Congreso Nacional 1990d).

After this heavy setback the Senator Pacheco fumed that "the result obtained is totally negative because the essence (of the bill) was the reduction of penalties and the transfer of processes from military justice to the ordinary courts," while an angry Francisco Cumplido grimly noted that the fundamental reforms had been rejected, and so the bill would go to a conference committee, complaining that "here they have simply rejected the most important (reforms) and they didn't propose anything." The Minister of Justice was particularly stung by what he viewed as the violation of an agreement reached between Concertación Deputies and their opposition colleagues. National Renovation Senator Diez responded that "we voted against the reduction of penalties and agains the transitory articles just as the UDI and RN did in the Chamber (of Deputies)..." (El Mercurio 1990a).

There were compelling legal and political reasons for wanting to change the "special laws" against the possibility of some political crisis in the distant and unforeseen future in which these laws might be invoked. However, as a practical matter, most of those affected by the special laws were already in prison for offenses already committed. This focused the Concertación on a Constitutional Reform that would enable the president to pardon those convicted of violating these laws, something the opposition were willing to give them, for those cases in which, in the words of National Renovation Senator Miguel Otero, President Aylwin "...considered it ethical, moral, and licit to pardon those whom they call 'political prisoners'" (El Mercurio 1990d). During the days following the committee votes, representatives of the Concertación and the National Renovation Party met privately at the home of Minister Cumplido, where they successfully hammered out an agreement giving the executive the opportunity to pardon political prisoners left over from the former regime (El Mercurio 1990c).

While Institutional Senators Thayer did not sit on the Constitution Committee, he did take a public position on the Cumplido laws, specifically on the question of the jurisdiction of the military courts, saying that while "one cannot pretend to have peace based on punishment for some and impunity for others...nevertheless this should not go to the other extreme of transferring to the ordinary courts mixed cases involving civilians and those in uniform..." (El Mercurio 1990b). While this Institutional Senator took a moderate position on labor issues (see Chapter 5), his position on human rights issues cannot have given former President Pinochet much cause to regret having appointed him Senator.

A cluster of three amendments offered by PPD Senator Soto met with an even chillier reception on the committee than did the attempts to restore the bill to the form approved by the Chamber of Deputies. Senator Soto proposed to authorize special benefits and conditional liberty for people imprisoned under special laws for acts committed during the period of military government.[11] Her amendment would have limited the application of the very controversial 1978 Decree Law No. 2,191, which granted amnesty to members of the armed forces for human rights violations during the initial years of military rule. Senator Soto's amendment would require judges to first investigate the deeds and prosecute those responsible before applying the amnesty. She also sought expeditious handling of cases in which someone had been kept prisoner during the "summary" stage of a criminal proceeding[12] for more than one year for violations of the State Security Law, the Weapons Control Law, or the Antiterrorism Law. Each

---

[11] September 11, 1973 through March 11, 1990.

[12] This corresponds roughly to the pretrial stage in the English Common Law system.

of these was defeated with Senators Diez, Guzmán, and Letelier casting negative votes, while Senators Pacheco and Vodanovic abstained (Biblioteca del Congreso Nacional 1990d). As with the amendment by Senator Lavandero to replace the word "offenses" against the armed forces with "injury," these amendments offered by Senator Soto seem in retrospect to have been doomed to defeat. Nevertheless, their author did not see herself as simply trying to stake out a position but instead offered them with some hope of success (Interview with Laura Soto, May 23, 1997).

Civil Military Relations. One of this slate of amendments cosponsored by the president and Senators Pacheco and Vodanovic, and defeated by Senators Diez, Guzmán, and Letelier, would have removed from article 416 of the Code of Military Justice special penalties for "violence against a Carbineer in service." PPD Deputy Jorge Molina, who was present for the committee's debate, expressed his view that the term "violence" must be interpreted in its natural and obvious sense, which is to apply violent means against things or people to defeat their resistance. Senator Guzmán added that one could not confuse an act of violence with whatever other that results in irritation, inconvenience, disgust, anger, or rage (Biblioteca del Congreso Nacional 1990d).

An amendment by Senators Diez and Feliú that received unanimous support dealt with the handling of confessions in cases that were moved from the military courts to the civilian ones, permitting the accused to make a new declaration. An amendment in the same spirit from the executive and Senators Pacheco and Vodanovic to allow a new opportunity to introduce evidence should a case be transferred from the military courts also passed unanimously (Biblioteca del Congreso Nacional 1990d).

The "Special Laws". During the second reading of the Human Rights Bill, Senators Diez and Feliú proposed a series of amendments designed to speed the processing of cases involving alleged violations of the "special laws,"[13] and to shorten the appeals process. Several of these met with the approval of Senators Guzmán and Letelier, who added their favorable votes to that of Senator Diez, while the Concertación Senators abstained. These included measures calling to increase the hierarchical stature of the courts hearing cases involving violations of the aforementioned laws, thereby shortening the appeals process, and allowing the Supreme Court to establish new tribunals to hear such cases when they had been kept waiting in the military courts for more than a year, though with the stipulation that for such "intercepted" cases, appeals would proceed through the military court system (Biblioteca del Congreso Nacional 1990d).

---

[13] These were the State Security Law, the Weapons Control Law, and the Antiterrorism Law.

An amendment requiring that cases involving violations of the "special laws" move to the top of the court calendar ahead of the queue of other cases waiting to be heard by the relevant magistrates in order to speed their resolution was approved by the same vote, save that Senator Pacheco voted "no" instead of joining his Concertación colleague Senator Vodanovic in abstaining (Biblioteca del Congreso Nacional 1990d).

Criminal Procedure. Senator Guzmán proposed a minor change in the wording of all Chilean laws to replace the word "prisoner" with "one who has been processed" in references made to an individual who had been accused of a crime, but not found guilty of it. He expressed concern that those accused of crimes not be stigmatized with references that made it sound as though they had been found guilty of something. This amendment received the unanimous approval of the committee, garnering the votes of Senators Diez, Letelier, Pacheco, and Vodanovic as well as that of its author (Biblioteca del Congreso Nacional 1990d).

A second modification was recommended by Senator Guzmán, in the form of two amendments to article 5 of the bill which contained reforms in the Code of Criminal Proceedings. These were designed to speed the criminal process; the first required that the "summary" stage of criminal proceedings, during which the magistrate must decide whether an accusation has merit, could not last for more than three years. The second amendment called for a four-year time limit on the time between the magistrate's endorsing the accusation against the accused and the initial sentence.[14]

The first of these amendments passed as written with the unanimous approval of the committee, with members noting that it would remedy injustices in which citizens accused of crimes spent long years deprived of basic liberties, such as the right to leave and reenter the national territory, while their cases languished in the courts. The second amendment also passed, though with a modification proposed by Senator Letelier to extend the time limit from four to five years, and another from Senator Vodanovic to require that denial of provisional freedom to the accused while the case was processed needed to be based on objective criteria. Francisco Cumplido, Minister of Justice, proposed an additional amendment to delay the implementation of this important change in the law for 120 days after the remainder of the law should be published. This suggestion also met with the support of the committee (Biblioteca del Congreso Nacional 1990d).

This was not the end of the discussion of this change in the law. While the amendments received easy approval in the Senate, they were rejected

[14] In Chile, rulings on appeal are also called sentences, and the amendment would allow these to continue past the five-year deadline.

by the Chamber of Deputies. A Conference Committee took the question up, along with other points of discrepancy between the two chambers. The Conference Committee voted in favor of the Senate time limits (as approved by the Senate Constitution Committee at the second reading), with Senators Diez, Guzmán, Letelier, and Vodanovic and Deputies Andrés Chadwick (UDI), Alberto Espina (RN), and Hernán Rojo (PDC) voting in favor, while Deputies Andrés Aylwin (PDC) and Jorge Molina (PDC) voted in contra (Biblioteca del Congreso Nacional 1990f). Senator Pacheco abstained, noting that while the measure might prevent undue delays in the judicial process, it could also be abused by the guilty, who could use dilatory motions to delay the process long enough to force dismissal of their cases. Jorge Molina argued against the measure on the grounds that it favored mainly those accused of white-collar crimes, and might also be used by narcotics dealers (Biblioteca del Congreso Nacional 1990f). Senator Guzmán defended the measure as preventing the indefinite imprisonment of someone without there ever being a sentence, adding that the threat of abuse was blunted by a measure excluding interruptions in the judicial process due to actions of the accused (Biblioteca del Congreso Nacional 1990f). Senator Vodanovic explained his favorable vote by noting that judicial delay could not be used as a form of punishment, and that the measure would in principal be of greatest use to people of limited means and those accused of political crimes (Biblioteca del Congreso Nacional 1990f).

While the Deputies accepted the changes, which were tied under a "closed rule" with other resolutions of discrepancies between the Deputies' and Senators' versions of the bill, the executive used his suppressive veto to eliminate the time limits on the judicial process. This veto was sustained in the Chamber of Deputies; however, the Senate was nevertheless required under the constitution to vote on the matter as well, even though given the decision of the Deputies the vote was redundant. Minister Cumplido explained that the veto came in the wake of internal government studies finding that the changes would primarily benefit those accused of violating the laws against tax evasion, smuggling, exchange rate manipulation, and bank fraud. In response to a question from Senator Pacheco, he added that narcotics traffickers were unlikely to be much affected by the change (Biblioteca del Congreso Nacional 1991c). The majority of the Senate Constitution Committee supported the presidential veto, although Senators Guzmán and Vodanovic voted to override (Biblioteca del Congreso Nacional 1991c). Senator Vodanovic explained that notwithstanding the reasons offered for suppressing the time limits, he was for overriding the veto, noting that the executive had not mentioned citizens whose cases were unnecessary prolonged by judicial inefficiency, nor had the executive mentioned the benefits the bill as passed by Congress would have for those accused of political crimes (Biblioteca del Congreso Nacional 1991c).

The remainder of the Constitution Committee's busy agenda included second readings of twenty bills, voting on a total of 693 amendments. These bills ranged in complexity from a motion by several members of the Chamber of Deputies[15] to facilitate the investigation and proof of injuries caused by criminal action, which gave rise to only three amendments voted during the second reading, to a complex presidential message governing the administrative careers of judges and other legal functionaries, which was the subject of 147 amendment votes at its second reading.

Preference Parameters

As discussed earlier, two voting Senators must be chosen to "anchor" the preferred positions of the legislators on the committee. To facilitate comparison with the committee's human rights votes, the Senators chosen are Socialist Hernán Vodanovic, whose position is normalized to equal -1, while Institutional Senators Letelier's preferred policy is set equal to 1.

In addition to Senator Vodanovic, the other two Concertación Senators voting often enough to permit separate estimation of their preferred outcomes are Senators Soto and Pacheco; see Table 11. The difference between the estimated preferences for Senator Soto and those of Senator Vodanovic is not statistically significant.[16] In contrast, Senator Pacheco is well to the right of both of these Concertación Senators, with estimated preference parameters that more closely resemble those of members of the opposition than they do those of either Senator Soto or Senator Vodanovic. This can be seen in Figure 7.2, which illustrates the Senators' preferred outcomes. The differences between the estimated preference parameters for Senators Pacheco and those of each of his colleagues Soto and Vodanovic are both large and statistically significant.[17] The slightly

---

[15] These were Deputies Espina, Taladriz, Rodriguez, Vilches, Prokuriça, Caminondo, Navarrete, Garcia, Cantero, and Ribera.

[16] The test statistic for the null hypothesis that the two Senators share the same values for x and b, which is asymptotically distributed as χ^2_2, equals 0.4686, corresponding to a p value of 0.7911 and indicating acceptance at all standard significance levels.

[17] For the null hypothesis that Pacheco and Vodanovic have the same preferred outcome, the χ^2_2 test statistic equals 11,847.966, while for the hypothesis that Pacheco and Soto have the same preference parameters the χ^2_2 test statistic of 8.5923 corresponds to a p value of 0.0136, corresponding to rejection at the $\alpha = 0.05$, though not at $\alpha = 0.01$.

Table 11. *Parameter estimates for the constitution committee, human rights votes excluded*

Participant	Parameter[a]			
	x	b	g	c
Partido Socialista			−0.090	−8.940
			(1.079)[a]	(0.990)
Hernán Vodanovic S.	−1.000	0.061		
		(0.320)		
Partido Por Democracia			−20.000	8.095
				(2.019)
Laura Soto G.	−0.679	0.112		
	0.619	(0.589)		
Partido Democrata Cristiano	−20.000	1.951	−2.738	−1.057
		(1.677)	(0.733)	(0.714)
Máximo Pacheco G.	0.533	1.460		
	(0.106)	(0.245)		
Executive Proposals			−3.392	4.344
			(0.775)	(0.756)
Renovación Nacional			0.000	0.000
Sergio Diez U.	1.252	2.025		
	(0.228)	(0.343)		
Miguel Otero L.	1.079	2.570		
	(0.117)	(0.335)		
Institutional Senators			0.033	0.513
			(0.116)	(0.338)
Olga Feliú S.	0.738	1.021		
	(0.199)	(0.420)		
Sergio Fernández F.	0.855	1.354		
	(0.149)	(0.275)		
Carlos Letelier B.	1.000	2.161		
		(0.330)		
William Thayer A.			−0.079	−0.890
			(0.440)	(1.036)
Union Democrata Independiente			0.272	−3.190
			(0.207)	(0.421)
Own Party Proposals		0.566		
		(0.227)		

[a] Estimated standard errors are show in parentheses; $\hat{\alpha} = 5.231$, $\hat{Sd}(\hat{\alpha}) = 0.360$, $\log(\text{lik}) = -714.853$, $n = 693$ amendments.

less decisive rejection of the hypothesis that Senators Pacheco and Soto have the same preferences is purely the result of Senator Soto's having voted less often on the committee, so that her preferences are somewhat less accurately estimated. The size of the gap is nevertheless substantial.

The Constitution Committee

Figure 7.2. Estimated Preferred Social Outcomes.

The preference parameters for the other Christian Democrats on the committee, Hormazábal and Paez, who voted very infrequently, cannot be precisely estimated. Nevertheless, the parameter estimates indicate that these Senators probably did not share Senator Pacheco's preferences on the social issues considered by the Constitution Committee. Estimating a common pair of preference parameters for these two Senators, the estimate for x, their preferred outcome, had to be constrained at -20:   the handful of votes cast by the two Senators were all "perfect" votes on the left. Because of the small number of observations available for these two Senators, the finding is only suggestive. However, an analysis of the debates from the Senate floor indicates that there is indeed a rift among the Christian Democrats on the social agenda considered by the Constitution Committee.

While there is a large gap between the estimated preference parameters for Senator Pacheco and the other Concertación members on the committee, he is much closer to the Senators of the opposition; see Figure 7.2. For example, the estimated breach between his preferred outcome and that of Institutional Senator Feliú is but one-seventh the size of the gulf separating him from Socialist Senator Vodanovic. Nor do the estimated differences between the preference parameters for Senator Pacheco and Institutional Senator Feliú exceed the threshold of statistical significance.[18]

The policy differences among the Senators on the right are less dramatic than among the Concertación Senators. Among the five opposition Senators on the committee for whom separate preference parameters could be estimated, three (National Renovation Senators Diez and Otero and Institutional Senators Fernández) take very similar positions at the right of the issue spectrum. The small estimated differences among the preferred outcomes for these three Senators are not statistically significant.[19]

---

[18] The test statistic for the hypothesis that Senators Feliú and Pacheco share identical preference parameters, x and b, is asymptotically distributed as χ_2^2, so that the realized value of 4.2517 corresponds to a p value of 0.1193, corresponding to acceptance at all standard significance levels.

[19] The test statistic of 5.4505 generates a p value of 0.2441 when compared with its asymptotic distribution, which is χ_2^2.

194

A second group of opposition Senators, Feliú and Fernández, have preferences estimated slightly to the left of the other three. The very similar preference parameter estimates for these two exhibit no statistically significant differences.[20] As mentioned above, the estimated preference parameters for Senators Feliú and Pacheco also fall below the threshold of statistical significance, while the estimated difference between the preference parameters for Senators Fernández and Pacheco is only marginally statistically significant.[21] A test of the null hypothesis that Senators Feliú, Fernández, and Pacheco all share the same preferences receives some support from the data.[22] This surprising affinity between Senator Pacheco and his institutional colleagues Feliú and Fernández contrasts with the difference between Senator Pacheco and his two fellow Concertación members, especially Senator Vodanovic, and with the significant difference between the rightmost Senator of this group, Senator Fernández, and the three opposition Senators, Diez, Letelier, and Otero, at the right end of the spectrum.[23]

The preference parameter estimates indicate that there are three groups of Senators who share very similar outlooks on the social issues considered by the Constitution Committee. The first of these consists of the Socialist and PPD Senators on the left. Some members of the Christian Democratic Party probably share their perspective, though these Christian Democrats from the left of their party cast so few votes on the committee that this conjecture about their preferences on the basis of their committee voting records must be considered speculative. The second group, on the right of the spectrum, consists of Senators Diez, Otero, and Letelier. Then there is a third group, Senators Feliú, Fernández, and Pacheco, who take positions somewhat more moderately on the right.

Proposal Parameters. Returning to the parameter estimates in Table 11, the National Renovation party is once again used as the "reference

[20] The χ_2^2 test statistic of the hypothesis of identical prefence parameters generates a test statistic of 0.6745, corresponding to a p value of 0.7137, indicating acceptance of the null hypothesis at all standard significance levels.

[21] The χ_2^2 test statistic for the null hypothesis that Senators Pacheco and Fernández share the same preference parameters equals 5.9048, corresponding to p value of 0.0522. This would lead to rejection of the null hypothesis at the $\alpha = 0.10$ significance level, but not at either $\alpha = 0.05$ or $\alpha = 0.01$.

[22] The χ_4^2 statistic for the hypothesis that all three Senators share identical preference parameters equals 8.4693, corresponding to a p value of 0.0758, and leading to acceptance at $\alpha = 0.05$ and $\alpha = 0.01$, though not at $\alpha = 0.10$.

[23] The χ_6^2 statistic for the hypothesis that all four Senators, Fernández, Diez, Otero, and Letelier, share identical preference parameters equals 21.061, corresponding to a p value of 0.0018, leading rejection at all standard significance levels. Compare this with the easy acceptance of the hypothesis that Senators Diez, Letelier, and Otero share a common set of preference parameters.

proposer," with its ideology and consensus quality parameters, g and c, both normalized to equal 0. The most accurately estimated ideological displacements are those of the UDI and Institutional Senators; see Table 11. Given the role played by Institutional Senator Thayer on the Labor Committee, a separate displacement is measured for this Senator. In contrast with the Labor Committee, the ideological content of this Institutional Senator's proposals does not statistically significantly differ from that estimated for the other Institutionals.[24] In fact, all of the estimated ideological proposal parameters for the opposition Senators shown in Table 11, those for Senator Thayer, for the other Institutional Senators, and the UDI Senators, are very similar to the values for the reference proposer, the National Renovation Party, and one cannot reject the null hypothesis that the true parameters are identical.[25] With the exception of the ideological proposal parameter for PPD Senator Soto, which had to be constrained at -20, the parameter estimates also indicate similarity among the proposal parameters for the Concertación members, though less than for the opposition Senators. The executive, the Radicals, and the Christian Democratic Senators all have estimated ideological proposal parameters near -3, while the estimated value for the Socialists, to the right of these, is very imprecisely estimated. A formal test for equality among the proposal Parameters for the three remaining members of the Concertación whose ideological proposal parameters were not constrained leads to borderline rejection.[26]

The consensus appeal parameters, the c, are reported in the fourth column of Table 11. The parameter estimates for the Radicals, the UDI, and especially those for the Socialists are all large and negative, indicating a low probability of acceptance, correcting for the ideological displacements for amendments sponsored by members of these parties. On the other side, proposals by PPD Senator Soto and by the executive had very high consensus appeal. In the case of proposals from the executive, this probably is due to the twin advantages of a large staff and the special proposal powers set aside for the executive in article 62 of the constitution. In the case of Senator Soto these factors clearly do not play a part. Nor can the estimate for Senator Soto be written off as a byproduct of collinearity with the estimated consensus quality for the Socialists, with whom she

[24] The χ_1^2 test statistic for the null hypothesis that $g_{Thayer} = g_{Instit}$ is 0.0742, corresponding to a p value of 0.7854 and leading to acceptance at all standard confidence levels.

[25] The χ_3^2 statistic is 2.0955, corresponding to a p value of 0.5528 and indicating acceptance at all standard significance levels.

[26] Comparing the test statistic of 8.0492 with its asymptotic χ_3^2 distribution leads to a p value of 0.0450, indicating rejection at $\alpha = 0.10$ and at $\alpha = 0.05$ but not $\alpha = 0.01$.

frequently coproposes amendments.[27] While it is possible that the high consensus quality of her amendments is due to her skill as a lawyer, an alternative hypothesis that deserves some consideration is the strong latent appeal of the women's rights element of her proposal agenda. Her proposals on social issues are often targeted toward particularly extreme elements of the status quo, such as legislation that made adultery a crime for women but not for men, so that the large leftward displacement of her proposals tends to start from a position to the right of the status quo elements targeted by the amendments of her Senate colleagues.

The positive and significant[28] "own party proposals" parameter indicates that Senators on the committee tended to defer to proposals made by members of their own parties, voting favorably on such proposals somewhat more often than they would have on purely ideological grounds. The value for α of 6.195 is precisely estimated, with a standard error of only 1.050, and it produces a high rate of unanimous voting on the committee.[29] This high degree of unanimity probably stems from the importance of "technical" legal concerns to the committee: badly written laws serve no one's policy interests, and despite their very real differences, committee members are all aware of the importance of avoiding judicial ambiguities and unintended side effects from the legislation they sponsor.

Implied Voting Probabilities. Before taking a closer look at the substantive questions considered by the committee, we can gain additional perspective on the parameter estimates by considering their implications for hypothetical amendments offered by various proposers. To facilitate comparison with voting on the committee's human rights agenda, the same set of hypothetical proposers used in Table 10 is used to construct a similar set of voting probabilities for committee votes on social issues; see Table 12. Because Senator Guzmán, who played an important part in the committee's deliberations, was assassinated before most of the committee's social agenda was voted, he is replaced in the simulations, as he was in the committee, by Senator Otero. Because the social issues led to more frequent votes than the human rights agenda, separate proposal parameter estimates are available for the Socialists and PPD, for which a common pair of proposal parameters was estimated on the human rights agenda.

---

[27] The estimated correlation between these estimated consensus quality parameters is -0.1070.

[28] The t ratio for this parameter is 2.4922, corresponds to a p value of 0.0127, which is significant at the $\alpha = 0.10$ and $\alpha = 0.05$ significance levels but not at $\alpha = 0.01$.

[29] Over 88% of the amendments considered by the committee were decided on unanimous votes. The correlation between Senators' voting errors, the $\alpha v_i + \eta_{vi}$, implied by this estimate for α is 0.965.

Table 12. *Hypothetical vote margins: social issues*[a]

Votes		Probability by proposer							
In favor	Against	PS	PPD	Exec.	PDC	Rad.	RN	UDI	Instit.
0	5	0.870	–	0.075	0.356	0.571	0.291	0.488	0.249
1	4	0.006	0.608	0.110	0.179	0.138	0.037	0.083	0.070
2	3	0.016	0.359	0.104	0.100	0.099	0.024	0.059	0.026
3	2	0.034	0.011	0.051	0.014	0.049	0.014	0.017	0.009
4	1	0.034	0.019	0.017	0.020	0.013	0.141	0.074	0.090
5	0	0.040	0.003	0.643	0.332	0.129	0.493	0.278	0.555

[a] Committee Consists of Senators Diez, Letelier, Otero, Pacheco, and Vodanovic. A dash indicates a probability of less than 0.0005.

The first column indicates that the low consensus appeal parameter for the Socialists has a chilling effect on their proposals. The estimated probability that an amendment proposed by the Socialists is unanimously rejected is 0.870, over twenty-one times greater than the probability it meets with unanimous acceptance. In contrast, the high consensus quaility of proposals from PPD Senator Soto combined with their heavy ideological content polarize the committee as no other proposer can. The ideological content of these proposals all but guarantees approval by Socialist Senator Vodanovic. Senator Pacheco is left on the margin; attracted by the high consensus quality of the PPD Senator's proposals, he is also repelled by their leftist ideological content. This balance goes in favor of the PPD Senator only about one time in three, while in the remaining cases the consensus quality of Senator Soto's proposed amendments is not enough to win the vote of her fellow Concertación Senator. The leftist ideological content of Senator Soto's proposals on social issues virtually guarantees rejection by the three Senators on the right edge of the ideological spectrum: Diez, Letelier, and Otero. Thus, while Soto's proposals get some favorable attention, their ideological content polarizes the committee, dooming the majority of them to defeat. Of course, with Senator Fernández or Senator Feliú on the committee instead of Senator Otero, the chances of a majority rise, but only somewhat.[30] Proposals by the executive are much less polarizing than on the human rights agenda and have an almost two-thirds probability of being unanimously accepted.

As with proposals by the executive, amendments offered by the National Renovation Party are less polarizing than on the human rights

[30] With Senator Feliú substituted for Senator Otero, the probability of winning support from a majority on the committee rises from 0.033 to 0.135, while with Senator Fernández the probability of majority support would be 0.081.

agenda, with a probability of unanimous approval of almost 50%. However, UDI proposals are much less likely to meet with unanimous approval than on the human rights agenda. An important factor at work in the case of proposals from the UDI party is their low consensus approval. In part this is undoubtedly due to that party's expert on the constitution, Jaime Guzmán, having been assassinated. Proposals by the Institutional Senators were somewhat less successful than on the human rights agenda, with a somewhat lower probability of unanimous acceptance, and a probability of unanimous rejection of almost one in four.[31]

Putting the Estimates in Context

To gain a clearer understanding of the substantive content of the issues that comprise the social dimension of the committee's agenda it is useful to take a closer look at some of these proposals. Many of the amendments voted on by the committee were aimed at a bill introduced late in the Aylwin administration to reform the laws governing marital assets. This is particularly important given that the parameter estimates indicate that these issues tap a different ideological dimension than the human rights bills do.

The Status Quo. The marriage laws in Chile are complicated by the lack of legal divorce. As a practical matter, this does not prevent marriages dissolving, but it does complicate the process. Chilean law includes provisions for marital annulment, though in practice this requires both parties to agree on terms and entails considerable legal expense. Because of the complexity and costliness of the legal procedures involved, annulment is not an option for people of limited means. The poor often simply continue with their lives without ever obtaining a legal annulment, sometimes even marrying again. A 1994 study by the Chilean government using tax records identified hundreds of such cases of "polygamy." For the middle class, marriages that break up are frequently annulled, though if the partners cannot agree to terms, lengthy separations can occur. In these cases the laws governing the division of marital property are very important.

Married couples in Chile can opt for one of two arrangements: separation of goods, in which the parties to the marriage administer their property separately, subject to certain qualifications such as the requirement that husbands economically "support" their families, or the pooling of marital assets, which is not uncommon. This pooling terminates at the end of a marriage. Ending the pooling arrangement is also common when one of the parties has incurred large debts. While creditors can pursue marital assets, they have a much harder time attaching the assets of a debtor's spouse when the couple has opted for a separation of goods. Moreover,

---

[31] The corresponding probability for the human rights agenda is estimated at 0.011.

the administration of marital goods is accorded special treatment under Chilean law, and disputes between partners over the disposition of the marital assets are not uncommon. This is particularly a problem when a couple has separated but has been unable to agree to dissolve the marriage or terminate the pooled property arrangement.

In cases of pooled assets, complex rules govern the allocation of property among the couple's "shared patrimony" and the "reserved patrimony" of each partner, and husbands' and wives' contributions are treated differently. As the Aylwin administration drew to a close, the laws regulating the disposition of marital assets had not been changed for decades.

Another element of the status quo that had become an embarrassment was the treatment of adultery in the criminal code, which made adultery a crime for women, while male marital infidelity only crossed the criminal threshold if it amounted to "concubinage": actually setting up a household with a woman other than one's wife and maintaining it for a period of at least seven days. As a practical matter the standard of proof needed to establish that a wife has committed adultery is sufficiently high that the law is almost never applied; application of the law against "concubinage" required more evidence still. Nevertheless, virtually everyone recognized that such outrageously asymmetric treatment of husbands and wives had no place in the law.

In response to this status quo the executive proposed a series of reforms, mostly designed to make the laws function more smoothly, and to reduce some of the asymmetries in the treatment of husbands and wives. These included reforms of the rules dealing with marital property. As part of the same bill, the government sought to apply the criminal penalty for adultery to men and women alike, while abolishing the crime of "concubinage."

The Criminal Status of Infidelity. Needless to say, not everyone agreed that Aylwin had taken the correct approach to making the criminal code gender neutral! The Chamber of Deputies voted instead to decriminalize marital infidelity, whether adultery or "concubinage," as the best means of resolving the asymmetry in the law. The Episcopal Conference of the Catholic Church disapproved of this measure, taking the unusual step of publicly warning Congress that if it decriminalized adultery it could send a signal legitimizing infidelity (El Mercurio 1994). Perhaps not by coincidence, the Senate was more sympathetic to the executive's version of the bill, and the Constitution Committee embraced an amendment offered by Christian Democrat Máximo Pacheco reinserting the language making adultery a crime for both husbands and wives (El Mercurio 1994). Socialist Senators Calderón, Nuñez, and Vodanovic, and PPD Senator Soto responded by offering an amendment restoring the Deputies' version of the bill, decriminalizing adultery (Biblioteca del Congreso Nacional 1993d).

The Socialist/PPD caucus took the view that the question of fidelity was a civil matter which did not belong in the criminal code at all. This approach did not meet with the approval of the Constitution Committee, and Senators Feliú, Letelier, and Pacheco voted to reject it, while Senator Soto abstained (Biblioteca del Congreso Nacional 1993d). But this was not the end of the Senate's deliberations on the subject.

When the bill arrived on the floor the decriminalization amendment was renewed, forcing a floor debate and one of the upper chamber's relatively rare recorded votes. Many Senators participated in this debate, and their remarks help to illustrate the links between the voting records of the committee members and the positions of their parties on the Constitution Committee's social agenda.

Senator Soto defended the proposed amendment, arguing as follows:

> In my judgement, the question is connected with the ambit of modernity, but it is absurd to conclude, on the grounds of agreeing with feminism and of opposing discrimination, that the appropriate means is to increase the penalty for the husband. This is really inadmissible.
>
> (Biblioteca del Congreso Nacional 1994a)

This basic point of view was shared by Senator Soto's Socialist colleagues, as well as by the members of the Radical Party and some of the Christian Democrats. The Radicals were historically the secular party of Chile's political center, while the Christian Democrats were the pro-religious center party. Radical Senator Gonzalez grasped the opportunity to differentiate his small party, with only three Senators, from its successful Christian Democratic competitor, outlining a very different social agenda than his coalition partners, even if he managed to wander considerably from the debate then at hand:

> We cannot permit ourselves to be characterized as assassins, those of us who want to study profound themes such as abortion or euthanasia. It is known that in our country there are 250 thousand or 300 thousand abortions a year, and women put their lives in danger for not being able to carry these out under adequate conditions. We aren't in favor of killing anyone; nor of destroying the family. Completely to the contrary, we believe, and profoundly, that this is the fundamental pillar of society, and that we must try to strengthen it at every opportunity. But this is not achieved through penal sanctions applied to conduct that belongs to human beings, through dispositions that appear absolutely anachronistic in our times.
>
> (Biblioteca del Congreso Nacional 1994a)

The central argument in favor of making adultery a criminal offense was made by Máximo Pacheco:

> Adultery harms both partners in a marriage, and the damage is very hard to repair. Moreover, among its principal, and innocent, victims are the children. Finally

201

the breakup of a family signifies the weakening of society, which is composed of families. As adultery is such a grave ill, it is important and just that society should establish a limit on personal actuation in the sphere of the sexual, clearly saying that this lack of marital faith is something against civil law, and something against the penal code.

(Biblioteca del Congreso Nacional 1994a)

Expressing a very different social vision than Radical Senator Gonzalez, Senator Pacheco went on to express his views more generally of a permissive legal system:

In effect, following this fundamental premise, society would arrive at a more corrosive individualism, then it would be obliged to tolerate conduct exercised with free choice, in the private sphere, as juridically intangible.

This would take us to the consequence of legalization of private consumption of drugs, and the acceptance of the cult of the private of every kind of aberration under cover of freedom of religion, among other sinister consequences.

(Biblioteca del Congreso Nacional 1994a)

The Senators of the right could do no more than agree with these sentiments. For example, Senator Diez:

With respect to the proposed amendment which we are voting, the words expressed by (Senator Pacheco) correspond faithfully to my own thinking. In my opinion, adultery is an illicit deed.

(Biblioteca del Congreso Nacional 1994a)

Senator Feliú also found herself in accord:

But in fact, the world of today, with all that it presents us, brings us (as has been made mention of on the floor, especially by the Honorable Mr. Pacheco) to analyze the values that we want to protect as legislators. In our quality as such, do we privilege the liberty of persons to do what occurs to them, or do we privilege the family?

(Biblioteca del Congreso Nacional 1994a)

Senator Prat of the National Renovation Party observed that the controversy was largely symbolic:

I understand that the proposed amendment claims to correct a norm that appears unequal and ineffective, but no one denies that it is in disuse, and moreover, in practice has almost no application.

Moreover, the proposition sends a signal that damages something valuable which we seek to protect: the family, which in our judgment should have priority at the moment of casting a vote.

(Biblioteca del Congreso Nacional 1994a)

Among the amendment's supporters, Senator Lavandero's reply to these criticisms was perhaps the most compelling:

I consider that maintaining the penalty for adultery will not resolve the problem of protecting the family. I believe that the husband who imprisons the mother of his children causes greater harm than that which he seeks to sanction, and cannot conclude that in this form he is defending the family. To the contrary, he is destroying it.

(Biblioteca del Congreso Nacional 1994a)

He went on to point out that decriminalizing adultery did not entail removing all legal consequences, observing that the Civil Code still provided considerable sanctions.

Others were less comfortable about being forced to take a public position on the issue, arguing that the subject matter might be better discussed in another context, rather than as part of a bill dealing with reforms to the laws dealing with marital property. Of course, as the president had himself attached the issue of adultery to the bill it would not have been easy to be rid of the amendment by declaring it was not germane.

Minister Alvear of SERNAM[32] sought to emphasize the movement toward equal treatment of men and women under the proposed new adultery law:

I reiterate that the basic idea of the government's project is to modify the situation with respect to marital property and also as it concerns the personal status of married people. That is why we opened the theme of fidelity and also why we introduced changes in the Law of Civil Marriage to equalize sanctions.

(Biblioteca del Congreso Nacional 1994a)

The minister of Justice, Mr. Cumplido, who noted that as the Deputies had approved a version of the bill consistent with the Socialists' proposal, rejecting the amendment in the Senate would all but guarantee that there would be a conference committee (something that would only be avoided if the Deputies surrendered to the Senate's demands), which could work out the details of a compromise more carefully (Biblioteca del Congreso Nacional 1994a).

Minister Cumplido's suggestion of passing the buck to the Conference Committee by voting "no" on the amendment appealed to some, for example Senator Zaldívar, who spoke in favor of rejecting the amendment: "...but not because we are in favor or against the article as it was proposed by the Committee, or in favor of or against sanctioning the man, but so that there shall be a Conference Committee that pronounces on the subject" (Biblioteca del Congreso Nacional 1994a).

While Senators seeking cover welcomed the excuse of voting down the amendment so that a Conference Committee could give the matter "careful study," those more willing to commit publicly to positions on the

---

[32] The National Women's Service, a government agency charged with promoting the welfare of women.

issue sought to characterize the likely results of a conference committee. For example, Senator Calderón provided the following analysis of the Conference Committee:

> I am uneasy about the mechanism of the Conference Committee, because it could result in maintaining discrimination against women, which is exactly what the government wants to correct through the bill. Certainly there would be no law in this part, but instead the current norm, which penalizes the wife, would persist.
> (Biblioteca del Congreso Nacional 1993d)

As cosponsor of the amendment, he clearly ranked the amendment to decriminalize adultery ahead of either the status quo, which discriminated against women, or the government's bill, which applied the criminal penalties equally to men and women. However, his argument seems aimed at persuading persons who rank the government's bill first, the Socialist/PPD amendment to decriminalize second, and the status quo last that voting against the amendment would result in a lottery between their most and least favored outcomes, while the amendment offered the safety of their second best result, to decriminalize adultery, as an assured outcome.

While National Renovation Senator Sergio Diez seems to have agreed with his Socialist Colleague's analysis of the game tree, he did not share Senator Calderón's preferences over outcomes: "...in the case of the crime of adultery that we are dealing with this morning, the worst solution is to eliminate it as an illicit deed" (Biblioteca del Congreso Nacional 1993d). Given the Senator's support for the government's amendment, his self-reported preference ranking placed the government's bill first, the status quo second, and decriminalization last, a preference ranking that made voting for the Socialist/PPD amendment a dominated strategy: the Conference Committee lottery could produce nothing worse, and might result in something better.

The Socialist/PPD amendment was defeated by a lopsided margin in what was, except for the Christian Democrats, a party-line vote (Biblioteca del Congreso Nacional 1994a). The Socialist/PPD and Radical/SD caucuses took the socially liberal position of voting to decriminalize adultery. The parties of the opposition took a very clear stand for the socially conservative position of keeping adultery a crime. No Senator from the opposition voted for the amendment: not from the UDI or National Renovation parties, not among the Institutional Senators, and not Independent Senator Alessandri.[33]

---

[33] While Senator Alessandri was "paired" and so unable to vote, he spoke against the amendment during the floor debate and actually tried to vote against it until he was reminded of the pairing arrangement by Senator Nuñez, who had also tried to cast a vote, leaving little doubt about where this Senator stood.

Yet it is worth noting that among the nine Senators listed as present for that day's debate (Biblioteca del Congreso Nacional 1993d) who did not vote on the amendment or announce that they were "paired" and so unable to vote,[34] six were from the National Renovation Party.[35] In fact, the silent nonvoters among the National Renovation Senate delegation were more numerous than the five National Renovation Senators who voted (See Table 13). The absence of these Senators did not go unnoticed in the press, with *El Mercurio* naming Senators who were "among those who took part in the debate, or part of it, but did not vote" (El Mercurio 1994), while *La Epoca* directly accused them of dodging the vote: "So sensitive was the theme, that several parliamentarians who were present in the chamber, preferred to leave in silence and not vote" (La Epoca 1994).While the press was somewhat cavalier about the identities of the nonvoters,[36] the speculation that some of the nonvoting was strategic is an interesting one. Perhaps some of the National Renovation Senators who did not vote quietly disagreed with their party's position, but were unwilling to break ranks on the floor.

While one may speculate about internal divisions among the National Renovation Senators, the divisions among the Christian Democrats are written across the record in bright scarlet letters. Senator Pacheco, identified by the parameter estimates as having preferences on social issues that are closer to the opposition than they are to his fellow Concertación members Calderón and Soto, was joined in support of the administration position by four other members of his party, each of whom gave a speech during the floor debate justifying his vote. Four other Christian Democrats opposed the measure, with two of them[37] participating extensively in the floor debate. The parameter estimates indicate that the rift within the Concertación on social issues is of virtually the same magnitude as the breach between the Socialist/PPD position and that of the opposition, and the debate is consistent with this, with opposition Senators Diez and Feliú agreeing with the social vision expressed by Senator Pacheco. The floor debate over the amendment to decriminalize adultery also supports the view that Senator Pacheco was not acting as a lone eccentric on the Constitution Committee, advocating preferences that were inconsistent with

---

[34] In addition to Senators Núñez, Alessandri, and Huerta, National Renovation Senator Ortiz and Radical Senator Sule announced that they were paired.

[35] These were Senators Cooper, Lagos, Larre, Otero, Pérez, and Rios. Also not voting were Senators Fernández, Carmen Frei, and Valdés. As President of the Senate, Gabriel Valdés frequently abstained when his vote would not have changed the outcome.

[36] Senator Sule, listed among the presumed vote dodgers, was paired with National Renovation Senator Ortiz, and so according to the Senate rules should not have voted.

[37] Senators Hormazábal and Lavandero.

Table 13. *Votes on amendment 107 to decriminalize adultery*

Party	In favor	Opposed
Rad.	González	
Rad.	Navarrete	
PPD	Soto	
PS	Calderón	
PS	Núñez[a]	
DC		Diaz
DC	Arturo Frei	
DC	Hormazábal	
DC	Lavandero	
DC		Pacheco
DC	Páez	
DC		Palza
DC		José Ruiz
DC		Zaldívar
RN		Diez
RN		Prat
RN		Romero
RN		Siebert
UDI		Cantuarias
UDI		Urenda
Indep.		Alessandri[a]
Instit.		Feliú
Instit.		Huerta[b]
Instit.		Letelier
Instit.		Martin
Instit.		Mc-Intyre
Instit.		Sinclair
Instit.		Thayer

[a] Senators Núñez and Alessandri were paired, but both were present and both cast votes, which were later subtracted from the respective totals in favor and against.
[b] Senator Huerta was also paired, with Senator Sule, and retracted his vote: (Biblioteca del Congreso Nacional 1994; Sesiones del Senado: Legislatura Extraordinaria 327 Sesión 21, 5 Enero, pp. 3,651–3,652).

the rest of his party. Instead he appears to have represented the preferences of an important faction of his party, including President Aylwin.

Limiting Judicial Power. An amendment by UDI Senator Cantuarias would have eliminated a section of the bill which proposed a new article of the Civil Code allowing judges to attribute rights to the use of marital property. Senator Feliú favored the proposal on the grounds that the article Senator Cantuarias sought to eliminate was redundant given judges' existing powers to order support payments. The proposed amendment received unanimous support from the committee, including the favorable votes of Senators Letelier and Pacheco as well as Senator Feliú.

The matter did not end there. During the discussion of the bill on the Senate floor, Ms. Alvear, Director of SERNAM, expressed the executive's concerns about the Senator Cantuarias's amendment. She argued that the article eliminated by Senator Cantuarias's amendment was a necessary tool allowing judges to protect the interests of the custodial parent in cases of marital separation. She noted that given existing procedures for administering housing subsidies, a woman with children who had been abandoned by her husband might be unable to reapply for a housing subsidy in light of her new circumstances, and she argued that judges should be given ample powers to allocate the use of marital assets to resolve such problems (Biblioteca del Congreso Nacional 1994b).

The response of Senator Otero to the Minister's remarks is especially interesting given the intense conflict between the Chilean right and left over income redistribution:

> It is a fact that in this country the woman is the one who maintains and protects the family, especially in the economically weak classes. At the same time, what the Minister says is right: in many cases a dwelling obtained with the help of the state remains in the husband's name. And when he abandons his wife, the family is left absolutely defenseless.
>
> (Biblioteca del Congreso Nacional 1994b)

After a speech of the same tone, Senator Otero ended by saying "I see neither reasons nor motives for voting in favor of the suppression of an article that simply gives judges a faculty" (Biblioteca del Congreso Nacional 1994b). In this instance compassion for the family and support for motherhood were in conflict with the budget, and for almost every Senator on the right motherhood won.

Senator Cantuarias carefully backed away from his proposal by saying "the elimination of this norm does not have the purpose of disprotecting the family, the children, nor – as has been indicated by the majority of the examples – the spouse or woman who lives with them." The amendment author added "...the objective of our[38] proposed amendment was exclusively to create a norm that would not provoke confusion" (Biblioteca del Congreso Nacional 1994b).

Senator Diez proposed a face-saving exit, suggesting a more elegant but substantively equivalent wording for the amendment Senator Cantuarias'

---

[38] The amendment was solo authored.

amendment had sought to eliminate. Because this suggestion amounted to an amendment proposed well past the deadline for new amendments (which expired before the committee had finished its second reading of the bill), this required the unanimous agreement of the Senate, which was forthcoming (Biblioteca del Congreso Nacional 1994b), although Senator Feliú, while not blocking the rewording proposed by Senator Diez, cast the lone vote in favor of Senator Cantuarias' amendment, insisting that the amendment would not add to judges' existing powers while she predicted it would distort the entire system of already existing judicial powers related to the allocation of family goods (Biblioteca del Congreso Nacional 1994b).

One of the Socialist/PPD amendments specified that if a married couple could not agree on a location for the family domicile between themselves, a judge could resolve the dispute. In a companion amendment, the same Senators would add as a cause for anullment the refusal to live with the other when there has been a judicial resolution of the location of the family domicile.

These amendments did not meet with the approbation of the committee, with Senator Pacheco joining opposition Senators Feliú and Letelier in unanimously voting to reject the amendments. The committee justified its position by contending that the decision of where to live was within the zone of privacy of the couple, and preferred the current language setting forth the right of both husband and wife to live in a common home except when there were grave reasons for not doing so. The committee report added that the proposed amendment would clutter the already crowded calendars of the courts (Biblioteca del Congreso Nacional 1993d). The amendment adding the refusal to live in the judicially decreed family domicile as a cause for anullment also included a switch to nonsexist language in a clause making an attempt at selling one's spouse into prostitution a cause for anullment, and this change in language met with unanimous approval, notwithstanding the rejection of the remaining, and more practically significant, portion of the amendment (Biblioteca del Congreso Nacional 1994b).

Streamlining Procedures. One amendment proposed by UDI Senator Cantuarias divided the committee's members on a technical legal question. Article 141 of the Civil Code allowed for the possibility that the household goods and primary residence of a married couple belonging to one or both of the spouses be declared part of the common family property, even if the couple had opted for a separation of goods. The article went on to specify that the court apply "brief and summary" procedures in such cases. These procedures, while more streamlined than the ordinary procedures used by the courts with their many opportunities for introducing and reviewing evidence, required that the spouse of the partner asking for the change be notified of the proceedings before a decision was taken.

Senator Cantuarias proposed to amend article 145 of the Civil Code, which dealt with the alienation of goods that were part of the family property, to include a similar guarantee that the spouse be notified (Biblioteca del Congreso Nacional 1993d). This requirement would make it more difficult for an unscrupulous husband to forge his wife's signature on an agreement to separate an asset from the family goods, as the court would nevertheless be obliged to notify the wife that proceedings were in process, giving her a chance to respond, and so to denounce the forgery. The proposal met with the approval of Senators Feliú and Letelier, who agreed that procedures designed to remove property from the shared family assets should use the same rules as procedures seeking to add property. Senator Pacheco disagreed, sustaining the position that the amendment was unnecessary, as notification of the other spouse was already an implicit requirement of summary procedures.

Senator Cantuarias proposed a similar requirement that when a judge allowed creditors to seize the family assets of a debtor, that the judge personally notify the debtor's spouse of the decision. This amendment again split the committee, despite the support of Senator Pacheco, it was nevertheless defeated by the negative votes of Letelier and Feliú, who based their opposition on the grounds that notification that creditors had been allowed to seize an asset left the spouse with scant legal recourse (Biblioteca del Congreso Nacional 1993d).

Equality. Senator Soto of the PPD and Senators Calderón, Nuñez, and Vodanovic of the Socialist Party jointly proposed a series of amendments designed to equalize the treatment of men and women under the marriage laws. The keystone of this group of proposals would have added a new article 132 to the Civil Code asserting the equality of husbands and wives in both rights and obligations. Senator Feliù noted that when the "potestad marital," a group of rights enjoyed by married men over the person and possessions of their wives, had been repealed, no one had taken advantage of the opportunity to pass a law asserting equality between husband and wife. The representative of SERNAM who was present at the Committee meeting, Carlos Peña, expressed his opinion that it was necessary to distinguish between equality outside the area of marital property, where in his perspective there was no doubt at all that there already existed clear equality between husbands and wives, and equality in the ambit of marital property, in which he acknowledged equality did not exist. He went on to argue that couples choosing to pool their assets in a "conjugal society," in which the law recognized the husband as the custodian of the family assets, had made a choice inconsistent with equal rights and obligations for husbands and wives, and that the law should not be reformed in ways that would be inconsistent with this option. The committee was persuaded by Mr. Peña's arguments, and unanimously rejected the proposed amendment, with the votes of Senators Feliú, Letelier, and Pacheco. The committee also stated for the record that it agreed with Senator Feliú's puzzling remark that it was rejecting the amendment because it was part of a series of proposals whose purpose was to change the system fundamentally, and not because they failed to recognize the equality of the rights and obligations between husbands and wives. This is odd because the arguments of Mr. Peña, with which the committee expressed wholehearted agreement, were precisely directed against equality of rights and obligations (Biblioteca del Congreso Nacional 1993d).

Conclusions

The most striking departure from the bipolar model among the three committees considered in detail is afforded by the Constitution Committee. When human rights issues are separated from the remainder of the Constitution Committee's agenda, two distinct patterns of alliance emerge. On human rights questions the committee divides as the country did in the 1988 plebiscite on Pinochet's continuation in power, with the Concertación Senators presenting a united block on the left, and the opposition Senators taking an equally cohesive position on the right. Moreover, the content of proposals from the left and the right is very different. Proposals from the Concertación tend to move policy leftward, although only in the case of executive proposals is the estimated policy impact statistically significant. Proposals from the opposition Senators tend to preserve the status quo policy position, while they enjoy substantial consensus appeal, which given their status quo preserving policy content indicates high valence. In contrast, the consensus appeal of proposals from the Concertación tends to be low, except for the executive. This low consensus appeal could be a byproduct of proposals having a midpoint far to the left, or of the proposals having low valence, or both. Consider the proposal by Senator Soto to require trials and convictions before the self-amnesty declared by the military government could be applied. This would certainly move policy well to the left of the status quo, while at the same time if it were implemented without prior negotiation with the armed forces it would create a real risk of military intervention, the epitome of a low-valence outcome.

A closer look at the issues that divided the Concertación and the opposition on human rights indicates that they disagreed about the treatment of those accused of crimes committeed for political reasons during the period of military rule, with politicians and journalists on the right always enclosing the term "political prisoners" in quotation marks when applied to these people. They disagreed as well about the correct course for investigating crimes committed by members of the armed forces during the coup and subsequent period of military rule, about the scope of the jurisdiction of the military courts, and about the leeway that should be accorded to freedom of expression. These issues were central to the campaign for the "No" that brought Pinochet to defeat in the 1988 plebiscite on his second term. The human rights issue agenda created the interparty alliance of the Concertación, and it continues to play a vital role in its maintenance.

In contrast with their unity on human rights questions, the Concertación split on the social issues that constitute the remainder of the Constitution committee's agenda. On the left of the social spectrum are PPD Senator Soto and Socialist Hernán Vodanovic. On the right of the spectrum we encounter National Renovation Senators Diez and Otero, and Institutional Senator Letelier. The surprise here is that the remaining Senators with preferred outcomes close to the right end of the spectrum include Christian Democratic Senator Pacheco as well as Institutional Senators Feliú and Fernández. This affinity of Senator Pacheco and some of his Christian Democratic coreligionists with the right on social issues is consistent with the Christian Democratic Party's deep roots in Catholicism. While the Chilean Catholic Church came to oppose the military regime and its persecution of political opponents, it takes a traditional position on a host of ethical issues such as abortion and divorce. Many Christian Democrats follow church teachings to the left on human rights and to the right on other social issues.

8

Legislative Politics and Chile's Transition Toward Democracy

This chapter draws together the evidence about legislators' policy preferences presented in Chapters 5–7 and then applies the model of executive legislative relations from the first two chapters to explain variation in the rate of policy change across issue areas. This analysis reveals that the policy guarantees left in place by the military government are not permanent; the existing institutional framework permits a gradual shift of policy toward the position advocated by the democratically elected president. However, the speed of change ranges from very slow in some policy areas down to glacial in others. In an ironic twist it is the strong presidency written into the Constitution of 1980, presumably in the expectation that Pinochet was the most likely occupant, that operates as the primary means by which policy responds to the electoral majority.

The first section of this chapter uses the committee roll-call votes to address the question of "dimensionality." Are the observed voting alliances the same across the four issue areas analyzed in depth during the preceding chapters, or is it meaningful to think about there being multiple issue dimensions, with some legislators locating on the left on issues involving income redistribution but on the right on questions of personal morality? Comparing Senators' estimated positions across the various issue areas reveals there are at least the two issue areas just mentioned: redistributive issues revolving around the welfare state, and issues involving personal morality that emerge from a divide in Chilean politics that has existed since the nineteenth century between secular parties and those closely aligned with the Catholic Church. Notably, the human rights issue does not exist in its own issue dimension. Instead Senators' issue positions on human rights are closely tied with their positions on the welfare state, with those on the left of the welfare state issues favoring human rights reform and a more aggressive stance toward human rights violators from the period of military rule, while those on the right oppose changes from the status quo.

212

Section 2 turns to the implications of these findings about legislative politics. Attention first turns to the implications of multidimensionality. On the one hand, the institutional structure has the effect of imposing strong proposal germaneness restrictions, whose practical effect is to keep each bill unidimensional, thereby avoiding the cycling behavior that might otherwise emerge in a multidimensional setting. On the other hand, the existence of a second issue dimension connected with personal morality means that in Chile's two-candidate legislative elections, socially conservative welfare liberals, the traditional Christian Democrats, can provide a serious challenge to candidates on the right, in some cases enabling the Concertación to capture both seats in a two-member electoral district. Because the depth of the Senate majority defending the status quo varies across issue areas, so too do the legislative tactics used by the executive.

The third section of this chapter returns to the model of legislative agenda setting set forth in the first two chapters and uses it to analyze the prospects for Chile's ongoing democratic transition. The speed of reform depends on the rate at which the executive is able to devise high-valence alternatives to the status quo, the relative salience of valence issues as compared with ideological positions, and the gap between the executive and the median member of the Senate, who wields a de facto veto over reforms proposed by the executive. The human rights issue is currently one of the most gridlocked because of the large gap between the executive and the highly united opposition in the Senate, the relatively low importance of valence in this policy area, and the relative immunity of human rights questions to a changing environment. It is on this last count that we might expect change. In another generation the principals involved in human rights abuses will be deceased, and the intensity attached to attribution of responsibility for the murders committed during the period of military rule will be greatly reduced.

Section 4 turns to the incentives for the right and the left to manipulate the political agenda, with the right trying to increase the salience of personal morality issues that divide the Concertación coalition, and the left keeping the focus on the human rights issues that created it.

8.1 BEYOND LEFT AND RIGHT

The analysis encompassed three committees, and four issue areas: labor, education, human rights, and the residual social and legal agenda of the Constitution Committee, which I'll continue referring to as "social issues." Within each of these issue areas the statistical estimator recovers legislators' preferred positions on an issue-specific continuum from left to right.

With the exception of working conditions for teachers, a question that overlaps the education and labor issue areas, these four issue areas are intrinsically unconnected with one another. There is no logical reason why a position on the left of the human rights issue, for example favoring a transfer of jurisdiction over violations of the arms laws to the civilian courts, should be inconsistent with a position on the right of the labor spectrum, for example favoring a reduced minimum wage, or higher maximums on working hours. Nor does a conservative position on drug abuse intrinsically relate to one's position on school vouchers or on municipal vs. Education Ministry administration of a school. However, logical connectedness is one thing; ideology is another. To what extent do issue positions on the left of one of the four issue dimensions identified here correspond to positions on the left of one or more of the others?

A partial answer to the question of how consistent Senators' positions are across issue areas can be had by comparing the estimated positions of Senators who serve on multiple committees. Of course, we would expect some of the parameters of the model to change as we move across issue areas, even if all four areas deal with the same ideological dimension. We might expect Máximo Pacheco, a former Education Minister, to make proposals with greater appeal, as measured by the $c_{Pacheco}$ parameter, on education policy that he would on labor relations. Likewise, former Supreme Court Justice Carlos Letelier might be expected to propose judicial reforms more successfully than education policy. Similar arguments provide potential explanations for differences in the g and b parameters. However, Senators' estimated positions, their x's, are another matter.

If Senators' positions in two issue areas, say human rights and social policy, are governed by the same ideological position, then we should see their issue positions relative to one another remain the same for both sets of issues. This requires us to use a common yardstick to measure positions on the two issue areas. A total of five Senators, Diez, Fernández, Letelier, Pacheco, and Vodanovic participated sufficiently often in the Constitution Committee's debates on human rights and social policy to permit estimation of their issue positions in both areas; see Figure 8.1. In order to compare Senators' positions across issue areas, two must be chosen to normalize the scale. This was done here by placing Socialist Senator Vodanovic at a position of -1 for both human rights and social policy, while the position of Institutional Senator Letelier is normalized to 1 on both issue scales. If positions on human rights and social policy actually reflect the same underlying ideological orientation, then we should see the issue position of each of the remaining Senators remain the same relative to Senators Vodanovic and Letelier on both issues. Theoretically the remaining three Senators' estimated ideal points, reported for human rights in Table 9 and for social policy in Table 11, should lie along the dotted line

214

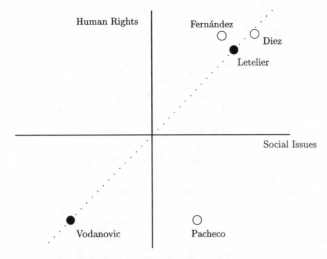

Figure 8.1. Positions on Human Rights and Social Issues.

that passes through the positions of Senators Vodanovic and Letelier. Of course, we would not expect this to be literally the case because of measurement errors in our estimates. However, if the hypothesis of a single underlying issue dimension is correct, then the differences between Senators' estimated positions and the 45° line passing through the issue positions of Vodanovic and Letelier should be small and statistically insignificant.

Examining the diagram shown in Figure 8.1, we see that the issue position of National Renovation Senator Sergio Diez is indeed very close to the predicted line: he is estimated to take an issue position somewhat to the right of Carlos Letelier on both human rights and social policy. Moreover, the very small departure of his estimated position from the 45° line, which is slightly farther right on social policy than it is on human rights, is statistically insignificant.[1] Similarly, the estimated issue position for Institutional Senator Sergio Fernández, who served as Pinochet's Minister of the Interior, is slightly farther right on human rights than it is on social policy, though again the data support the hypothesis that the estimated departure is entirely due to measurement error.[2]

---

[1] Under the null hypothesis that Senator Diez's human rights position, x^{HR}_{Diez}, and his position on social policy, x^{SP}_{Diez}, are equal, the test statistic will be asymptotically distributed as χ^2_1. The realized value for the test statistic of 0.0265 corresponds to a p value of 0.87064, leading to acceptance at all standard significance levels.

[2] Under the null hypothesis that Senator Fernández's human rights position, $x^{HR}_{Fernandez}$, and his position on social policy, $x^{SP}_{Fernandez}$ are equal, the test statistic will be asymptotically distributed as χ^2_1. The realized value for the test statistic of 0.6625 corresponds to a p value of 0.41565, leading to acceptance at all standard significance levels.

215

In stark contrast with the findings for Senators Diez and Fernández, Senator Pacheco's estimated human rights issue position of -1.002 is virtually identical with that of Senator Vodanovic, while his social policy position of 0.533 is much closer to that of Institutional Senator Sergio Fernández than it is to that of his fellow Concertación Senator Hernán Vodanovic. Not only is this departure from the 45° line large, it is highly statistically significant.[3] Moreover, if we subject the hypothesis of one ideological dimension spanning both human rights issues and social policy to the more appropriate test of the hypothesis that all five Senators simultaneously satisfy the constraint of a single issue dimension, the result remains statistically significant.[4]

The rejection of the hypothesis of a common ideological position across the human rights and social policy issue areas is driven by the large departure of Senator Pacheco's preferred policy from the 45° line. This Christian Democratic Senator did not appoint himself to the committees on which he served, and instead required the support of a substantial portion of his party's Senate delegation. This Christian Democratic Senator was simultaneously a faithful advocate of the human rights agenda he pursued during the period of military rule as cofounder of the Chilean Human Rights Committee and a committed social conservative. Pacheco, who had been President Frei's Secretary of Education, was a member of the Christian Democratic Party during its early years, when the influence of the Catholic Church on that party was strongest. His position on left for human rights but on the right on social issues is very consistent with that of Chile's Catholic Church. As the discussion of the substantive content of the social issues considered by the Constitution Committee makes clear, Senator Pacheco is not alone in this position. An important part of the Christian Democratic Senate delegation[5] share his adherence to a conservative position on moral issues, such as divorce and the decriminalization of adultery.

---

[3] Under the null hypothesis that Senator Pacheco's human rights position, $x_{\text{Pacheco}}^{\text{HR}}$, and his position on social policy, $x_{\text{Pacheco}}^{\text{SP}}$ are equal, the test statistic will be asymptotically distributed as χ_1^2. The realized value for the test statistic of 12.6068 corresponds to a p value of 0.000384, leading to rejection at all standard significance levels.

[4] Recall that $x_{\text{Vodanovic}}^{\text{HR}} = x_{\text{Vodanovic}}^{\text{SP}} = -1$ and $x_{\text{Letelier}}^{\text{HR}} = x_{\text{Letelier}}^{\text{SP}} = 1$ as a byproduct of the normalization; thus the hypothesis that all five Senators positions are identical across the two issue areas requires that we simultaneously have $x_{\text{Pacheco}}^{\text{HR}} = x_{\text{Pacheco}}^{\text{SP}}$, and $x_{\text{Diez}}^{\text{HR}} = x_{\text{Diez}}^{\text{SP}}$, and $x_{\text{Fernandez}}^{\text{HR}} = x_{\text{Fernandez}}^{\text{SP}}$. Under the null hypothesis the test statistic will be asymptotically distributed as χ_3^2. The realized value for the test statistic of 13.349 corresponds to a p value of 0.0034, leading to rejection at all standard significance levels: a single issue dimension does not capture Senators' underlying ideological positions.

[5] See the list of Christian Democrats who opposed a proposed amendment to decriminalize adultery shown in Table 13.

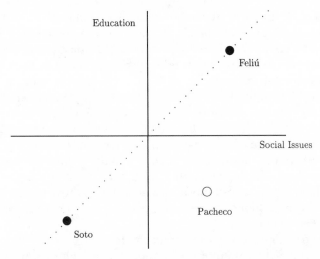

Figure 8.2. Positions on Education and Social Issues.

Similar tests can be performed by comparing the social agenda of the Constitution Committee with the Education and Labor Committees. Three Senators vote frequently on both the social agenda of the Constitution Committee and on the Education Committee. They are Senators Feliú, Pacheco, and Soto. Normalizing the preferred issue position for Senator Feliú to equal 1 while setting the preferred position for Senator Soto equal to −1, we can test the unidimensional hypothesis by checking for movement in the estimated preferred outcome for Senator Pacheco. After renormalizing the preferred outcomes reported in Table 11 by placing Senator Soto at −1 and Senator Feliú at 1, we see that the estimated preferred outcome for Senator Pacheco on the social agenda considered by the Constitution Committee[6] becomes 0.710, closer to the preferred outcome of Senator Feliú on the social issues than the Christian Democratic Senator's estimated location of −0.664, reported in Table 6, is to that of Senator Soto on the Education issues. Not only is this distance large, as can be seen from Figure 8.2; it is statistically significant.

In the case of the Labor Committee, matters are a bit less straightforward, for only two Senators, Feliú and Otero, overlap both committees. However, the Socialist party displays a high degree of cohesion, both in the coauthorship of proposals and in its daily operations. If one is willing to maintain the very reasonable hypothesis that the Socialist delegation to the Senate consists not of four policy mavericks each on his or her own

[6] The difference between the renormalized value of 0.710 and the parameter estimate of 0.533 reported in Table 11 stems from the use of Senators Feliú and Soto to normalize the ideological axis instead of Senators Letelier and Vodanovic.

policy crusade, but instead comprises highly disciplined advocates of the same policy, then one can obtain the third position by treating Socialist Senator Calderón, of the Labor Committee, and Constitution Committee Chairman Hernán Vodanovic as both advocating the same Socialist position, here normalized to equal -1. If we normalize the issue position of Senator Feliú to equal 1 in both issue areas, then the estimated preferred outcome for Senator Otero on labor policy of -0.012, reported in Table 2, differs significantly[7] from his estimated ideal policy of 1.392 on the Constitution Committee's social agenda, as reported in Table 11. As with Senator Pacheco, Senator Otero did not hold the committee assignments he did without considerable support from the remaining members of his party. Had his policy positions not coincided with those of an important segment of the National Renovation party, he would not have remained long on his committees.

It is interesting to speculate about the reasons for the difference between the unified position of the right on human rights issues, and their heterogeneity on labor relations questions. While some of this might be explained away as the result of differences in the composition of the committees, Senator Otero voted on both the human rights agenda of the Constitution Committee as well as the labor relations agenda of the Labor Committee. Why are his issue positions relative to those of Senator Feliú on the right and the Socialists on the left so different in the two settings? One possibility is that the elected Senators of the right face heterogeneous electoral constraints, so that some must compromise more than others. Perhaps in most districts no one can get elected, even in the binominal electoral system, without the support of at least some working-class voters, voters who will punish an extreme anti-labor policy. This is consistent with the unity of the right on the Education Committee. While that committee considers many labor issues, all of them deal with teachers, one of the few occupational groups to have a national union[8]; working-class voters on the right may have an easier time supporting a tough line against the teachers in particular than with employees in general.

The difference between the welfare state policies of the socially conservative Christian Democrats, and their positions on social issues such as divorce and drug abuse, can be traced to the close links between the Christian Democratic Party and the Catholic Church, and to the historical importance of Church vs. state issues in Chilean politics going back over a century.

---

[7] The χ_1^2 test statistic of 9.544 corresponds to a p value of 0.002, leading to rejection of the null hypothesis of a single dimension at all standard significance levels.

[8] Chilean labor law basically restricts unions to organize at the firm level. Because the public schools are run by the Ministry of Education, the "firm" is national, and thus the union is allowed to be as well.

Comparisons among the other three pairings of the four issue areas; between human rights and education, human rights and labor relations, and education and labor relations, are hampered by the lack of Senators overlapping the committees in each pair. However, as the preceding discussion indicates, the evidence is largely consistent with the hypothesis of a two-dimensional issue space, with one dimension corresponding to the welfare state issues that divide the left from the right throughout the industrialized world, and a second secular vs. religious dimension that deals with issues of personal morality, such as divorce and drug abuse.

There is one point at which this hypothesis fails: the issue positions of the Senators on the right are more heterogeneous on labor relations issues than they are on human rights or education policy. It may be that labor relations issues should be thought of as tapping a different ideological dimension than education policy and human rights. An alternative interpretation, which is consistent with the united position of the Concertación Senators across all three of these issue areas, is that the Senators of the right are electorally constrained by the need for support from members of the working class on the ideological right, people whose ideological loyalties come into direct conflict with self-interest on the labor relations agenda of the Labor Committee.

The heterogeneity of the issue positions taken on labor relations questions is even greater among the Institutional Senators than it is for the remaining Senators on the right, but it is perhaps easier to explain. Institutional Senators Feliú and Thayer both participated frequently in the deliberations of the Labor Committee and took dramatically distinct issue positions: while Senator Feliú was significantly to the right of the other opposition Senators, the estimated position of William Thayer is to the left of all of the National Renovation Senators.

With the death of Institutional Senator and former Air Force General Cesar Ruiz Danyau, the balance in the Senate Chamber was twenty-four Opposition and Institutional Senators, to twenty-two Concertación Senators. Of course, not every Senator was present for every vote, and not every absentee was covered by a pairing arrangement. On many polarized votes Thayer's support tended to carry amendments. When Thayer proposed an amendment to loosen the requirements imposed on firms for putting changes in the conditions in contracts into writing, a measure rejected by the Labor Committee, it was renewed and passed on the Senate floor on a fifteen to thirteen vote despite concerted opposition from the government (Biblioteca del Congreso Nacional 1993c). As a well-known moderate on labor issues, support from Thayer made it easier for opposition defectors to deflect charges that they were in the pockets of the labor unions by using Thayer's vote, and his stated arguments for political cover. By the same token, persuading an opposition defector becomes harder once Thayer has declared a position against a government initiative.

Thayer's more moderate position on labor issues has not passed unnoticed by the Concertación. From the perspective of Christian Democratic Senator Hormazábal "Willy Thayer still has a little bit of a heart" (Interview with Ricardo Hormazábal, May 20, 1997) when it comes to labor issues, adding quickly that on the question of constitutional reform he marches in lockstep with the other Institutionals. Asked why he thinks Thayer takes what seem to be ideologically inconsistent positions on labor policy and constitutional reform, Hormazábal observes that as a former Minister of Labor for Eduardo Frei, the Institutional Senator is a "prisoner of his history" (Interview with Ricardo Hormazábal, May 20, 1997), a history Senator Hormazábal is quick to recall in Senate debates by quoting pro-labor passages from Thayer's *Manual de Derecho del Trabajo* (Biblioteca del Congreso Nacional 1993e).

That the Institutional Senators do not represent a unified ideological position causes little alarm among the Institutionals themselves. In Thayer's words, "I seek that I should have the most reasonable position" (Interview with William Thayer, May 22, 1997), rather than looking to defend a particular ideology. Discussing the ideological position of the Institutionals, Olga Feliú comments "there is not exactly, I would say, a clear position coinciding with the parties of the right." While recognizing that "we Institutional Senators are not neutral"(Interview with Olga Feliú, May 26, 1997), Senator Feliú describes an intellectual basis for her policy outlook favoring free markets and the ideal of a noninterventionist state. But it is clear that she does not view promoting this policy outlook as the fundamental mission of the Institutional Senators.

While Senator Thayer sees himself as a nonideological pragmatist, his colleague Senator Feliú is correct in recognizing that the Institutional Senators are not ideologically neutral. Instead, Thayer's self-perception is a part of his ideology. Near the center of the political spectrum on labor issues, pragmatic considerations will often serve to break "ties" between a status quo on the right and proposed reforms on the left, and so Thayer, like most ideological moderates, sees himself as making practical choices. Yet he is very much a creature of ideology, and it is his moderate outlook on labor relations that makes him pivotal on labor legislation.

It is unclear why Pinochet appointed Thayer to the Senate. Thayer's sympathies for labor unions were neither concealed nor of recent vintage. A former Christian Democrat, Thayer served in the cabinet of President Eduardo Frei, his former law school professor, during the 1960s, both as the Minister of Labor and subsequently as Minister of Justice. He is also coauthor of one of the standard references on Chilean labor law (Novoa and Thayer 1997). Despite this background, Thayer supported the coup in 1973, and when the leadership of the Christian Democratic Party withdrew its early lukewarm support for the military government, Thayer remained an enthusiastic supporter. He had become a personal friend of Pinochet, whom he met when as a young man he was drafted for a brief period of military service, and he served as Chile's representative to UNESCO during the military government. For all his relative moderation on labor issues, William Thayer stands shoulder to shoulder with the other Opposition Senators on human rights questions. [9] It may be that Pinochet was primarily concerned with appointing a Senator whom he could trust to take a hard line on human rights and constitutional reform, and that labor relations was simply not as important to Pinochet as to some of his civilian allies.

Whatever interpretation one assigns to the heterogeneous labor relations positions of the Senators of the right, the results indicate that there are at least two ideological dimensions underlying the four issue areas examined here. One of these dimensions does a good job of capturing Senators' positions on both education policy and human rights, and it seems to correspond to questions about the welfare state. The association between positions on the welfare state and human rights is probably a result of the military government having used human rights violations as a weapon against their ideological opponents. A second clear dimension emerges dealing with social issues such as divorce and drug abuse. While the Socialist and PPD Senators are on the left on both the welfare state and social issues spectrums, and the Opposition Senators are consistently on the right for both, several of the Christian Democratic Senators simultaneously take welfare state positions on the left while siding with the right on social issues. This is also the position of an important element of the Chilean Catholic Church. This second dimension taps a longstanding cleavage in Chilean politics between religious and secular parties that has existed since the late nineteenth century, when Chile's political parties split over the role of the Church. Later divisions over the welfare state created a second dimension of cleavage among the parties. When Chile's Christian Democratic Party formed it had close connections with the Catholic Church, and although its party manifesto declares that it is not a confessional party, its close connections with Catholicism remain to this day.

8.2 LEGISLATIVE TACTICS

The preliminary analysis of the decision of whether to delegate power to a constitution in Chapter 2 relied on an a priori characterization of the institutions and preferences. Chapter 3 provided more detail on the

[9] See, for example, his public criticism of the Cumplido Laws quoted in Chapter 7.

workings of the legislative institutions written into the Constitution of 1980, and it showed that these institutions were well approximated by the agenda-setter model applied in Chapter 2. Chapters 5–7 provided evidence about Senators' issue positions, and with this information we can now return to the analysis of executive–legislative relations to ask about the sorts of policies the executive is likely to be able to push through. The answer to this question depends in part on the effects of the multidimensionality identified in the preceding section. The ability to bundle intrinsically unrelated policy reforms can provide the executive with a powerful advantage, as suggested by the influential analysis of McKelvey (1976). This section begins by considering the impact of multidimensionality on the legislative environment. The analysis then goes on to examine the somewhat different dynamics of executive–legislative relations in the four policy areas considered in detail in the preceding chapters: labor relations, human rights, education, and social policy.

Multidimensionality: Cycling and Duplicating

The multidimensionality of the political terrain revealed by Senators' issue positions opens up some important questions about the executive's legislative tactics. If the president is able to face Congress with bills that move policy simultaneously on both the welfare state dimension and on social policy, then the "cycling" results of McKelvey (1976) suggest the president's ability to control the outcome will expand considerably. But the opportunity to propose bills that move policy on more than one issue dimension at a time is more elusive in the rough and tumble world of Chilean politics than it is on the pages of McKelvey's famous article.

While the constitution permits the executive to make multidimensional proposals, for example a bill to raise the minimum wage and increase the resources devoted to preventing drug abuse, such a bill would have several important drawbacks. First there are the proposal germaneness restrictions offered by article 66 of the constitution, which prevents members of Congress from introducing amendments that are not directly relevant to the bill. This can keep a bill that moves policy on one dimension from being amended into a multidimensional "Christmas tree" bill festooned with ornamental amendments. By presenting a bill that crosses issue areas, the president would open the gates to multidimensional amendments as well. Then there are the constraints of having to explain proposed legislation to the voters. In McKelvey's analysis of cycling in multidimensional issue spaces (McKelvey 1976), the agenda setter can make a series of proposals, each of which commands a majority against the former, and which leads to whatever policy outcome the agenda setter wants, subject to some technical conditions on the distribution of voters' preferences that are virtually guaranteed to hold in a legislative the size of the Senate. However, in McKelvey's analysis the agenda setter is only concerned with making proposals that implement his or her desired policies. The agenda setter does not have to explain his or her activities to constituents without simultaneously alerting the legislators that they are being manipulated. There are no political opponents waiting to attack the sequence of intermediate positions McKelvey's argument calls for. Also key to the McKelvey result is a degree of myopia on the part of the voters, who do not anticipate that they are being driven through a sequence of proposals like so many cattle. If a Concertación president actually attempted to make a series of policy proposals of the sort contemplated in McKelvey's cycling argument, it is very likely the opposition would catch on quickly, and instead of voting myopically, they might unite to defeat the proposals. Moreover, some of the proposals contemplated by McKelvey can result in moving at least one dimension of policy further from the agenda setter's preferred outcome.

This could be very hard to explain to the voters, especially if one sought to do so without alerting the opposition that the eventual goal of the proposal was actually to move policy closer to the president's preferred outcome on all dimensions!

While making a sequence of insincere multidimensional proposals to manipulate the eventual outcome may not be politically viable, taking a once and for all sincere position that exploits the multidimensionality of the issue space is another matter. The binominal electoral system requires the top party list to outpoll its competitor by a two-to-one margin before it gets the second seat. This means that in a typical Senate district in which something like four-ninths of the voters supported Pinochet on the 1988 plebiscite, one of the Concertación candidates needs to receive votes from a substantial fraction of former Pinochet voters in order for the Concertación to "duplicate," winning both seats.

In a one-dimensional issue space, competing for the critical voter on the political right would entail nominating a candidate with an issue position not unlike that of the two candidates on the opposition party list, a self-defeating strategy that would result in little gain in terms of policy results even if it were to succeed, while at the same time clouding the Concertación's image in the minds of voters, leaving them confused about what issues the Concertación stood for.

But with a second issue dimension open for competition, a very effective tactic emerges: nominating candidates who are on the left on the human rights and welfare state issues central to the Concertación's policy agenda, but conservative enough on social issues such as divorce and drug abuse to appeal to a significant fraction of the former Pinochet voters. The Concertación duplicated in three Senate districts. Two of these winning tickets involved a partnership between a Christian Democrat and a Socialist,[10] while the third involved a Christian Democrat and a member of the socially liberal but electorally moribund Radical Party.[11] All three of the Christian Democrats from these duplicated districts, including Máximo Pacheco, whose estimated preferences were key in identifying the second issue dimension, were among the five Christian Democrats listed in Table 13 as voting against decriminalization of adultery. Senator Pacheco, with his position on the left for the social welfare issues and on the right for social questions, epitomizes these "duplicating" Senators.

The social conservatism of these duplicating Christian Democrats was sufficient to win over the former Pinochet voters needed to capture the second seat for the Concertación. By nominating social conservatives to pursue the second seats, the Concertación slimmed the opposition's margin in the Senate on welfare state and human rights issues at the price of conceding a Senate majority to the right for social issues, which would be seen as a cost only by the socially liberal members of the coalition. The duplicating Christian Democrats have had more success with the voters than they have enjoyed in the internal politics of their own party. In 1993, when Máximo Pacheco was up for reelection, his own party did not renominate him, instead nominating Eugenio Ortega, the brother-in-law of the Party's presidential candidate Eduardo Frei. Ortega failed to capture the second seat in the general election, which instead went to opposition candidate Fransísco Javier Errazuriz. In 1997 the Concertación did not renominate Nicolas Diaz and failed to duplicate in the Senate district he had represented, ceding one seat to UDI candidate Andrés Chadwick Piñera, who had been serving in the Chamber of Deputies. Senator Ruiz had somewhat better luck. After he was renominated he went on to survive a serious electoral challenge from Institutional Senator Sergio Fernández, who succeeded instead in displacing Socialist Rolando Calderón. While the socially conservative Christian Democrats have considerable appeal[12] to the voters, their conservative social positions make them unpopular within their own party. For social liberals within the Concertación the choice is sometimes straightforward; by not renominating Máximo Pacheco they probably conceded a seat to opposition candidate Fransísco Errazuriz, obtaining a conservative position on both social issues and the welfare state rather than on social issues alone. But the choice is not always so simple.

---

[10] In the tenth circunscripción the Concertación elected Christian Democrat Máximo Pacheco and Socialist Jaime Gazmuri, while in the nineteenth they elected Christian Democrat José Ruiz de Giorgio and Socialist Rolando Calderón.

[11] In the ninth circunscripción the Concertación elected Christian Democrat Nicolas Diaz and Radical Alma Sule.

[12] Another of the five voting against decriminalizing adultery was Andrés Zaldívar, the Christian Democratic Candidate in the 1999 Concertación presidential primary.

Had the Concertación offered a weaker candidate than José Ruiz in the nineteenth Senate district, Socialist Rolando Calderón might well have prevailed, giving the social liberals in the Concertación more of what they wanted. Of course, for socially conservative members of the Concertación, socially conservative welfare liberals always make ideal candidates.

Legislative Siege Tactics

While electoral politics may produce differently sized legislative minorities for the Concertación president in different issue areas, unless he or she is willing to bear the costs and the chaos of attempting to ram through multidimensional bills that span issue areas, he or she must approach the agenda one dimension at a time. Returning to the model of legislation developed in Chapters 1 and 2, consider again the effects of the president's advantage at being able to make high-valence proposals.

Figure 2.1 from Chapter 2 depicted the key elements of the military government's decision whether to delegate. The figure illustrated the lottery over policy during the first years after a return to civilian rule, at a time when new executive initiatives would enjoy a small advantage over the status quo. The parameter estimates from the preceding chapters show that the actual electoral outcome differed somewhat across issue areas. For labor relations the result has been a president on the left, at x_p^L, as illustrated in Figure 8.3. To gain approval in the Senate, which the opposition controlled by a margin of two votes,[13] the Concertación needed to hold on to all of its own Senators while bringing over at least two opposition Senators. Thus on labor policy the defection of Senator Thayer plus one other member of the opposition (or fewer depending on the partisan balance of absentees on the day of the vote) would suffice to win. While there were large divisions among the opposition on the Labor Committee, revealed in Table 2 and Figure 8.5, the government did not need the votes of Senators like Miguel Otero or Olga Feliú to pass its bills; it needed only to tempt one or two of the Senators on the left edge of the opposition. The preference parameters shown in Table 2 reveal considerable heterogeneity among the preferred policies of the Senators of the right, so to pass a bill the Concertación only needs the support of one or two Senators from the left edge of the opposition, at a point like x_c^L in Figure 8.3. This lies within region F_2, an area of legislative executive compromise where

---

[13] Before the November 21, 1990 death of Institutional Senator Ruiz Danyau, the opposition had twenty-five Senate seats, and the Concertación twenty-two, so that if all Senators were voting the Concertación could prevail with the support of all of its own Senators and the defection of two opposition Senators. After Ruiz Danyau died the margin went to twenty-four seats against twenty-two, so that all the government Senators plus one defector would lead to a tie vote, while the government contingent plus two would carry the question.

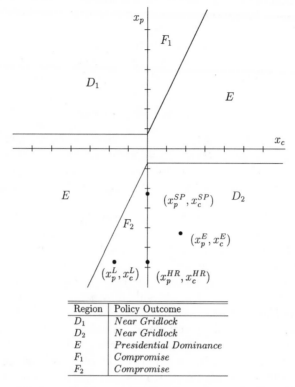

Region	Policy Outcome
D_1	Near Gridlock
D_2	Near Gridlock
E	Presidential Dominance
F_1	Compromise
F_2	Compromise

Figure 8.3. Issue Positions and Policy Outcomes: the Short Run.

the president is able to "leapfrog" the position of the median member of the "blocking chamber," in this case the Senate, to propose reforms to the left of the median. The result is a fairly rapid leftward evolution of labor relations policy, with legalization of unions, increased minimum wages, and expanded grievance procedures.

If, as suggested here, the labor policy equilibrium is one of executive-legislative compromise, with the executive essentially picking off the vote of Senator Thayer, then we should see the president's legislative tactics tailored to the idiosyncrasies of this one Senator. That is, we should see the president pay especially close attention to Senator Thayer's "preference shocks" that might lead him to support a measure despite its ideological content having been slightly farther than the status quo from his preferred outcome. Such tactics would enable the president to move labor policy farther leftward than he could if he had to deal with a united opposition, determined to vote as a block on key bills, as we observe on human rights questions.

226

How would these idiosyncratic tactics work? The process will be essentially the same whenever the president needs the support of only one or two key legislators who are not subject to party discipline, and it is useful to illustrate it for the case of William Thayer on labor relations policy. To begin with, we know that not all proposals with the same ideological characteristics are accepted by a given voter. Instead of there being a deterministic relationship between the ideological content of the proposal, the ideological orientation of the legislator and the legislator's vote, legislative approval becomes more likely as the ideological affinity between legislator and proposal rises. Instead of always voting for the closer alternative, legislators sometimes depart from this rule for idiosyncratic reasons. These departures are represented in the model by idiosyncratic preference shocks, but they can be thought of as corresponding to numerous idiosyncratic factors, such as personal contacts with lobbyists, special expertise, and nonideological idiosyncratic aspects of a legislator's world view. This means that instead of the success probability for observations being equal to 1 if they are closer to the preferred point of the median Senator than is the status quo, falling to 0 if they are any distance farther, success probabilities respond more smoothly. The random preference shocks soften the lines of the political landscape.

In the case of the Labor Committee we can work with the parameter estimates presented in Table 2 to infer how executive proposals would have fared had their displacement from the status quo been changed.[14] The parameter estimates are subject to estimation error, calibrated by their standard errors. However, if they were exact, and there were no preference shocks, then given the ancillary assumptions discussed in footnote 14, any executive proposal moving policy leftward to a smaller degree than -11.04, that is with $g_{exec} > -11.04$, would meet with approval from Senator Thayer, while he would balk at any leftward proposal past this threshold. In contrast with this stark prediction, the probabilistic model maintains that the probability of an affirmative vote responds more smoothly to changes in the leftward displacement of the executive's proposals from the status quo; see Figure 8.4. There we see that as the executive makes increasingly leftward reforms, the probability falls that an idiosyncratic preference shock, or an unusually high draw on quality,

---

[14] To do this we must make a conjecture about the location of the status quo. Recall that the c_{exec} parameter depends on two unknown parameters, the executive's valence advantage, va_{exec}, and the midpoint of the status quo and the proposal. Normalizing the status quo to equal 1 makes sense given that in sixteen and a half years of rule the military government had probably brought policy in line with its preferences, which might reasonably be expected to coincide with the right edge of the political spectrum, which for the Labor Committee coincides with the preferred policy of Senator Feliú. Given this value for the status quo, straightforward calculations reveal that the "valence advantage" for the executive over the status quo is 1.67.

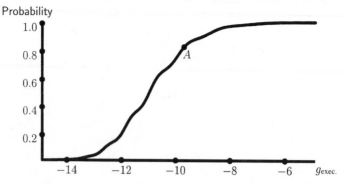

Figure 8.4. Probability Thayer Approves an Executive Proposal as a Function of g_{exec}.

will garner Senator Thayer's support. These calculations indicate that the estimated leftward displacement for executive proposals of -9.69 will meet with the support of Senator Thayer with a probability of 0.83; see the point marked "A" in Figure 8.4. This is not far from the value of $g_{exec} = -11.04$ that would guarantee success as predicted by the simpler version of the model that ignores idiosyncratic preference shocks and variation in the consensus quality of proposals from a given sponsor. Randomness means that if the executive pushes farther leftward from -11.04, he or she might get lucky, and win approval for the proposal, while if the executive draws back a bit he or she buys insurance.

If the executive could make an infinite number of proposals, he or she could in effect ignore the Senate median, making proposal after proposal at his or her own most preferred outcome, x_E, knowing that eventually the idiosyncratic shocks of the pivotal voter would exceed the threshold at which the proposal of x_E would gain approval. Of course, the executive does not have infinite resources, but the executive can use the ones he or she has to "lean" in his or her preferred direction, proposing a torrent of legislation and accepting a somewhat lower success rate, thereby obtaining more advantageous policies. This strategy has a second aspect: with a busy calendar and the use of "urgencies" provided in article 71 of the constitution and articles 26–28 of the Organic Law of Congress, the executive can overwhelm opposition Senators with a flood of bills, using his or her urgency powers to limit the time they have to evaluate each. This approach hardly fosters open and democratic deliberation, but it can be an effective means for the executive to pry policy concessions from a reluctant median Senator. This fact has not been lost on either the executive or the opposition, with Institutional Senator Feliú complaining that there are far too many laws proposed to permit full and careful deliberation (Interview with Olga Feliú, May 26, 1997).

In the case of the Labor Committee, the executive is very attentive to the opinions of Senator Thayer. The Labor Minister precleared proposals with this pivotal opposition Senator in a search of reforms that would move policy leftward and coincide with positive preference "shocks" for this legislator, thereby getting more ideological mileage out of a given bill. Thus in 1997, when the executive decided to reform the laws governing collective negotiation, he was careful to arrange an academic conference on the subject, at which various options for reform were discussed, and Professor William Thayer Arteaga (a.k.a. the median Senator on labor policy) gave an invited presentation on "collective negotiation and the challenges of the new economy for businesses and unions." The three-day conference (Universided de Las Condes 1997) ended in a round-table discussion which included the members of the Labor Committee, with Senator Thayer among the moderators! Having thus scouted the minefield, the government had advance notice of the idiosyncratic preference "shocks" of the Senate median and could make the most of its reform bill.

In contrast with the preceding discussion of labor legislation, when the two sides are each united and disciplined, so that adherents share similar preferred outcomes, the executive will have a hard time luring just the one or two opposition Senators the executive needs to vote for his or her project. Instead the executive will have to persuade the entire opposition. This is what we observe for bills related to human rights, where the Concertación and the executive share a preferred outcome on the left, a point like x_p^{HR} in Figure 8.3, while the opposition are united in defense of the status quo at x_c^{HR}. The combination (x_p^{HR}, x_c^{HR}) lies on the edge of region D_2 in Figure 8.3, corresponding to near gridlock. Given a valence advantage for his or her proposals over the status quo, the president can still move policy slightly in his or her preferred direction, but the payoff will be limited. This is what occurred with the Cumplido laws. Because the opposition were united, the government could not cut a separate deal with a few key Senators, so when the Cumplido laws were gutted by the opposition-controlled Senate Constitution Committee, Minister Cumplido had to hold meetings with the leaders of the National Renovation Party to identify amendments that would make key aspects of the laws acceptable to them (El Mercurio 1990c). Because the RN leaders involved in the negotiations were constrained by the need to maintain the approval of a substantial fraction of their party, Minister Cumplido was not in a position to take advantage of the leaders' idiosyncrasies in the way the Concertación was able to do with Senator Thayer.

The situation of near gridlock for human rights measures is very similar to the near deadlock over education policy. There again the government and the opposition each cleave to united positions at opposite ends of the spectrum. However, because technology is changing faster in education than in human rights, the president enjoys a greater valence advantage. For example, he can take advantage of the need to introduce computers into the schools to favor the public schools over the subsidized private ones and induce grudging acceptance from the opposition Senators. Education policy is an example of an area in which the opposition Senators would like to see reform, rather than continuation of the status quo. This configuration is illustrated as (x_p^E, x_c^E) in Figure 8.3, to the right of the vertical axis, and inside region D_2. The educational reforms sought by the opposition Senators, in the form of added support for schools in the subsidized sector, are in the opposite direction from the pro-public school reforms sought by the government. The Senators of the right are unable to get their proposed reforms through the double hurdle of the Chamber of Deputies and the executive veto. The result is near gridlock, but with somewhat faster movement leftward, caused by the somewhat higher advantage in consensus quality for the president's proposals in this issue area.

Social legislation, dealing with the divorce laws, drug abuse, and other related moral concerns, is a more complicated case. There the opposition are joined by a significant contingent from the Christian Democratic party. While some of these Senators have had trouble getting renominated within their own party, it is worth noting that the party's candidate in the 1999 Concertación primaries for the presidency, Andrés Zaldívar, is also a social conservative. The combination of a welfare state position on the left and a moral position on the right is still appealing to many of Chile's voters, and this gives the socially conservative Christian Democrats some staying power within the Concertación, even if many party leaders are not comfortable with it. To be sure, the youngest of the voters who propelled Eduardo Frei to the presidency in 1964 during the heyday of the Christian Democrats' fusion of Catholicism and leftward reforms on the welfare state are now well past age fifty. It may be that over time a younger and more worldly generation of Chileans will embrace social conservatism less enthusiastically, but for now the socially conservative wing of the Christian Democratic Party is an important part of the Concertación, and it acts as a constraint on how far the government can move policy leftward in this area. At the same time, these social conservatives are not confined to the Congress; many of them participate in the cabinet and help the president to decide what sort of reforms to propose. This has the effect of bringing the executive rightward on these issues as well. Returning to

Figure 8.3, we see that the configuration for social policy may correspond to a point like (x_p^{SP}, x_c^{SP}), with a congressional median near the status quo and a president who seeks only modest leftward reforms. This is on the edge of the region of near gridlock, and so while the president will move policy leftward over time, he will do so slowly.

8.3 POLICY REFORM AND THE INSTITUTIONAL ENCLAVES

The bulwark of institutional enclaves built into the Constitution of 1980 by the military government creates a powerful status quo bias. For the time being this bias is a source of great frustration for the Concertación coalition, even though they occupy the president's palace and run many of the executive agencies; though not the armed forces, their hands are tied: the policies they implement were chosen by the military government, and the Concertación have thus far made little progress in modifying them – thus the exasperated comments about having "Pinochet without Pinochet."

The analysis of four policy areas, labor, education, human rights, and social policy, indicates that the pace of change ranges from slow to glacial. In labor relations the Concertación was able to exploit divisions on the right to shift policy leftward at a faster rate than in the other areas. At the opposite end of the spectrum, both the Concertación and the opposition Senators are galvanized by the human rights issue, which lies at the core of each group's political alliance. Fundamentally, this issue area captures attitudes toward the former military government more clearly than any other. The Concertación began as an alliance against continued military rule between former political enemies, the Christian Democrats and the Socialists. The human rights issue touches the core of this coalition's agenda. The opposition Senators, both the elected Senators of the right and the Institutional Senators put in place by Pinochet, are similarly united on the other side of the issue. For them the military government represented salvation from Communism, and protecting participants in the former military government is a top priority. Not only is the opposition united on the human rights issue, but in contrast with the changing workplace, which is continually adapting to technological progress, there is less scope for valence considerations in the ambit of human rights. All might recognize the importance of improved workplace safety standards that incorporate recent advances in the understanding of the link between chemical exposure and cancer, changes that the government can exploit to shift policy leftward, forcing the right to choose between no safety standards and standards biased somewhat in favor of workers. But on human rights, advances in the analysis of DNA evidence will do little to tempt the opposition to vote for a more aggressive approach to the human rights issue. Thus progress on human rights has been glacial.

In all policy areas the Concertación has had some legislative success. While the pace of change varies across issue areas, it is nonetheless in the direction preferred by the Concertación. Moreover, this slow movement in policy toward that favored by the government is also encountered in the Concertación's gradually increasing control over the bureaucracy, the courts, and the institutional enclaves, even including the armed forces. As in the legislative arena, each of these elements of the government has been the object of a patient, sustained, and often quiet campaign by the executive. Through the careful manipulation of appointments the Concertación is very slowly gaining control of the government. As in the legislative arena, the pace of change varies across issue areas. The judiciary has proven particularly difficult to control, as judges from the period of military rule have promoted their friends within the judiciary while proving reluctant to retire. During the Frei administration, which began in March 1994, the judiciary became the object of a major proposed reform. This would involve a reorganization that would make the slow and often inefficient legal system more expeditious, and not incidentally, it would create a number of new positions and promotion ladders within the judiciary, positions creating a way around the Maginot line of judges left over from the Pinochet period.

Of all the enclaves, military appointments have proven least permeable to presidential influence. Article 93 of the constitution requires that the president choose the heads of the armed forces from a list of the five most senior members of their respective branches of the armed forces, and they serve four-year nonrenewable terms, during which the president cannot dismiss them without the approval of the National Security Council, which is itself dominated by the commanders in chief of the armed forces.[15] This leaves the president with scant leverage over the heads of the armed forces, and gaining the ability to dismiss recalcitrant generals is a top legislative priority for the Concertación, though the needed votes for changing the constitution to allow this are nowhere in sight. Of course, the president can choose among the five most senior candidates, and this gives him or her some leverage ex ante over ambitious officers climbing the promotion ladder, but this is an awfully slender reed by which to hang civilian control over the military!

---

[15] The eight-member National Security Council includes the commanders of the Army, the Navy, the Air Force, and the Carbineers, plus the president of the Republic, the controller general of the Republic, and the presidents of the Senate and Supreme Court. The Supreme Court is itself an institutional enclave insulated from presidential or electoral control, and so the four heads of the armed forces plus the president of the Supreme Court constitute an absolute majority of the National Security Council.

Across the board the involvement of the courts, the armed forces, and the office of the controller general in the selection of the Institutional Senators, and in the case of the courts and the armed forces, in the selection of the Constitutional Tribunal, has tended to politicize appointments within these institutions. This tendency toward politicization subsequently led one former member of the Ortúzar Committee that drafted the constitution, Sergio Diez, to favor abolition of the Institutional Senators. From his perspective, the Institutionals had done their job well; they had prevented an outbreak of revenge against participants in the former military government and had given Chile time to adapt to the return of civilian rule, but he opined that the cure was becoming worse than the disease, and that the continued existence of the Institutionals was beginning to entail a destructive politicization of the institutions selecting them (Interview with Sergio Diez, May 27, 1997).

On one count Senator Diez is absolutely right: political criteria for promotion in the courts and the armed forces are destructive. Of course, the promotion process within the courts and the armed forces during the Pinochet government was not politically neutral.[16] Indeed, as Institutional Senators Feliú observed, "We Institutional Senators are not neutral" (Interview with Olga Feliú May 26, 1997). What is ever so slowly changing is not the existence of political bias within the institutional enclaves, but its direction. As time passes the Concertación are gaining control over the institutional enclaves built into the constitution. Even as they slowly succeed in shifting the status quo in their desired direction, so too they are slowly acquiring the ability to preserve the new status quo by using the same institutional enclaves that have caused them so much grief until now.

As the Concertación gain control of the enclaves, and as they succeed in moving the status quo in their direction, the heavy status quo bias built into the constitution will become more to their liking. Consider the lottery over policy outcomes illustrated by Figure 8.5, where the Concertación have already succeeded in moving the status quo in their direction, for the sake of illustration, from the initial status quo at 0, as illustrated in Figure 2.1 of Chapter 2, to a position of -2, still somewhat to the right of the most preferred outcome of the Concertación. As at the outset there are two likely outcomes. First, the Concertación may remain in control of the presidency and have to pass their bills through the opposition-controlled Senate. Then there is the second possibility that the Concertación will lose the presidency to the opposition. Given some uncertainty about the exact ideological positions of the future Concertación president, for the sake of illustration suppose his or her position is uniformly distributed

---

[16] For a careful analysis of Pinochet's use of the Army promotion ladder to consolidate his power within the military government, see Arriagada (1989).

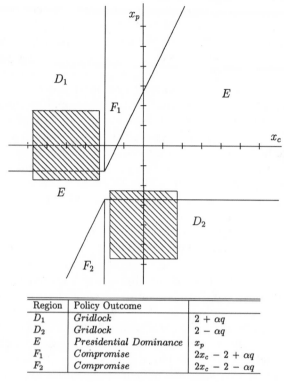

Region	Policy Outcome	
D_1	*Gridlock*	$2 + \alpha q$
D_2	*Gridlock*	$2 - \alpha q$
E	*Presidential Dominance*	x_p
F_1	*Compromise*	$2x_c - 2 + \alpha q$
F_2	*Compromise*	$2x_c - 2 - \alpha q$

Figure 8.5. Policy Outcomes with a Status Quo of -2 and $\alpha q = \frac{4}{5}$.

with mean -4 and variance 1, and for the median Senator, suppose his or her position is distributed uniformly with mean 0 and variance 1; the preferred outcomes of the president, x_p (on the vertical axis), and the median member of the Senate, x_c (on the horizontal axis), will correspond to a point in the shaded square located in the lower center of the diagram. It is also possible, though less likely, that the opposition will gain control of the presidency. In that case, barring an even more major and less likely reversal of electoral fortunes, the opposition president would face a legislative veto by the Concertación in the Chamber of Deputies. Given uncertainty about the precise policy preferences of the potential future opposition president and Concertación contingent in the Deputies, the set of possible combinations of x_p and x_c corresponds to a point somewhere in the shaded square on the left of Figure 8.5.

In contrast with the "medium run" prospects for policy at the end of the period of military rule, illustrated in Figure 2.1, the medium term lottery facing the Concertación after a decade or so in power is much more favorable. Should the opposition regain control of the presidency the most likely outcome corresponds to a point in region D_1, with the opposition president facing a situation of near gridlock against a Concertación-controlled Chamber of Deputies. The president would only be able to roll back the policy gains of the Concertación very slowly. In the more likely outcome of continued Concertación control of the presidency the likely outcome would be a point somewhere in region D_2, corresponding to near gridlock and a continued slow drift of policy toward the preferred outcome for the Concertación. In either case the expected policy outcome will be somewhere in the neighborhood of the new status quo. Only a very leftward-leaning opposition in the Senate (not out of the question if the Concertación can appoint enough of its own Institutional Senators) combined with a rightward-leaning Concertación president, or a rightward-leaning Concertación Chamber of Deputies combined with a leftward-leaning opposition president (a much less likely outcome), would result in outcomes in region E, corresponding to executive dominance.

In December 1997 the Concertación were less successful in the electoral arena than they had hoped, ending up with only twenty seats in the Senate in contrast with the twenty-two Senate seats they won in the 1989 elections. At the same time, the selection of the Institutional Senators was more favorable to the Concertación than one would have expected. In addition to two presidential appointees, Edgardo Boeninger and Augusto Parra, the Supreme Court appointed Enrique Silva, a long-standing member of the Radical Party. Silva is likely to sympathize with the Concertación, while another Institution Senators, Enrique Zurita, caucuses with the three Senators just mentioned rather than with the larger group of Institutional Senators aligned with the opposition. This suggests that there are at least three, and maybe four, Institutional Senators sympathetic to the Concertación. The additional success of the Concertación at influencing the appointment of the Institutionals was predictable, and they may enjoy even more success in another eight years. The current group of Institutionals includes Augusto Pinochet, now in his eighties and in exile, to whom the Constitution awards a Senate seat as a former president. The language of the Constitution precludes such a Senate seat for Patricio Aylwin, the first civilian president of Chile since military rule, but not for the current president, Eduardo Frei, who will be eligible to occupy a Senate seat when his presidential term expires in March 2000. Over time the bias of the Institutional Senators toward the former military regime is likely to fade.

In contrast, the electoral setbacks for the Concertación in the December 1997 elections seem to be part of an adaptation of party competition to the electoral system. The 1997 contest was complicated by the Communist Party's backing a third-party list of protest candidates, who took votes from the Socialists. However, the Communists failed to elect any of the candidates they backed, and the maneuver may have been part of an attempt to broker their way into the Concertación. It seems unlikely that they will be either willing or indefinitely able to continue to running protest candidates who garner enough votes to hurt the Socialists. The underlying pressure in the binominal electoral system is toward policy divergence. Parties near the political center run the risk of losing voters on both sides. While during the initial elections after the return to civilian rule individuals' preexisting party loyalties had a large influence on their votes, with the passage of time voters have adjusted their support toward new parties, like the PPD on the left and the UDI on the right, while older loyalties have faded. This suggests that over time the surviving legislative parties will adapt to the binominal electoral system. To the extent that competition takes place on a single dimension, running from left to right, there will be a group of parties seeking the allegiance of the critical voter needed to ensure a vote share of one-third coming from the left of the political spectrum, and another group competing for the pivotal voter needed to garner the rightmost third of the electorate. Thus we should see a tendency toward partial polarization, with parties like the UDI and the PPD that do not strive for the support of the median voter doing well in legislative elections. While the effect of the electoral system has not worked instantly, over several electoral cycles the face of party competition is adapting to the new rules.

The net effect of the changes has been to keep the Concertación from achieving a majority in the Senate, with their gains in influence over the selection of the Institutionals being counterbalanced, for the time being, by the electoral gains of the right. In this environment, corresponding to the lower central shaded square in Figure 8.5, the Concertación can count on a slow leftward drift of policy toward their preferred outcome. This means that over time their stake in the status quo policy, and so in the system that preserves it, is increasing. This raises the very real possibility that the Concertación will be coopted by the system of institutional enclaves, preferring to take it over rather than to dismantle it. Of course, there is relatively little practical difference between being coopted and trapped. Dismantling the system would be no trivial undertaking; the Senate supermajority needed to amend the constitution is likely to elude the Concertación for some time to come, meaning that constitutional reform would be difficult even if the Concertación parties remain committed to it.

8.4 HUMAN RIGHTS, SOCIAL ISSUES, AND THE DEMOCRATIC TRANSITION

The Concertación and the opposition divide over the welfare state, with the Concertación on the left and the opposition on the right of questions about taxes, income redistribution, labor unions, minimum wages, and public education. Two other issue areas exist alongside this classic division: human rights and social issues. Questions surrounding the legacy of deaths and disappearances left behind by the military government, and questions about the extent of special powers that should be delegated to the president and the armed forces in case of future emergencies, sharply divide right from left, while they create powerful unity within each group.

Senators' positions on human rights closely resemble their positions on the welfare state, with a strong bipolar structure emerging. This is true even though there is no intrinsic connection between the two issue areas. Limiting the jurisdiction of the military courts, or bringing members of the armed forces to account for past misdeeds, has very little to do in principal with the setting of the minimum wage, or with the level of the top tax bracket. Nevertheless, as Table 1 illustrated, human rights violations were systematically related to the political issues dividing the right from the left. The military government targeted members of the political parties of the left for torture and murder. Such policies leave changed political attitudes in their wake. To use the terminology of Carmines and Stimson (1989), human rights is an "easy" issue. While the details of tax policy and labor regulation may be complex, the argument that the policies of the military government are the policies of murderers is easy to understand. The logic of this argument is flawed; one might just as well say that Volkswagen owners are war criminals because Hitler's government introduced the VW. However, this does not rob the argument of its visceral appeal. While it began along the lines of what Carmines and Stimson might classify as an "external disruption," created by the military government's blundering cruelty, the human rights issue was was seized as a potent political weapon against the military government and its policies. Not only does the issue galvanize Socialists and Communists, who bore the brunt of the repression; the Christian Democrats are also swayed by the power of the issue, and they can be spurred to vote against policies that are identified as the "policies of oppressors" and not merely to vote against the repression. This makes the human rights issue a powerful one for supporters of the welfare state, though it simultaneously keeps open a potentially very dangerous area of conflict.

The capacity for human rights abuses to galvanize more general agendas is by no means peculiar to Chile. In China the cold indifference of the

Chinese government toward the "great leap forward famine" spawned by its own agricultural collectivization policies reshaped political attitudes toward Communist Party doctrine in the areas of China most severely scoured by famine (Yang 1996). For a generation after the U. S. Civil War, Republican candidates in the northern U. S. would "wave the bloody shirt," reminding supporters of the participation of many Democrats in the southern rebellion. While this tactic had powerful political appeal, it did little to reconcile postwar animosities!

The second issue area deals with issues of personal morality, such as drug abuse and divorce. While the political right are united in support of a morally conservative traditional approach to these issues, the Christian Democrats are deeply divided. With its roots in Catholicism, the Christian Democratic Party has many members who are simultaneously with the left in support of the welfare state and with the right on matters of personal morality. This constellation of issue positions is in keeping with an important strand of teaching in the Catholic Church, but it creates an important source of division within the Christian Democratic Party and the Concertación. The Socialists, the PPD, and the Radicals, all coalition partners of the Christian Democrats, take a more libertarian stance on questions of personal morality, even including drug abuse. While the Christian Democrats are loath to go as far as that, an important segment of the party nevertheless favors a much less traditional approach to issues of personal morality. Consider the amendment discussed in Chapter 7 to decriminalize adultery. Some of the most impassioned speeches on both sides of the issue came from Christian Democrats, and the Christian Democratic delegation was the only one to divide its votes on that question.

The importance of the human rights and social issues, the former knitting the Concertación closer together, the latter with the potential to pull both the Christian Democratic Party and the Concertación apart, has not been lost on the politicians. Legislators on the left know that one of the most reliable ways to hold the loyalties of wavering voters (and the politicians who represent them) is to keep reminding people of the human rights issue at every turn. They invoke the name of Pinochet more often than the former general's supporters, and continually inject reminders of the military government into the public debate. To an important extent this undoubtedly stems from heartfelt anger. Yet it is also a very effective means of rallying their supporters. The Concertación was formed to combat Pinochet, and combat him they will.

Perhaps the clearest statement of the nature of the appeal of the human rights issue to people on the left comes from Ronald Ramm, an activist campaigning for a "no" vote against Pinochet in the 1988 plebiscite: "If you vote yes, you are approving all the murders they have committed since 1973" (Constable and Valenzuela 1991). Barbed references to the military government also tended to boil up during legislative debates. During the debate on the teacher's statute,[17] President Aylwin and Senator Vodanovic introduced an amendment to require private schools using former municipal school buildings that had been "privatized" during the period of military rule to return those facilities to the municipalities. During the discussion Senator Hormazábal quipped, "I certainly value the opinion of the Senators of the Opposition, who also posses the comparative advantage of having participated in the drafting of the Constitution of 1980, while others of us could not enter the debate"(Biblioteca del Congreso Nacional 1991a). The debate turned on the standing of the private schools as "legal persons." In response to arguments that according to general principals of law the private schools, as "legal persons," could not be deprived of property without due process, Senator Hormazábal retorted "I would have liked it if the rights and attributes that converted human beings into fictitious persons during the previous regime [18] had also been applied in accord with the general principals of the law"(Biblioteca del Congreso Nacional 1991a). While these remarks, and a host of similar ones made by Concertación Senators during legislative debates, were not germane to the technical issue at hand, they were politically effective, linking the substantive question at hand with politically important beliefs about the illegitimacy of the military government.

The potential for social issues touching on personal morality to divide the Concertación has not escaped the attention of politicians on the right. Chile remains a socially conservative country, where the Catholic Church wields considerable influence. This means that on social issues the traditional position of the opposition and some of the Christian Democrats appeals to more voters than the more libertarian position of the parties of the left. National Renovation Deputy Teodoro Ribera optimistically predicts the declining salience of the issues surrounding the democratic transition, with the political debate coming to revolve around issues of personal morality such as abortion, drug abuse, and homosexuality (Interview with Teodoro Ribera, May 1997). He is certainly right that such a shift of emphasis would favor the right and divide the Concertación, as it does whenever such issues come up for legislative debate. However, as a prediction it probably represents a certain amount of wishful thinking on the part of this opposition legislator. While the Institutional Senators and the binominal electoral system remain, the Concertación will almost certainly be able to ensure that the specter of Pinochet continues to haunt legislative debates and election campaigns. Moreover, this prognosis ignores the importance placed on the traditional conflict between left and right

---

[17] This subsequently became Law No. 19.070.

[18] The armed forces on some occasions used the legal maneuver of insisting that people whom they had abducted and killed were fictitious, and thus had never existed.

on the welfare state. The commitment of the morally conservative Christian Democratic Senators to a position on the left on questions involving the welfare state is real. Any electoral alliance or coalition government involving the National Renovation Party on the right and the morally conservative Christian Democrats on the left, a possibility that is occasionally discussed in the press and around dinner tables in Chile, would be a very uneasy marriage indeed. While disagreements about income redistribution and free markets are much less severe than they were during the democratic breakdown of the early 1970s, that is hardly the right standard by which to measure consensus! On a host of substantive issues, from public education to unions, to minimum wages, to tax policy, the differences between the National Renovation Party and the more socially conservative Christian Democrats are substantial and would work against any long-term political alliance.

The ongoing importance of the human rights issue raises some important questions about the durability of the transition. While the left are committed to holding individuals in the armed forces accountable for the human rights violations that took place during the period of military rule, the military is equally determined to prevent any such thing. In 1994 the Army staged what has been called the *boinazzo*,[19] a show of force in which the army took to the streets of Santiago in combat fatigues for "maneuvers" while Pinochet and the other generals lobbied for the executive to intervene in legal proceedings against Pinochet's son and members of the armed forces for their activities during the period of military rule. Behind the many layers of institutional guarantees there remains the simple stark fact that the armed forces have the weapons. As long as they are able to remain somewhat independent of civilian control, the potential for trials and investigations that go farther than the military would like is limited. The military retreated into the barracks, but they did not surrender.

The situation that prevails today in Chile is somewhat reminiscent of the Cold War during the 1970s, by which time the likelihood of nuclear war had dropped to a very low level. However, this low probability was not the result of the weapons' being ineffective. Had either side crossed the other's threshold of tolerance, missiles would have flown and millions would have died. But by the 1970s each side had learned enough to avoid overstepping the bounds. Something similar seems to be happening in Chile. The hunger for retribution has grown less intense among those on the left, and the level of fear among those leading the armed forces is lower that at the beginning of the transition.

While it is unlikely that any Chilean politicians would have probed the boundaries of this equilibrium, as this book was going to press Spanish Judge Garzón did just that, issuing a warrant for Pinochet's arrest while he

---

[19] The name comes from the red caps or *boinas* worn by the soldiers.

was recuperating from surgery in a London hospital. Pinochet's arrest has heightened the polarizing human rights issue in Chile, even displacing the Latin American financial crises from the front pages of Chile's newspapers.

Thus far there have been no great surprises. Immediately after Pinochet's arrest many legislators on the right boycotted Congress, but this achieved nothing, and they have stopped. The Concertación, which formed around a shared opposition to military rule, has maintained a united front in the Senate. When dual resolutions about the handling of the Pinochet affair came to a vote in the Senate in late 1998, the chamber divided along party lines, with the Concertación all voting in favor of one and against the other, and the Senators of the elected opposition parties voting in block against the Concertación position, while the Institutional Senators split according to their loyalties, with the Frei appointees siding with the Concertación. Likewise, the Frei administration has worked very hard to avoid panicking the heads of the armed forces. Nevertheless, the crisis has revealed some cracks within the Concertación, with some members of the Socialist and PPD parties essentially arguing in favor of Pinochet's extradition to Spain, while others adhere to the official position of the Concertación that Pinochet should be returned to Chile to face justice. Thus far the leadership has managed to hold the Concertación together on this vital issue.

The policy of the Concertación has been that Pinochet should return to Chile to face justice, and they have worked very hard to secure his return. What would happen if Pinochet were returned to Chile and the Concertación had to make good on its now-avowed policy of subjecting Pinochet to Chilean justice is an open question. Also unclear at this writing is how the Chilean right would react if Pinochet were in fact extradited to Spain and put on trial. One suspects that should Pinochet return to Chile the Concertación would respect the military's auto-amnesty for crimes committed in 1978 or earlier, but would find some way to bring charges under international law that would leave Pinochet tangled in the courts for the rest of his life. With Pinochet back in Chile stirring up the general staff, it would prove very risky to actually jail him. Likewise it seems most likely that the right would not back a sustained, and very costly, boycott of commerce with Spain were Pinochet to be extradited, while the left would probably continue to support symbolic efforts to return Pinochet to Chile. Regardless of where Pinochet spends the remainder of his days, we can expect heightened divisions between the left and the right as the polarizing human rights issue is kept in the public spotlight. The more time the Concertación must spend defending their former tormentor in foreign courts, the greater the danger that the military will interpret the course of events as evidence of the importance of retaining their independence from civilian control, in order to preserve the credibility of their threat to seize power.

Conclusion

When aircraft encounter turbulent storm conditions, the principals of aerodynamic design are not suddenly suspended. In the same way the dynamic political equilibrium during a democratic transition depends on the interaction of political actors' objectives and beliefs with the institutional constraints, just as it does in more normal times, notwithstanding the emotionally charged content of objectives that include victims' quest for justice and despite sudden changes in institutional constraints. The Chilean transition is notable for its reliance on a set of temporary policy guarantees that the former military government imposed as the price of transition. These policy conditions are protected by a series of institutional checks on a powerful and democratically elected executive. If one were to simply import the state-of-the-art models of gridlock used to analyze the U. S. Congress, this arrangement would seem to provide a permanent framework for indirect military rule. However, the family of models based on the agenda-setter model of Romer and Rosenthal (1978) ignores the potential for the agenda setter, in this case the Chilean president, to exploit the valence component of policy to pry acceptance from the veto player, in this application the median member of the Senate, for policy positions closer to the agenda setter and farther from the Senate median.

In the Chilean transition the president's ability to couple high-valence policy reforms with movements in the ideological content of policy has profound implications for the long-run effects of the constitution imposed by the military government. The preceding analysis has shown that the president's ability to use this lever implies that policy will gradually come into line with the outcome preferred by the executive, and the electoral majorities that sustain him or her in power. This alignment will be more rapid in policy areas in which legislators' positions are less polarized, with relatively greater weight on the valence component of policy compared with its ideological position, and for which the pace of change is more rapid, so that opportunities for reform open more frequently.

242

Conclusion

In the Chilean case this means that all of the policy guarantees imposed by the Pinochet government are temporary, but, as George Orwell might say, some are more temporary than others. In case of the human rights issue, which is shared in some variant by virtually every transition from Eastern Germany to South Africa, the position issue is the treatment of those involved in the human rights abuses committed under the auspices of the Pinochet government, while the valence component of policy deals with the guarantee of no future human rights abuses. For the present the Chilean solution involves virtually no change from the policy left in place by the Pinochet government. The two sides are polarized, and the valence issue has relatively low salience relative to the position issue of prosecutions. There are those on the left willing to risk another round of military intervention in their pursuit of the guilty, and those on the right who would sooner see the military intervene again than tolerate accusations and trials. Nor is the valence element of policy affected by rapid changes that might open an avenue for executive proposals with high valence relative to the status quo. The conditions identified by the model all point to near complete gridlock, which is what we have observed for the decade since civilian rule resumed.

In another generation, when the principals are no longer on the scene, the salience of the position component of the human rights issue will presumably decline; a history written a few decades from now that accuses deceased members of the CNI will divide Chileans, but it will not have the immediacy an indictment of those same still living men would have today. If another generation goes by without a new round of military intervention or civil war, we may expect that the unexploded human rights bomb will become less of a threat.

What does this model tell us about dealing with the toxic human rights legacy of authoritarian governments in particular and about the degree to which constitutions delegate discretion to future decision-makers in general? Turning first to the question about human rights, the Chilean solution effectively prevents punishment for those involved in the human rights abuses committed by the authoritarian government. After the fact this is a painful concession, especially for those close to the victims. But without a credible guarantee that they will not be brought to justice, the leaders of a ruling authoritarian government are unlikely to relinquish power, grimly fighting to the last surviving subordinate. Neither continued military rule nor civil war offer much chance for justice; the former contains no prospects for punishing the guilty, while the latter is likely to result in a new and grisly round of human rights violations.

Guarantees for the guilty may be the least among the unpalatable evils among which democrats must choose during the early stages of a democratic transition. But will such guarantees really prevent future bloodshed?

Conclusion

The model of gridlock developed here identifies three considerations: the intensity with which attitudes are polarized, the relative salience of valence and position aspects of policy, and the pace at which the agenda setter can formulate high-valence alternatives to the status quo. The last of these three is not likely to be an important consideration in most cases of human rights violations, and so we must focus our attention on the first two. Even with the passage of time attitudes about past human rights violations can remain polarized. After more than two centuries the left and the right in France commemorate the fall of the Bastille in very different ways. Time has not produced consensus. What has happened, in the case of France, is a reduction in the intensity of hatred: the position issue of assigning blame is now much less important than the valence issue of avoiding civil war. But the relative salience of blame and retribution fade more slowly for some conflicts than for others. In cases in which victims and perpetrators held different ethnic, religious, or linguistic identities, collective blame and hatred may persist long after the individuals actually involved are dead and gone. In these cases the Chilean solution may actually backfire. By protecting individuals from responsibility for their acts, amnesty may actually help to create a belief in collective responsibility for individual misdeeds. It is this risk that the South Africans are attempting to reduce with their more aggressive approach to truth and reconciliation. By insisting that the perpetrators identify themselves and describe their crimes before being given amnesty, the South Africans may succeed in at least partially separating culpability for crimes from group identities. However, to the extent that the taint of human rights abuses is applied to groups rather than individuals, and to the extent that people's belief systems assign collective guilt for the cruelties of an authoritarian government, the salience of the human rights issue will remain high for generations, and the Chilean approach will offer at most a suspension of hostilities, rather than a road to reconciliation.

The model used here to understand the Chilean transition identifies a tradeoff faced by all constitution writers, however legitimate their democratic pedigree. On the one hand, constitutions can delegate to future decision makers so that they can adapt the valence elements of policy to changing circumstances. On the other hand, constitution writers will want to prevent future policy makers who do not share their ideological outlook from changing policy by locking in the details of the status quo. The tension between delegation and constraint arises because of the simultaneous concern for valence aspects of policy, about which all agree, and for the ideological position of policy, about which there is no consensus. Here the focus was on one type of constitution, with the president as agenda setter, but the tradeoff is much more general.

244

At one end of the spectrum constitutions can fully delegate to a dictator, or to an unconstrained parliamentary majority. This will provide flexibility in dealing with valence issues, whether in the form of a national security crisis or a chronic public health or public safety problem, such as cancer or crime, about which all agree, but it may also create considerable uncertainty for the constitution writer. At the other end of the spectrum, the constitution can make it difficult to change the particulars of the law, either by including detailed legislation as part of the text of the constitution itself, or by making it easy for a legislative minority to block reform, as with the two-thirds cloture rule that used to prevail in the U. S. Senate.

The model developed here identifies three features of the political environment at the time a constitution is written that will influence the choice of options along the continuum running from constraint to delegation. First, there is the distance between the constitution writer and the political actors considered likely to hold power. In systems with regular alteration of the major parties in power, this corresponds to the degree of polarization, but if there is an extreme party that is virtually guaranteed to remain out of power, then this extremeness becomes irrelevant. Conversely, even if all of the major parties are close together, if the constitution writer is extreme we may expect little delegation. Nor is this tradeoff between delegation and constraint restricted to "constitutional moments." During the early days of the cold war, when there was considerable consensus in the U. S. that communist countries posed a national security threat, the U. S. Congress delegated considerable power to the president, power it partially withdrew at the end of the Vietnam War, as the consensus crumbled.

A second key factor is the salience of valence vs. policy position. The more salient the valence aspect of policy, the greater the level of delegation. Many constitutions provide for greater delegation to a president or a prime minister in cases of national emergency. This applies to wartime threats to national security, but it can also be important during economic crises that tend to affect all citizens in the same direction, such as a sudden increase in the price of a raw material like petroleum, or a sudden drop in the price of a major export. Since citizens of small open economies will tend to share these interests to a greater extent, we may expect that the constitutions of such countries will tend to delegate more flexibility.

A third factor identified by the model is the ability of future decision makers to formulate high-valence alternatives to status quo policy. The more rapidly changing the environment, the quicker the existing laws and institutions will fall out of sync with the policy environment. We may expect that constitution writers in countries with volatile economies, such as those based on the export of primary products, will delegate more flexibility so that future decision makers can adjust to trade shocks. We might also expect to see more delegation during periods of technological change, subject to the major caveat that this change leaves the degree of ideological polarization unchanged.

We may expect constitution writers to try to differentiate among policy areas, delegating more flexibility in some areas than others. However, this is an area in which they are likely to encounter only limited success. Many policies can be disguised as undertaken to safeguard "national security" or to provide "economic stabilization." Policymakers probably recognize that policy flexibility can readily metastasize across specific subject areas. Like it or not, the decision to delegate is largely a global one that crosses specific policy areas.

The model developed in the preceding chapters has the potential to be applied across a wide variety of settings. It is by no means restricted to the peculiar mix of concerns surrounding the Chilean transition toward democracy. However, in applying formal models such as the one exposited here, the preceding pages contain a warning: one must attend carefully to the details! A superficial reading of the U. S. and Chilean constitutions reveals many similarities between the legislative processes in the two; both are bicameral, both use conference committees, both allow presidential vetos. However, in Chile the president's constructive veto and agenda monopolies combine to make him or her the agenda setter, whereas in the U. S. system it is at least *de jure* Congress which acts as the agenda setter. In applying the model of constitutional delegation to Chile, a careful study of the institutional details was not enough; considerable work was needed to identify the issue positions of the executive and of key legislators. In tracing out the implications of this model for other democratic transitions, and more generally, for the way that constitution writers choose between delegation and constraint, considerable attention must go to the details. Ideological polarization and the degree of flexibility a constitution delegates to subsequent decision makers require careful measurement. Bicameralism may correspond to a high degree of delegation when a single disciplined party controls both chambers and the executive, whereas with a divided government and a high cloture threshold in one chamber the very same written constitution can correspond to a high degree of constraint. Whether institutions arise from democratic deliberation or result from Faustian bargains with an authoritarian regime, the devil is in the details.

Appendix A

Estimating Preferences from Voting Records

Obtaining an accurate measure of legislators' preferences is no mean task because of the powerful incentives politicians often have to misrepresent their objectives strategically. Thus campaign literature often emphasizes the putatively high "valence" of a candidate's character, and of the party's issue positions. In the 1990 election, candidates for the Concertación and the opposition alike were in favor of economic prosperity, high-quality education, good health care, and a clean environment, and they were opposed to poverty and civil disorder. Special interests will allege their projects represent tremendous gains in efficiency over the status quo, and denounce policies they oppose as having low valence. Similar incentives are widespread throughout the political process.

Situations that require politicians to take public positions on issues can overcome these incentives to dissimulate. This is part of the function of the press; by asking questions they set a hypothetical agenda and let political candidates and officeholders respond. However, successful politicians are masters of the rhetorical gymnastics and social acrobatics used to deflect and evade difficult questions. Another institution designed to force politicians into the open is the roll-call vote in which each legislator must register his or her vote of "yes," "no," or "abstain," which becomes part of the public record. This restricted vocabulary limits the space for semantic maneuver, and so can do much to clarify a politician's position. Moreover, even when the vote is not brought to immediate public attention it may return in the next election to haunt the legislator who cast it, as political opponents and news reporters have powerful incentives to identify and publicize controversial or unpopular positions a legislator may have taken (Kingdon 1981; Arnold 1991), while the legislator himself will be quick to point to popular public votes.

The requirement that Senate committees take public roll-call votes on all amendements considered at the second reading of a bill, combined with the difficulty of predicting the details of the agenda under which the bill will be considered, creates incentives for committee members to vote sincerely. This is useful to other members of the Senate because of the information it provides about the amendments being considered to those who are already acquainted with the committee member's ideological orientation. It is useful to outside observers in a second and perhaps unintended way: the roll-call voting records of committee members provide considerable information about their policy preferences. It is to the task of unraveling this important information from roll-call votes that our attention now turns.

The first section of this Appendix examines how we could estimate the preference parameters from the spatial voting model introduced in Chapters 1 and 2 if the committee votes cast by Senators sincerely reflected consistent issue positions. The subsequent section addresses the question of whether we should expect sincerity, while the third section of the Appendix turns to the question of party loyalty.

A.1 RECOVERING INFORMATION FROM SINCERE VOTES

The following discussion is an overview of the statistical model, and it should be more than adequate for interpreting the statistical results presented in the following three chapters. Interested readers will find a much more detailed and complete discussion of the statistical model in Londregan (2000).

Starting with the utility function given in Equation (4.1) and substituting into the condition for voting in favor of proposal i over the status quo given in Equation (4.2), we have[1]

$$c_i + g_i x_v > \epsilon_{vi} \tag{A.1}$$

[1] Expanding the square terms on both sides and multiplying by two, we have
$$-x_v^2 + 2x_v p_i - p_i^2 + 2\alpha v \epsilon_{vi} + 2\epsilon_{vi} > -x_v^2 + 2x_v p_{sq} - p_{sq}^2 + 2\alpha v \epsilon_{vsq}.$$
Here $\epsilon_{vi} = \xi_{vi} - \xi_{sq}$. The "$-x^2$" terms on both sides cancel. Next collect all terms save ϵ_{vi} on the left-hand side:
$$p_i(2x_v - p_i) - p_{sq}(2x_v - p_{sq}) + 2\alpha(v_i - v_{sq}) > -2\epsilon_{vi}.$$
Dividing by two on both sides this becomes:
$$(p_i - p_{sq})\left(x_v - \tfrac{p_i + p_{sq}}{2}\right) + \alpha(v_i - v_{sq}) > -\epsilon_{vi}.$$
Collecting terms, this becomes:
$$(p_i - p_{sq})x_v - \left[(p_i - p_{sq})\tfrac{p_i + p_{sq}}{2}\right] + \alpha(v_i - v_{sq}) > -\epsilon_{vi}.$$
Letting
$$g_i = p_i - p_{sq} \qquad c_i = \alpha(v_i - v_{sq}) - \left[(p_i - p_{sq})\tfrac{p_i + p_{sq}}{2}\right]$$
we can rewrite this condition as
$$g_i x_v + c_i > -\epsilon_{vi}.$$

248

where the random term ϵ_{vi} measures the net effect of the legislator's idiosyncratic reactions to the status quo and the proposal

$$\epsilon_{vi} = \xi_{vsq} - \xi_{vi}. \tag{A.2}$$

Higher values for the terms on the lefthand side of Equation (A.1) increase the likelihood that legislator v will vote in favor of proposal i. While the parameter x_v represents the preferred outcome for legislator v, the remaining parameters g_i and c_i require some explanation. The g_i parameter measures the distance between the position of the proposal and the status quo:

$$g_i = p_i - p_{sq}. \tag{A.3}$$

Notice that the ideological content of the proposal will affect different voters differently, something captured in Equation (A.1) by the interaction of the g_i and x_v terms. Recall that ideological preferences on the left are represented by low and even negative values for x_v, while positions on the right correspond to high values for x_v. Holding all else equal, including the midpoint of the proposal and the status quo, consider a proposal moving policy to the right, with $g_i > 0$. The farther a legislator is to the right, represented by a high value for x_v, the larger will be the value of $g_i x_v$, and the more likely it is that legislator v will vote in favor of proposal i. The farther x_v is to the left, the smaller the value of $g_i x_v$ and the smaller the probability v will vote in favor of the measure. For proposals moving policy leftward from the status quo, for which $g_i < 0$, the value of $g_i x_v$ becomes larger for more negative values of x_v, that is, for those farther to the left. In this case the effects of individual legislators' ideological preferences are reversed, with those on the left being more likely to vote in favor than those on the right.

The c_i parameter is connected to the underlying model by a more circuitous path, and it is worth taking a moment to trace this out. This parameter essentially measures what we may think of as the "consensus appeal" of a proposal, including the proposal's valence, and some of its ideological characteristics as well. Essentially we may see unanimous approval of a proposal either because it yields high valence for everyone, or because it offers relief from an ideologically extreme element of the status quo.

While ideological extremism can repel legislators, it differs from valence in that it repels different legislators to different degrees. An extreme proposal on the left will bother legislators on the left to a lesser degree than those on the right, although all may join in voting against it and in favor of the status quo. This is different than a policy that would, for example, increase crime, or reduce highway safety, outcomes that would be seen as equally undesirable by individuals across the ideological spectrum.

249

In the context of the quadratic model of preferences the impact of ideology breaks neatly into two distinct parts. The first of these, captured by the $x_v g_i$ term in Equation (A.1) discussed above, differs across voters. The second part of the impact of ideology on voting corresponds to $m_i g_i$, where m_i denotes the midpoint of proposal i and the status quo.[2] This second part of ideology's voting impact affects everyone equally. Some straightforward but tedious algebra reveals that

$$c_i = \alpha(v_i - v_{sq}) - g_i m_i. \qquad (A.4)$$

The first terms in Equation (A.4) pertains to the difference between the valence of proposal i and the status quo: $v_i - v_{sq}$, while the second represents the common part of the reaction to the ideological content of a proposal.

What all of the elements of the c_i term have in common is the absence of the preference parameters, x_v, that are specific to particular voters. Thus we can think of c_i as measuring the "consensus appeal" of proposal i. This is slightly different than measuring its valence. While valence does affect the value of c_i, there are some subtle but important differences between valence, represented by v_i, and the c_i parameter. First, c_i responds not to the valence of a proposal but to the difference between a proposal's valence and that of the status quo. This response is greater the larger the value of α. Second, c_i also responds to ideological features of the proposal and the status quo that affect everyone in the same way, the $g_i m_i$ term in Equation (A.4) that we might think of as capturing the part of ideological extremism that affects all legislators equally. Given the quadratic spatial preferences set forth in Equation (4.1), these factors have identical effects on voting, and so we cannot empirically disentangle the various components of c_i from one another.

It is convenient to reformulate the model in Equation (A.1) to allow for the possibility of a nonzero mean for ϵ_{vi}. This is what we might expect if there was a systematic bias in favor of the status quo. To allow for this possibility, it is useful to define b_v and η_{vi} as follows:

$$b_v = -E\{\epsilon_{vi}\} \qquad \eta_{vi} = \epsilon_{vi} - E\{\epsilon_{vi}\}.$$

This means that b_v is negative one times the expected preference shock for legislator v, while η_{vi} is what remains of the idiosyncratic error corresponding to legislator v's assessment of proposal i. This new error term now has a mean of zero. Introducing this new notation, we can rewrite Equation (A.1) as Equation (4.3), which is reproduced here for convenience:

$$c_i + b_v + g_i x_v > \eta_{vi}.$$

---

[2] Formally we can define $m_i = (p_i + p_{sq})/2$.

Estimating Preferences from Voting Records

At this point, one way to complete the model would be to simply posit a probability distribution for η_{vi}, with common choices including the standard normal, the uniform, and the extreme value distribution which gives rise to logit probabilities. Unfortunately, maximum likelihood estimates of this whole family of models are inconsistent. The inconsistency results from what is known as the "parameter proliferation problem." Stated loosely, statistical consistency means that if we add enough data our estimates will "close in" on the true parameter values. As the size of the data set grows arbitrarily large, our estimates will come arbitrarily close to the true parameter values.[3] The problem with models such as that in inequality (4.3) is that as we add more data, for example by observing more proposals, we also add more parameters, for example, the c_i and g_i corresponding to the new proposals. As the data set grows, the complexity of the problem increases. In this case it can be shown (Londregan 2000) that the estimated parameters do not converge to the true parameters, and that this failure to converge is especially severe when the number of legislators casting votes is small, as in the case of Senate committees.

One solution to this problem is to reformulate the model in terms of a finite set of underlying parameters. Instead of attempting to estimate the location parameters for each proposal individually, we can model the stream of proposals that share a set of observable characteristics. Thus we can posit that the displacement parameter for proposal i, g_i, depends on a vector of observable characteristics, $\vec{w}_{gi}$, which might include the proposal's subject matter, the list of its authors, and so forth, plus an idiosyncratic error term specific to proposal i:

$$g_i = \vec{g}'\vec{w}_{gi} + \zeta_{gi}. \tag{A.5}$$

We can build a similar model of the consensus appeal c_i parameters, where the observable explanatory variables may differ from those used to explain the proposal displacement:

$$c_i = \vec{c}'\vec{w}_{ci} - v_i^*. \tag{A.6}$$

A similar framework could be used to capture the voter specific parameters, with

$$x_v = \vec{x}'\vec{w}_{xv} + \zeta_{xv} \qquad b_v = \vec{b}'\vec{w}_{bv} - \zeta_{bv}. \tag{A.7}$$

These explanatory variables might include the party of the legislator casting a vote, or some measure of the law maker's district characteristics, such as the fraction of the labor force employed in agriculture.

[3] See Cox and Hinkely (1974) for a detailed discussion of statistical consistency.

Substituting into inequality (4.3) and rearranging terms, we obtain the condition for legislator v to vote in favor of proposal i:

$$\vec{c}'\vec{w}_{ci} + \vec{b}'\vec{w}_{bv} + (\vec{g}'\vec{w}_{gi})(\vec{x}'\vec{w}_{xv}) > \eta_{vi} + v_i^* + \zeta_{bv} - \zeta_{gi}\zeta_{xv} - (\vec{g}'\vec{w}_{gi})\zeta_{xv} - (\vec{x}'\vec{w}_{xv})\zeta_{gi}.$$

(A.8)

In the application to the Senate committees this formulation can be simplified somewhat. First of all, notice that the voting condition in inequality (A.8) includes the condition in Equation (A.1) as a special case, when the explanatory variables are all voter- and proposal-specific dummy variables, and the corresponding proposal- and voter-specific error terms, the ζ and the v, are all set equal to zero.

Here I move partially back in the direction of inequality (A.1) by estimating different preferred outcomes for each of the voters. Even with rotating committee assignments, the number of voters for whom preference parameters x_v and b_v have to be estimated is bounded above by the number of Senators, forty-eight, who served during the Aylwin administration. With a full set of senatorial dummies the associated error terms will all equal zero, and the condition for favoring a proposal simplifies to

$$\vec{c}'\vec{w}_{ci} + \vec{b}'\vec{w}_{bv} + (\vec{g}'\vec{w}_{gi})(\vec{x}'\vec{w}_{xv}) > \eta_{vi} + v_i^* + (\vec{x}'\vec{w}_{xv})\zeta_{gi}.$$

(A.9)

The model for proposals used here recognizes that the streams of proposals from a particular author within a particular committee jurisdiction will typically be made in pursuit of a stable set of legislative objectives. This is a reasonable expectation as political opponents and journalists can hold a legislator accountable for amendments he or she has offered even more easily than they can take him or her to task for his or her public votes.

The v_i^* term measures the idiosyncratic variation in the consensus appeal of proposals with identical observed characteristics as discussed in Chapter 4; most legislators come up with a mixture of "good" and "bad" ideas. Furthermore, it is notoriously difficult for people to recognize their own "bad" ideas, so that despite the public nature of legislative proposals many of these unsuccessful ideas are included on the agenda. In contrast, we might expect legislators to be good judges of the ideological content of their proposals, so that all of the proposals made by a particular author during a particular legislative session will be made in pursuit of a stable set of ideological goals and offered against an overall policy status quo that changes very slowly. In this setting we might expect the variance among the ζ_{gi} to be small, with all proposals from the same author trying to move policy by about the same amount and in the same direction.[4] If we treat all of the proposals in the same area by the same author as attempting to

---

[4] Initial experimentation with data from the Senate Labor Committee indicates that the variance of the ζ_{gi} in that setting is very close to zero.

move policy by the same distance, and of course in the same direction, so that ζ_{gi} is equal to zero, the condition for voting in favor of the proposal simplifies to

$$\vec{c}'\vec{w}_{ci} + \vec{b}'\vec{w}_{bv} + (\vec{g}'\vec{w}_{gi})(\vec{x}'\vec{w}_{xv}) > \eta_{vi} + \upsilon_i^*. \tag{A.10}$$

To estimate the model in inequality (A.10) we need to posit probability distributions for η_{vi} and υ_i. Here I treat η_{vi} as normally distributed with mean 0 and variance 1, the standard normal distribution. Likewise, υ_i^* is normal with mean zero. The variance of υ_i^* might be greater or less than that of η_{vi}, depending on the relative importance of variation in the consensus appeal of proposals and the idiosyncratic preference "shocks" of the individual legislators. To calibrate this variance it is sufficient to replace υ_i^* with $\alpha\upsilon_i$, where υ_i is normally distributed with mean 0 and variance 1, while the parameter α, which needs to be estimated, measures the variance of υ. The model to be estimated is

$$\vec{c}'\vec{w}_{ci} + \vec{b}'\vec{w}_{bv} + (\vec{g}'\vec{w}_{gi})(\vec{x}'\vec{w}_{xv}) > \eta_{vi} + \alpha\upsilon_i. \tag{A.11}$$

Let $\mathsf{V}(i)$ denote the set of legislators who voted on proposal i while the function yes (v, i) is equal to 1 if legislator v voted in favor of the proposal, while it equals -1 if instead he or she voted against it. Let $\Phi(.)$ be the standard normal cumulative density function, while $\phi(.)$ is the standard normal probability density function. We can write down the contribution of proposal i to the log of the likelihood function. It is a function of the parameter vector $\vec{\psi}$:

$$l_p(\vec{\psi}) = \ln\left(\int_{-\infty}^{\infty} \prod_{v \in \mathsf{V}(i)} \Phi\{\mathrm{yes}(v, i)[(\vec{g}'\vec{w}_{gi})(\vec{x}'\vec{w}_{xv}) + \vec{b}'\vec{w}_{bv} + \vec{c}'\vec{w}_{ci} + \alpha\epsilon_i]\}\phi(\epsilon_i)d\epsilon_i\right)$$

$$\tag{A.12}$$

where

$$\vec{\psi} = \begin{bmatrix} \vec{x} \\ \vec{b} \\ \vec{g} \\ \vec{c} \\ \alpha \end{bmatrix}. \tag{A.13}$$

Some Practicalities

In addition to the usual probit normalization that the η_{vi} have mean 0 and variance 1, four other normalizations are required to identify the model. Two of these amount to an arbitrary selection of origin and scale for legislators' preferred ideologies. We could measure most preferred outcomes on a scale from 0 to 100, or on a scale of -1 to 1, or on any scale we liked.

In fact we could reverse measures, putting the political left on the right of the scale, that is, by giving them higher numbers, as is done in the U. S. by organizations like Americans for Democratic Action, whose ADA score places political liberals at 100 (on the right of the scale) and political conservatives at 0, on the left of the scale. In this setting, a change of the units used to measure $\vec{x}$ can simply be offset by changes in $\vec{g}$ and $\vec{c}$. To avoid ambiguities, it is sufficient to normalize the locations of two legislators. Thus for each committee a legislator generally thought to be on the political right, such as Institutional Senator Olga Feliú, is normalized to have a location of 1, while a Senator thought to be on the left, such as Socialist Senator Rolando Calderón, is normalized to have a location of -1.

The remaining normalizations have the effect of choosing a "reference proposer," or when explanatory variables are used in place of dummy variables for the proposers' identity, a "reference proposal type." For this proposal type the corresponding element of $\vec{c}$ and the corresponding element of $\vec{g}$ are set equal to zero. Substituting these normalizations into Equation (4.4) we see that the condition for supporting proposals of the reference type is

$$\vec{b}'\vec{w}_{bv} > \eta_{vi} + \alpha v_i.$$

This means that the probability that voter v supports a proposal of the reference type depends on the level of $\vec{b}'\vec{w}_{bv}$, so that the $\vec{b}$ parameters measure the tendency to vote for proposals of the reference type.

As with the selection of two legislators to normalize the ideological preference parameters, the choice of reference proposer is arbitrary. Changes are simply offset by changes in the estimated values of the remaining parameters.

Given our identifying normalizations, the parameters of the model set forth in Equation (4.4) can be estimated consistently by using maximum likelihood estimation.[5] By fixing the number of parameters, that is, the lengths of the vectors $\vec{x}$, $\vec{b}$, $\vec{g}$, and $\vec{c}$, we no longer add parameters to estimate whenever we add data, and so we avoid the parameter proliferation problem. As already noted, the number of legislators voting in a given committee is small, and so we may still choose to estimate preference parameters x_v and c_v for every legislator who participated in a committee's votes. This choice is readily encompassed in the framework of Equation (4.4) by letting $\vec{w}_{xv}$ and $\vec{w}_{bv}$ correspond to vectors of legislator-specific dummy variables. However, as we add votes the key is not to try to estimate a separate parameter for each proposal. While the Constitution Committee voted on over 800 proposed amendments during the sample period, no attempt is made to measure correspondingly many proposal

---

[5] See Londregan (2000) for details.

parameters. Instead proposals are identified with their authors, or in some cases, with the party affiliations of their authors by using author-specific or party-specific indicator variables. While it would be very useful to have detailed information about which of a proposed amendment's cosponsors was the real author, and what the relative contributions of the cosponsors really was, this information is simply not available. While one might hope to learn something about it from the legislators themselves, and those who have retired might be willing to speak frankly, there is little hope of obtaining comprehensive and reliable data of that nature. Instead multiply authored amendments are taken to be weighted averages of the characteristics of their authors, with each of N authors' characteristics receiving a weight of $1/N$. Thus if legislator i was among five cosponsors of amendment p, and the model includes a proposer "dummy" variable for legislator i, then the elements of $\vec{w}_{gp}$ and of $\vec{w}_{cp}$ corresponding to legislator i would equal $1/5$.

As a practical matter it would be convenient to estimate characteristics of all proposers, whose number is bounded above by the membership of the Senate plus the President of the Republic. Likewise, it is convenient to work with the set of legislators voting on a committee. But this approach entails difficulties for voters and proposers who seldom participate.

Consider the case of Institutional Senator Fernández, who participated in but one proposal in the data from the Senate Labor Committee. This proposal was rejected, and so Labor Committee proposals by Senator Fernández have an observed failure rate of 100%. If one were to include a proposer-specific parameter for Senator Fernández in the specification, maximum likelihood estimation would attempt to set the c parameter corresponding to that Senator equal to $-\infty$, attributing all of the "blame" for the proposal's rejection to the participation a Senator making proposals with infinitely poor consensus appeal. Of course, this would be a classical case of overfitting the data, with the sparse participation of Senator Fernández in the work of the Labor Committee essentially creating a stray parameter corresponding to a single data point. For this reason it is impractical to attempt to estimate individual-specific parameters for proposers and voters who participate infrequently, and so these are grouped with other members of their parties. Individual-specific preference and proposal parameters are only calculated for frequent participants.

A.2 SINCERE VOTING IN SENATE COMMITTEES: A FORMAL MODEL

To better understand the factors at work in the context of the Chilean Senate the simple formal model introduced in Chapters 1 and 2 provides useful guidance. Suppose that a committee member's constituents expect him or her to advocate a policy position of x. Let a public vote cast by the member be represented by the variable $\eta \epsilon \{0, 1\}$, where $\eta = 1$ represents a vote in favor of the proposal under consideration, while $\eta = 0$ is a vote against the proposal, and hence implicitly in favor of the status quo. If the member votes on a proposal of p_P when the status quo alternative is p_{SQ}, the member's electoral payoff is

$$V(\eta; x, p_P, p_{SQ}, q_P, q_{SQ}) = -\eta(p_P - x)^2 - (1 - \eta)(p_{SQ} - x)^2 \\ + \alpha[\eta q_p + (1 - \eta)q_{SQ}].$$

(A.14)

Suppose the legislator has "true" policy preferences represented by

$$U(p, q; z, \alpha) = -(p - z)^2 + \alpha q. \qquad (A.15)$$

where z is the member's "true" preferred policy outcome. Letting $\pi(\eta)$ denote the probability the bill is enacted, the expected value of the member's overall well being resulting from the bill is

$$V(\eta; x, p_P, p_{SQ}, q_P, q_{SQ}) + w\{\pi(\eta)U(p_P, q_P; z) + [1 - \pi(\eta)]U(p_{SQ}, q_{SQ}; z)\}.$$

(A.16)

In Equation (A.16) the w term corresponds to the weight the legislator attaches to his or her actual policy preferences, as opposed to those he or she is expected to advocate.[6] The dependence of $\pi(\eta)$ on η recognizes that the Senator's vote at the second reading of the bill in the committee may affect the probability the policy is eventually adopted. Some straightforward manipulation reveals that the Senator will vote in favor of the proposal if the following condition is met:

$$\left[2(p_P - p_{SQ})\left(x^* - \frac{p_P + p_{SQ}}{2}\right) + \alpha(q_P - q_{SQ})\right]\{1 + w[\pi(1) - \pi(0)]\} > 0$$

(A.17)

where

$$x^* = \frac{x + zw[\pi(1) - \pi(0)]}{1 + w[\pi(1) - \pi(0)]}.$$

Provided $1 + w[\pi(1) - \pi(0)] > 0$ the Senator behaves "as if" his or her most preferred outcome was x^*. The value of z represents the legislator's "true" policy position. Research on retiring members of the U. S. Congress (Lott 1992) indicates members' actual preferred points, the z's, are very similar to the positions they advocated throughout their tenure,

---

[6] Since this term calibrates the weight the legislator places on his or her own agenda, we can restrict our attention to non-negative values of w.

the x^*'s. Whether this finding would generalize to other legislatures is, of course, an open question, but it is suggestive. The w values are inversely proportional to the importance of maintaining an ideological posture for electoral reasons. The greater the weight a member places on reelection, the smaller will be the member's value for w, and the closer x^* will approach x, the position that favors the member's electoral chances. The value of $[\pi(1) - \pi(0)]$ is the impact of the member's vote in the committee on the probability the amendment is actually part of the legislation that is finally enacted. It is conceivable that this impact is negative, that is, that by voting against an amendment in the committee the Senator actually increases the probability the amendment will be adopted. However, it seems very unlikely that this effect will be large enough to make the $1 + w[\pi(1) - \pi(0)]$ term negative.[7]

If the other members of the legislature know the value of x^* then they can learn from the legislator's public committee vote. For this to work it is not necessary that x, the preferred policy of the constituents, be close to z, the preferred policy of the member, nor is it essential that w, the weight the member places on his or her own policy preferences, be small. It is not even necessary that the effect of the member's vote on the probability the amendment is eventually enacted is constant, as long as other Senators know what it is. Even if this last condition is not satisfied, if w is small, or z is close to x or the absolute value of $[\pi(1) - \pi(0)]$ is bounded above by a small number, then the value of x^* will be nearly constant across amendments, and we may expect other Senators to learn what it is.

As a practical matter a committee member's impact on the final passage of the amendment, $[\pi(1) - \pi(0)]$ is probably small. Both the conference committee and the president are informed, and so they will recognize the deceptive vote for what it was. The conference committee bill, and presidential "observations," must be voted under a closed rule, that is, the amendment will be bundled together with the rest of the bill. Moreover, the other committee members votes already provide additional information to the uninformed members of the parent chamber; to change the outcome through a deceptive vote a committee member needs to change the information possessed by the pivotal voter in one of the parent chambers by enough to change his or her vote on the entire bill, or his or her vote must change the conference committee's decision of whether to offer the amendment.

Two factors identified by this model, the probability of affecting the ultimate outcome, $[\pi(1) - \pi(0)]$, and the relative weight a legislator accords

---

[7] A sufficient condition is that the legislator places more weight on the reelection motive than he or she does on his or her personal ideological agenda, so that $w < 1$.

to his or her own preferences in casting a vote, w, are both likely to be small for Senate committee votes on amendments during the second reading of a bill. The unpredictable agenda keeps $[\pi(1) - \pi(0)]$ low, while the public nature of the votes gives constituent preferences relatively larger weight, keeping w small as well.

A.3 PARTY COHESION

This framework permits a careful assessment of the degree to which members of the same political party share the same preferences. The most straightforward approach to doing this is to compare the estimated x_v's and b_v's for members of the same party. On most committee votes a party is represented by at most a single Senator. The ideal point estimates for a particular committee are based mostly on nonoverlapping votes, and we seldom observe Senators from the same party voting on the same proposed amendments.

While multiple votes from members of the same party are rare, they do occur, and they provide us with additional important information about Senators' preferences. We seldom observe Senators from the same party voting differently when they vote on the same measures. Some of this similarity is surely attributable to the tendency for Senators from the same party to have similar preferred outcomes. Yet party pressures may also play a role. On key votes the party leaders may demand loyalty, pushing Senators to shift from their most preferred outcomes with promises of rewards and threats of punishments. While most legislative scholars readily acknowledge that some degree of party discipline occurs, it is also part of the common view that, at least for Congressional parties in the U. S., this discipline is applied selectively.[8] Moreover, neither the press nor academic observers are regularly invited to attend when party leaders twist the arms of the membership. Thus, we are not in a position to measure directly which votes, if any, were in fact party whip votes. Even if we are prepared to accept that all votes labeled party whip votes in fact are, we will miss any that involved more discreet pressure. Moreover, there is always the concern that the party leadership will attempt to exaggerate its ability to twist arms by claiming some votes as "whip votes" when members were all inclined to vote for them anyway.

In the precoup Chilean setting, observers noted considerable heterogeneity in the level of discipline among parties, with discipline tending to

---

[8] See, for example, the discussion of "party leadership votes" in Cox and McCubbins (1993).

be tighter on the left than on the right (Agor 1971). During the Aylwin years that are the focus of this study, the proposal behavior of the Socialists is extremely disciplined, with many amendments from Socialists Senators being cosponsored by the party's entire Senate delegation. Patterns of coauthorship exhibit much looser cohesion among members of the other parties. However, the Socialists' Senate delegation is sparse, with only four members distributed across the various committees, and in the data analyzed here we do not observe pairs of Socialists in committees voting on the same amendments. In fact, when we remove legislators' votes on proposals they themselves have written or coauthored, we never observe more than two members of any party voting on the same proposal in any of the committees studied here.

For pairs of proposers from the same party voting on the same proposal, we can augment the voting equation (4.4) to allow the idiosyncratic preference shocks, the η_{vp} to be correlated between the two party members, thereby allowing for party whip behavior. While we may not be able to identify which votes the party attempts to influence, we will nevertheless observe a closer affinity in the voting records of members subject to the same party whip than would be expected from the similarity in their preferred policies alone. This approach is similar to the statistical analysis of carcinogenic environmental hazards. Statistical analysis can often tell us whether people living near a nuclear power plant contract cancer at a higher rate than the general population, though if the cancer rate is higher for power plant neighbors statistical analysis cannot tell us which of the cancers resulted from proximity to the power plant, and which would have occurred anyway. Likewise, by allowing for correlation between the preference shocks, the η_{vp}, for members of the same party voting on the same proposal, we are still unable to identify which votes are in fact whip votes, though we can detect whether some whip voting is taking place. Another possibility is that the correlation between the η_{vp} for members of the same party is in fact negative. This might emerge if members of the same party coordinated their committee attendance to avoid sending largely redundant signals with their identical votes, showing up only when at least one of the party's committee members wanted to highlight a proposal about which the party members disagreed.

The likelihood function (A.12) is readily extended to deal with this case by including the correlation between votes cast by members of the same party. Thus, letting ω_{vp} represent the nonrandom influences on the vote of member v on proposal P,

$$\omega_{vp} = (\vec{g}'\vec{w}_{gp})(\vec{x}'\vec{w}_{xv}) + \vec{b}'\vec{w}_{bv} + \vec{c}'\vec{w}_{cp},$$

the contribution to the likelihood function of proposal p becomes

$$l_p(\vec{\psi}, \vec{z}) = \ln\left[\int_{-\infty}^{\infty} \prod_{v \in V_1(p)} \Phi(\text{yes}(v)\{\omega_{vp} + \alpha\epsilon_p\}) \prod_{r \in W(p)} \Phi^b(\text{yes}[v_1(r)]\{\omega_{vp} + \alpha\epsilon_p\}, \right.$$

$$\left. \text{yes}[v_2(r)]\{\omega_{vp} + \alpha\epsilon_p\}, 2\tan^{-1}(z_r)/\pi)\phi(\epsilon_p)d\epsilon_p \right] \tag{A.18}$$

where

$\Phi^b(a, b, \rho)$	is the bivariate normal cumulative density function with discriminants a and b, and correlation ρ.
$V_1(p)$	is the set of all voters who are the only members of their party to vote on proposal p.
$W(p)$	is the set of all parties, r, that have two members voting on proposal p
$v_i(r)$	are members of party r, $i \in \{1, 2\}$, voting on proposal p.
z_r	is a parameter that gauges the correlation between the η_{vp} for members of party r with $\rho = 2\tan^{-1}(z_r)/\pi$.

While this new formulation introduces some additional notational complexity, the only real change here is to allow for correlation between the η_{vp} for members of the same party. Because the correlation coefficient is theoretically bounded on the interval $[-1, 1]$, it is convenient first to estimate the parameter z_r for each party with members casting simultaneous votes and then to recover the corresponding value for ρ. This so-called arctangent transform is convenient because it simplifies the mechanics of maximizing the likelihood function.[9]

A final technical question which must be addressed before proceeding with the analysis of the committees has to do with votes on one's own proposals. It is only under odd circumstances that Senators ever vote against their own proposals, and very little is lost in treating the probability a Senator votes in favor of his or her own proposal as being equal to 1, so that its contribution to the log of the likelihood function is $\ln(1) = 0$. This is tantamount to dropping such votes from the data set, before estimating the model.

---

[9] A further complication arises in that, in some cases, when the number of votes cast by members of the same delegation is very small, there are no disagreements between members of the same party. When this occurs the maximum likelihood estimator wants to make the corresponding z_r arbitrarily large, coming as close as possible to $\rho = 1$. I deal with these cases by restricting the value of ρ to the interval $[-0.999, 0.999]$, which corresponds to restricting the value of z_r to the interval $[-636.62, 636.62]$.

Table 14. *Party whip parameter estimates*

Issue area	Party	z^a
Labor	PDC	−8.975
		(204.446)
Labor	SI	636.62
Education	PDC	636.62
Human Rights	SI	636.62
Social Issues	RN	636.62
Social Issues	SI	2.099
		(1.423)

[a] Estimated standard errors are shown in parentheses.

A somewhat different approach is possible for votes on proposals from members of one's own party. In this case we can include an element of $\vec{w}_{bv}$ that is equal to 1 if legislator v is voting on a proposal from a member of his or her own party. In this case the corresponding element of $\vec{b}$ measures another aspect of party loyalty, that is, it measures how much more likely a member is to vote for a proposal if it comes from a member of his or her own party, controlling for the member's ideology and the proposal's ideological and valence characteristics. This complements the party whip parameter, z_r, that measures the correlation between the preference disturbances of members of the same party voting on the same proposal. A positive significant value for this parameter would indicate that members give preference to proposals from fellow party members even after controlling for their ideological content. Including this parameter has the added advantage that it purges our ideological estimates of party loyalty effects. However, to avoid of high collinearity with the other elements of $\vec{w}_{bv}$, a single-party loyalty parameter common to all the legislators voting on a given committee is estimated.

The party whip parameters corresponding to the estimates reported in Tables 2, 6, 9, and 11 appear in Table 14. In no case is the estimate statistically different from 0. In most cases the parties' Senators only cast a handful of votes on the same amendments, and agreed on all of these. There were two cases, the Christian Democrats (PDC) on the Labor Committee and the Institutional Senators (SI) on the social agenda considered by the Constitution Committee, in which two members of the same delegation cast sufficiently many divided votes to permit unconstrained estimation of their party whipping parameter. For the Christian Democrats the estimated value for z of −8.975 corresponds to a correlation coefficient of

−0.929 for the Senators' idiosyncratic shocks. However, this surprising negative value is imprecisely estimated, and it does not differ significantly from 0. Likewise, the estimated party whip parameter of 2.099 for the Institutional Senators voting on the Constitution Committee's social agenda corresponds to a correlation of 0.717 between the idiosyncratic preference shocks for these Senators, but as with the Christian Democrats on the Labor Committee, the estimate is imprecise, and does not differ significantly from 0. None of the estimates reported in Table 14 permits us to reject the null hypothesis of no significant party whipping once Senators' most preferred outcomes have been accounted for.

Bibliography

Agor, W. H. (1971). *The Chilean Senate*. Austin: University of Texas Press.

Alberto Alesina, J. Londregan, and H. Rosenthal (1993). A Model of the Political Economy of the United States. *American Political Science Review 87*, 12–33.

Alessandri Palma, A. (1967). *Recuerdos de Gobierno*. Nascimento.

Allamand, A. (Ed.) (1989). *Discursos, Entrevistas, Y Conferencias*. Chile: Editorial Andante.

Arnold, R. D. (1991). *The Logic of Congress*. New Haven: Yale.

Arriagada Herrera, Genaro. (Ed.) (1989). *La Politica Militar de Pinochet*. Santiago: Salesiones.

Biblioteca del Congreso Nacional (1973, August 2). *Sesiones del Senado*. Biblioteca del Congreso Nacional. Tomo 318, Sesión 53.

Biblioteca del Congreso Nacional (1990a, June 30). *Sesiones del Senado*. Biblioteca del Congreso Nacional.

Biblioteca del Congreso Nacional (1990b, June 26). *Sesiones del Senado*. Biblioteca del Congreso Nacional. Legislatura Extraordinaria 320, Sesión 11.

Biblioteca del Congreso Nacional (1990c, August 14). *Sesiones del Senado*. Biblioteca del Congreso Nacional. Legislatura Extraordinaria 320, Sesión 24.

Biblioteca del Congreso Nacional (1990d, November 15). *Sesiones del Senado*. Biblioteca del Congreso Nacional. Legislatura Extraordinaria 320, Sesión 14.

Biblioteca del Congreso Nacional (1990e, September 4). *Sesiones del Senado*. Biblioteca del Congreso Nacional. Legislatura Extraordinaria 320, Sesión 29.

Biblioteca del Congreso Nacional (1990f, December 20). *Sesiones del Senado*. Biblioteca del Congreso Nacional. Legislatura Extraordinaria 321, Sesión 28.

Biblioteca del Congreso Nacional (1991a, May 15). *Sesiones del Senado*. Biblioteca del Congreso Nacional. Legislatura Extraordinaria 321, Sesión 51.

Biblioteca del Congreso Nacional (1991b, May 16). *Sesiones del Senado*. Biblioteca del Congreso Nacional. Legislatura Extraordinaria 321, Sesión 52.

Biblioteca del Congreso Nacional (1991c, January 16). *Sesiones del Senado*. Biblioteca del Congreso Nacional. Legislatura Extraordinaria 321, Sesión 34.

Biblioteca del Congreso Nacional (1992, January 22). *Sesiones del Senado*. Biblioteca del Congreso Nacional. Legislatura Extraordinaria 323, Sesión 36.

Bibliography

Biblioteca del Congreso Nacional (1993a, March 30). *Sesiones del Senado.* Biblioteca del Congreso Nacional. Legislatura Extraordinaria 325, Sesión 37.

Biblioteca del Congreso Nacional (1993b, August 3). *Camara de Diputados.* Biblioteca del Congreso Nacional. Legislatura Ordinaria 326, Sesión 22.

Biblioteca del Congreso Nacional (1993c, April 6). *Sesiones del Senado.* Biblioteca del Congreso Nacional. Legislatura Extraordinaria 325, Sesión 39.

Biblioteca del Congreso Nacional (1993d, December 15). *Sesiones del Senado.* Biblioteca del Congreso Nacional. Legislatura Extraordinaria 327, Sesión 19.

Biblioteca del Congreso Nacional (1993e, April 7). *Sesiones del Senado.* Biblioteca del Congreso Nacional. Legislatura Extraordinaria 325, Sesión 40.

Biblioteca del Congreso Nacional (1994a, January 4). *Sesiones del Senado.* Biblioteca del Congreso Nacional. Legislatura Extraordinaria 327, Sesión 20.

Biblioteca del Congreso Nacional (1994b, January 5). *Sesiones del Senado.* Biblioteca del Congreso Nacional. Legislatura Extraordinaria 327, Sesión 21.

Blanc Renard, Neville, Humberto Nogueira Alcala, Emilio Pfeffer Urquiaga Mario Verdugo Marinkovic (1990). *La Constitución Chilena.* Valparaíso: Ediciones Universitarias de Valparaíso.

Brown, Charles, Curtis Gilroy and Andrew Kohen (1982). The Effect of the Minimum Wage on Employment and Unemployment. *Journal of Economic Literature 20,* 487–528.

Card, D. E. and A. B. Krueger (1995). *Myth and Measurement: The New Economics of the Minimum Wage.* Princeton: Princeton University Press.

Carmines, E. and J. Stimson (1989). *Issue Evolution: Race and the Transformation of American Politics.* Princeton: Princeton University Press.

Comisión Chilena de Derechos Humanos (1978). *Derechos Humanos Y Plebisato* Santiago.

Comisión Chilena de Derechos Humanos (1982). Acta de Amplificación del Consejo de la Comisión Chilena de Derechos Humanos. Unpublished mimeo, archives of the Comisión Chilena de Derechos Humanos, Santiago.

Comisión Nacional de Verdad y Reconciliación (1991). *Informe Rettig.* Santiago: Ediciones del Ornitorrinco.

Constable, P. and A. Valenzuela (Eds.) (1991). *A Nation of Enemies: Chile Under Pinochet.* New York: W. W. Norton.

Contador, A. M. (Ed.) (1989). *Continuismo y discontinuismo en Chile.* Santiago: Bravo y Allende.

Cooke, J. E. (Ed.) (1961). *The Federalist.* Middletown: Wesleyan University Press.

Cox, D. and D. Hinkely (1974). *Theoretical Statistics.* New York: Chapman and Hall.

Cox, G. and M. McCubbins (1993). *Legislative Leviathan: Party Government in the House.* Berkeley: University of California Press.

De la Barra, O. P. (Ed.) (1982). *El Pensimiento de Eduardo Frei.* Santiago: Editorial Acocangua.

Denzau, A. W. Riker and K. Shepsle (1985). Farquharson and Fenno: Sophisticated Voting and Home Style. *American Political Science Review 79,* 1117–1133.

Bibliography

Downs, A. (1957). *An Economic Theory of Democracy*. New York: Harper and Row.

El Mercurio (1978, November 1). *Comisión Chilena De Derechos Humanos Con Funcionario de ONU.*, Santiago: El Mercurio.

El Mercurio (1990a, November 1). *Formula se Restringe A Facultad de Indultar.*, Santiago: El Mercurio.

El Mercurio (1990b, November 11). *Comisión Rechazó Beneficios Legales para Presos Politicos*, Santiago: El Mercurio.

El Mercurio (1990c, November 11). *En 'Leyes Cumplido' Y "Presos Politicos": Acuerdos Sustantivos Lograron Anoche RN y la Concertación*, Santiago: El Mercurio.

El Mercurio (1990d, November 12). *Criticos Juicios Sobre 'Presos Politicos': Plateamientos de Senador Thayer a 'Leyes Cumplido*, Santiago: El Mercurio.

El Mercurio (1991, May 15). *El Senado Vota Hoy Proyecto de Estatuto Docente*, Santiago: El Mercurio.

El Mercurio (1994, January 6). *Senadores Rechazaron Despenalizar Adulterio*, Santiago: El Mercurio.

El Mercurio (1997, April 6). *Medio a Medio: Los Dichos de Aylwin.*, Santiago: El Mercurio.

Farnsworth, E., R. Feinberg, and E. Leenson (1973). *Chile: El Bloqueo Invisible*. Buenos Aires: Ediciones Periferia.

Finer, S. (1962). *The Man on Horseback*. London: Pall Mall.

Frieden, J. A. (1991). *Debt, Development, and Democracy: Modern Political Economy and Latin America*. Princeton: Princeton University Press.

Garretón., A. (1983). The political evolution of the chilean military regime and problems in the transition to democracy. In G. O'Donnell, P. Schmitter and L. Whitehead (Eds.), *Transitions from Authoritarian Rule: Latin America*, pp. 95–122. Baltimore: Johns Hopkins University Press.

Gilligan, T. and K. Krehbiel (1987). Collective Decision-Making and Standing Committees: An Informational Rationale for Restrictive Amendment Procedures. *Journal of Law, Economics, and Organization 3*, 287–335.

Haberman, S. (1977). Maximum Likelihood Estimates in Exponential Response Models. *Annals of Statistics 5*, 815–41.

Hersh, S. (1983). *The Price of Power: Kissinger and the Nixon White House*. New York: Simon and Schuster.

Hinich, M. J. and M. C. Munger (1994). *Ideology and the Theory of Political Choice*. Ann Arbor: University of Michigan Press.

Hotelling, H. (1929). "Stability in Competition" *The Economic Journal 39*, 41–57.

Huber, J. D. (1996). *Rationalizing Parliament: Legislative Institutions and Party Politics in France*. Cambridge: Cambridge University Press.

Huidobro, S. (1989). *Decisión Naval*. Valparaíso: Imprenta de la Armada.

Junta Militar (1973). *Algunos Fundamentos de la Intervención Militar en Chile*. Santiago: Editorial Nacional Gabriela Mistral.

Kingdon, J. W. (1981). *Congressmen's Voting Decisions*. New York: Harper and Row.

265

Bibliography

Krehbiel, K. (1988). Spatial Models of Legislative Choice. *Legislative Studies Quarterly 13*, 259–319.

La Epoca (1991, May 15). *Paro y marcha al Congreso en jornada nacional de protesta de los prefesores*, Santiago. La Epoca.

La Epoca (1994, January 6). *Senado mantuvo la penalización del adulterio*, Santiago. La Epoca.

La Tercera (1991a, May 15). *80 mil docentes adhieren al paro.*, Santiago. La Tercera.

La Tercera (1991b, May 16). *Masiva protesta frente al Congreso*, Santiago. La Tercera.

La Tercera (1998, November 13). *Caso Pinochet, presente en estada de Frei en Sudáfrica.*, Santiago, Internet Edition. La Tercera.

Londregan, J. B. (2000). Estimating Preferred Points in Legislatures. *Political Analysis 8*, 35–56.

Londregan, J. B. and T. Romer (1993). Polarization, incumbency, and the personal vote. In William Barnett, Melvin Hinich, and Norman Schoefield (Eds.), *Political Economy: Institutions, Competition, and Representation*, pp. 355–77. New York: Cambridge University Press.

Londregan, J. B. and J. M. Snyder (1994). Comparing Committee and Floor Preferences. *Legislative Studies Quarterly 19*, 233–66.

Lott, J. R. (1992). Political Cheating. *Public Choice 52*, 169–186.

MacRae, D. (1958). Dimensions of Congressional Voting. Technical report, University of California Publications in Sociology and Social Institutions.

Maira, L. (Ed.) (1984). *Chile: Autoritarismo, Democracia Y Movimiento Popular*. Méjico: Centro de Investigación y Docencia Económicas.

Martinez, J. (1989). Leyes electorales: Sin prudencia ni equidad. *Mensaje* (37).

McClosky, H. and J. Zaller (1984). *The American Ethos: Public Attitudes Toward Capitalism and Democracy*. Cambridge: Harvard University Press.

McGraw, K. M. (1991). Managing Blame: An Experimental Test of the Effects of Political Accounts. *American Political Science Review 85*(4), 1133–1157.

McKelvey, R. D. (1976). Intransitivities in Multidimensional Voting Models and Some Implications for Agenda Control. *Journal of Economic Theory 2*, 472–82.

New York Times (1973, September 20). *CIA Is Linked to Strikes In Chile That Beset Allende*, New York: New York Times.

North, D. C. (1990). *Institutions, Institutional Change, and Economic Performance*. New York: Cambridge University Press.

North, D. C. and R. Thomas (1973). *The Rise of the Western World: A New Economic History*. New York: Cambridge University Press.

Novoa Fuenzalida, P. and W. Thayer Arteaga (1997). *Manual de Derecho del Trabajo*. Santiago: Editorial Juridica de Chile.

Otano, R. (1995). *Cronica de la Transición*. Santiago: Planeta.

Poole, K. T. and H. Rosenthal (1985). A Spatial Model for Legislative Roll Call Analysis. *American Journal of Political Science 28*, 357–384.

Przeworski, A. (1991). *Democracy and the Market: Political and Economic Reforms in Eastern Europe and Latin America*. New York: Cambridge.

Bibliography

Roll, R. (1977). A Critique of the Asset Pricing Theory's Tests. *Journal of Financial Economics*, 129–76.

Romer, T. and H. Rosenthal (1978). Political Resource Allocation, Controlled Agendas, and the Status Quo. *Public Choice 33*, 27–43.

Schultz, T. W. (1968). Institutions and the Rising Economic Value of Man. *American Journal of Agricultural Economics*.

Senado de Chile (1990). Boletín de Indicaciones. No. 27-06.

Senado de Chile (1994). *Reglamento del Senado*.

Shepsle, K. (1979). Structure Induced Equilibrium in Multidimensional Voting Models. *American Journal of Political Science 23*, 27–60.

Sigmund, P. E. (1974). Allende in Retrospect. *Problems of Communism*.

Sigmund, P. E. (1978). *The Overthrow of Allende and the Politics of Chile, 1964–1976*. Pittsburgh: University of Pittsburgh Press.

Sigmund, P. E. (1993). *The United States and Democracy in Chile*. Baltimore: Johns Hopkins University Press.

Simon, H. (1982). *Models of Bounded Rationality*. Cambridge: MIT Press.

Smith, B. H. (1986). Old allies, new enemies: The catholic church as opposition to military rule in chile, 1973–1979. In J. S. Valenzuela and A. Valenzuela (Eds.), *Military Rule in Chile: Dictatorship and Oppositions*. Baltimore: Johns Hopkins University Press.

Spooner, M. H. (1994). *Soldiers in a Narrow Land: the Pinochet Regime in Chile*. Berkeley: University of California Press.

Stokes, D. (1963). Spatial Models of Party Competition. *American Political Science Review 57*, 368–77.

Universided de Las Condes (1997). Seminario: Negociación Colectiva en Chile.

Urzua, P. B. (1975). Inflation: Chile's Experience. CEMLA Monthly Bulletin 21.

U. S. Congress, Senate. (1976). Staff Report of the Select Committee on Intelligence Activities: Covert Action in Chile, 1963–1973. 92nd Congress, 1st Session. Washington D.C.: Government Printing Office.

Valenzuela, A. (1978). *The Breakdown of Democratic Regimes: Chile*. Baltimore: Johns Hopkins University Press.

Viera-Gallo, J. A. (1989). El acuerdo constitucional. *Mensaje*, 237–39.

Yang, D. L. (1996). *Calamity and Reform in China: State, Rural Society and Institutional Change Since the Great Leap Forward Famine*. Stanford: Stanford University Press.

AUTHOR INTERVIEWS

Sergio Diez, May 27, 1997, Valparaíso, Chile.
Olga Feliú, May 26, 1997, Santiago, Chile.
Juan Hamiltón, May 1997, Santiago, Chile.
Carlos Hoffmann, May 1994, Valparaíso, Chile.
Ricardo Hormazábal, May 20, 1997, Valparaíso, Chile.
Jorge Lavandero, May 20, 1997, Valparaíso, Chile.
Mariana George Nacimiento, 1994, Valparaíso, Chile.

Bibliography

Maxímo Pacheco, June 1994, Santiago, Chile.

Teodoro Ribera, May 1997, Valparaíso, Chile.

Laura Soto, June 1994, Valparaíso, Chile, and May 23, 1997, Viña Del Mar, Chile.

William Thayer, May 22, 1997, Santiago, Chile.

Index

269

Index

Index

dimensionality, 20–21, 48, 117–118, 218–219, 221, 223, 225
DINA. *See* National Directorate of Intelligence
disappearances, 50, 51, 56–57, 75, 237
distribution of income, 139
districts, 84–91, 93, 102, 109, 123, 213, 223, 251
disturbance term, 111
divergence, 35, 180, 236
divorce, 118, 173, 199, 211, 216, 218, 221, 223, 230, 238
DNA, 231
domain of regulation, 31
domestic violence, 172, 174
domestic workers, 140
Downs, Anthony, 14
draft, 94
drug abuse, 118, 214, 218, 221–223, 230, 238–239
drug enforcement, 172
due process, 169, 239
duplication, 87–90, 222–224

E

earnings, 141
Eastern Germany, 243
economy, 35, 53–54, 68, 74, 76, 139
Ecuador, 75
Education Committee, 6, 119, 146–159, 163, 166, 168, 170–171, 175, 177, 217–218
education. *See also* Education Committee; Teachers, 8, 60, 105, 114, 123, 146–171, 180, 213–222, 247
  policy, 8, 52, 118, 146–148, 171, 214, 219, 221, 230
Edwards Bank, 53
efficiency, 34–35, 40, 100, 247
Eisenhower, Dwight, 67
El Mercurio, 205
elections. *See also* Electoral system, 1, 7, 31, 45, 57, 64, 76–93, 103, 104, 155, 213, 218, 231, 235–236, 241–242, 247
electoral system, 2–3, 5, 7, 31, 51, 61–63, 76, 82, 89, 93, 212–213, 218, 225, 232n, 236, 242, 255, 257
  electorate, 7, 67–68, 236
  fraud, 62
employees, 106, 140–143, 159, 165, 218
employers, 105, 137–146, 169
enforcement, 106
Enriques, Miguel, 54
environmental policy, 20

Episcopal Conference of the Catholic Church, 200
equilibrium, 42, 45–46, 226, 240, 242
Errazuriz, Fransísco Javier, 224
error terms, 111, 250–252
Espina, Alberto, 191, 192n
Estación Central, 86
estimators, 6, 100, 108–119, 124–133, 135, 144–169 passim, 175–176, 180, 192–199, 197n, 210, 214–215, 224, 227, 248–262
  preferred outcomes, 8, 149–150, 172, 217
ethnic groups, 10–11, 244
Euclidean preferences, 14
euthanasia, 201
executions, 9, 57, 75, 162
executive, 1–5, 8, 13, 31–47, 52, 54, 60, 62–63, 67–70, 82, 94, 100, 102, 123, 132–133, 139– 142, 144, 153–168, 172–200, 207, 210, 213, 222, 240, 242–243, 246
  bargaining, and, 33
  compromise, and, 36–38, 41, 43, 46, 225–226
  dominance of, 13, 34–35, 37, 100, 235
  legislative relations, 32, 212, 222
  proposals, 33, 152, 154, 165, 179, 228
exiles, 120
expected utility, 29
expenditures, 165
experts, 57, 103, 107, 227
explanatory variables, 251–252
external disruption, 237
extremism, 35, 43, 83, 111, 129, 197, 249
Eyzaguirre, Rafael, 162n, 186

F

factory ships, 29, 47
family, 201–203, 207–208, 209–210
Fantuzzi, Angel, 142
farmworkers, 106
Faustian bargain, 7, 9, 246
Federación Nacional de Tripulantes de Naves Especiales de Chile, 29
federal systems, 148
Feliú, Olga, 85, 124–128, 135–139, 143–150, 155–170, 175, 189, 194–233, 254
Fernández, Sergio, 85, 123, 175–178, 182–186, 194–198, 205n, 211–216, 224, 255
filibusters, 66
finance, 95
Finance Committee, 119, 168
Finer, Samuel, 2, 57

Index

Index

Index

Index

279